THE WESTERN HERO IN HISTORY AND LEGEND

The Western Hero
IN HISTORY AND LEGEND

By *Kent Ladd Steckmesser*

UNIVERSITY OF OKLAHOMA PRESS
NORMAN

Library of Congress Catalog Card Number: 65–11226

Copyright 1965 by the University of Oklahoma Press, Publishing Division of the University. Composed and printed at Norman, Oklahoma, U.S.A., by the University of Oklahoma Press. First edition.

For George and Carol

Preface

THE FAR WESTERN FRONTIER of the nineteenth century still exists —in the American imagination. And it is the hero of that frontier, the trapper, outlaw, soldier, and gunfighter, who personifies the period and the place. In his biography Americans have found all the action and color needed for a great national myth.

The Western hero is typically a product of legend as well as of history. Legends are so inevitable in the hero's biography that they come to have an inherent social truth of their own. The average reader accepts them along with facts, not only because he generally lacks the time or knowledge to separate the two, but also because legends seem to have a universal appeal. To ignore legends simply because they are by definition historically unfounded is an error which too many professional historians have made. Legends are of great importance in any interpretation of our national past.

The four heroes in this book are classic examples of how history and legend mingle in our picture of the Far Western frontier. They represent trade groups commonly identified with this frontier, and each of them became a type-figure of the group to which he belonged. But despite their occupational differences, a common pattern emerges, and a common hero-type is created by the fusion of history and legend. The purpose of this volume is to explain how and why these heroes were created.

A vast body of popular literature lies between the actual historical experience of the frontier and the reading public's conception of that experience. Americans have generally learned about the frontier West, not through firsthand accounts or well-researched reconstructions, but through popular and secondhand interpretations. Dime novels, biographies, magazine articles, novels, movies, and television plays have told them what they know about the West. Since a legend involves all these forms, an investigation of the Western hero becomes a study in history, fiction, and folklore. An analysis of the evolution of legends in these media should serve as a guide to the hero as he was and to what people have thought he was.

KENT LADD STECKMESSER

Pasadena, California
March 3, 1965

Acknowledgments

THE AUTHOR HAS RECEIVED the benefit of aid and counsel from many writers, scholars, and librarians. He is especially indebted to David Lavender, of Ojai, California; Dr. Philip J. Rasch, of Camp LeJeune, North Carolina; Professor Norman Maclean, of the University of Chicago; and Nyle H. Miller and Joseph W. Snell, of the Kansas State Historical Society; all of whom were generous enough to read and comment upon portions of the manuscript. He also owes intellectual debts to Henry Nash Smith, Walter Blair, James C. Malin, and Don Russell. Among the many librarians who rendered assistance, he is especially grateful to those of the Huntington Library, San Marino, California, who have helped make research at that institution an extremely pleasant experience. The staffs of the Western History Room at the Denver Public Library and the Library of the Museum of New Mexico at Santa Fe were also very helpful. To these and to the many others who offered suggestions for this book, *gracias*.

Contents

Illustrations

THE WESTERN HERO IN HISTORY AND LEGEND

The Origins of a Tradition

FRONTIER HEROES SPRANG UP as soon as America had a frontier. Typically they were men who had actually performed some notable and verifiable exploit. Then through literary elaboration and the workings of the folk imagination, their deeds were expanded to epic proportions, and new exploits and traits were added to their names. As this process was repeated, the individuals who benefited from it came to personify the frontiers of which they had been a part.

The John Smith legend lies at the source of this heroic tradition. The Smith of history was in many respects an ideal type-figure for the Western heroes who followed him. He was of humble origin, loved to travel the unknown wilderness, and made his reputation as a fighter and man of action. His *A True Relation* (1608) is a brief but valuable narrative of the Jamestown colony. By dictatorial methods within the colony, and by strong-handed dealings with the Indians outside it, Smith saved the infant settlement from extinction. He thus occupies an important place in both Colonial historiography and history.

But Smith's historical importance became buried beneath the grandiose legends which were incorporated into his later opus, *A Generall Historie of Virginia* (1624). Here he appears as a great lover and an epic Indian fighter as well as an accomplished leader. Simple incidents in the 1608 narrative are expanded into hair-raising tales in 1624. A meeting with a single Indian becomes a hand-to-hand combat with six or eight of them.[1] Battles, escapes, and captivities which were unreported in 1608 are enthusiastically

[1] Bradford Smith, *Captain John Smith: His Life and Legend,* 105–106, 149.

added. And Smith remembered how the intervention of the beauteous Pocahontas had saved him from the chopping block: "At the minute of my execution, she hazarded the beating out of her brains to save mine, and not only that, but so prevailed upon her father, that I was safely conducted to Jamestown." All these literary embellishments made Smith a hero to readers in England who were fascinated by the romance of the New World. They were also instrumental in converting Captain Smith into a figure remembered more as a legendary hero than as a Colonial leader and chronicler.

The successive Indian wars of America's Colonial period produced other heroes on the Smith model. One remembers the Indian-fighting and scouting exploits of Robert Rogers in the French and Indian War. Rogers, like Smith, was known to sophisticated audiences in London. His *Journals* of the war, published in 1765, were a pioneer effort at commercial exploitation of frontier heroism. Yet no frontier character gained a national audience in this country until after the Revolutionary War. Perhaps Americans were not far enough removed from the frontier for it to appear glamorous to them. A comfortable and literate "East" protected from the harsh realities of the frontier seemed to be necessary before the Western hero could become a vital figure in American legend.

In 1784, a Pennsylvania schoolteacher named John Filson published a thirty-three-page sketch called *The Adventures of Col. Daniel Boon* [*sic*] as an appendix to a longer work on the settlement of Kentucky.[2] The sketch made Boone the representative hero of the trans-Appalachian frontier and helped to define the tradition of the Western hero. Boone himself was a simple woodsman who had explored the Kentucky bluegrass region in 1769–70 as the employee of North Carolina land speculators. He had been in several Indian scrapes and had spent four months as a captive of the Shawnees in 1778. He had escaped to lead the defense of

---

[2] *The Discovery, Settlement, and Present State of Kentucke* [*sic*], with an Appendix containing *The Adventures of Col. Daniel Boon* (Wilmington, Del., printed by James Adams, 1784).

Boonesborough against the longest siege in the history of Indian warfare. After the war, Boone had worked as a farmer and hunter but was continually ejected from his lands by lawsuits.

Filson represented Boone as a sensitive philosopher and furnished him with ornate language. The pioneer delivers grandiloquent speeches on his discoveries in Kentucky: "No populous city, with all the varieties of commerce and stately structures, could afford so much pleasure to my mind, as the beauties of nature I found here." Boone's presumed preference for nature rather than society struck the right chord in both Europe and America, since Rousseau's "natural man" was an intriguing subject for discussion. The actual Boone lived to denounce the antisocial legend that sprang from Filson's interpretation.[3]

Filson's brief sketch was the foundation of a prototypic Western legend which grew to elephantine proportions in biographies, poems, histories, novels, dime novels, periodical articles, and other media. Although later writers all condemned the *Adventures* as poor history, they were forced to copy from it since it was for one hundred years the only well-known source of information about Boone's career. Biographers continued to depict the woodsman as a profound and articulate philosopher. They described his successive removals westward as the expression of a passion for the picturesque wilderness and a desire for "elbow room," rather than as a penalty for incompetence in legal and business affairs. They made epic claims for their hero by comparing him with Adam, Columbus, Balboa, and even Luther.[4] They described him as the discoverer and founder of Kentucky, although hundreds of

---

[3] Lyman C. Draper MS, Wisconsin State Historical Society, Madison: "Nothing embitters my old age but the circulation of the absurd and ridiculous stories that I retire as civilization advances; that I shun the white man and seek the Indians. . . . You know all this false. Poverty and enterprise excited me to quit my native state, and poverty and despair my native land."

[4] For these allusions see Humphrey Marshall, *History of Kentucky,* I, 20; William Gilmore Simms, "Daniel Boon, the First Hunter of Kentucky," *Views and Reviews in American Literature, History, and Fiction,* 125; Emerson Hough, *The Way to the West,* 88.

white men had actually preceded him there.[5] To match the exploits attributed to him, many writers described Boone as a physical giant. While the Boone of history was five feet, eight inches tall and weighed 175 pounds,[6] the Boone of legend became a "tall man of powerful frame."

Daniel Boone also became the hero of exciting tall tales in which he fights Indians and wild animals, makes breath-taking escapes, and performs incredible exploits of marksmanship or woodsmanship. He fights a huge bear using only a knife. He encounters two Indians and manages to kill both of them with one bullet. He escapes the savages by swinging from grapevines to confuse his trail, or by jumping off a sixty-foot cliff. In one story Boone is trapped in his tobacco shed by four Indians. As they taunt him and gloat over their success, he gathers an armful of dry tobacco leaves and hurls it in their faces, blinding them with the dust. They choke and curse while Boone races gleefully to the safety of his cabin. This tale was repeated in many books, despite the fact that the real Boone had never even raised tobacco.[7]

Many of these tales are clearly generic or traditional rather than historical. The story of Boone's sixty-foot leap off a cliff was denounced by Boone's son and other relatives. Equally important, the sixty-foot leap was a traditional tale in the Ohio River country, being attached to numerous individuals.[8] The story was simply assigned to Boone to symbolize his ability to outwit pursuers. In this manner many of the heroic deeds of Harrod, McAfee, and other Kentucky pioneers were attributed to the better-publicized Boone.

Boone also became a stock figure in fiction. In poems and novels such as Lord Byron's "Don Juan" (1823), James Kirke Paulding's

---

[5] Clarence Alvord, "The Daniel Boone Myth," *Journal of the Illinois State Historical Society,* Vol. XIX (April, 1926), 16–29.

[6] Lyman C. Draper MS.

[7] *Ibid.*

[8] Morgan Neville in his 1828 story, "The Last of the Boatmen," reported the same episode for a man named Huling. See Walter Blair, *Half Horse, Half Alligator,* 55. The same tale appeared as "Ulin's Leap" in the New York *Mercury,* March 28, 1832 (clipping in Lyman C. Draper MS).

Westward Ho! (1832), and Robert Montgomery Bird's *Nick of the Woods* (1837), he symbolizes the solitary adventurer fleeing from civilization and its corruptions. Later, in paperback stories and lurid dime novels, he personifies the bloodthirsty Indian fighter. Surrounded by piles of dead savages, he occasionally philosophizes about his role, as he does in this passage from an 1853 novel: "Why, thar's more real satisfaction in sarcumventing and scalping one o' them red heathen, than in all the amusement you could scare up in a thick-peopled, peaceable settlement in a life time."[9]

The most famous literary adaption of the Boone legend was to be found in James Fenimore Cooper's Leatherstocking tales. Reviewers of the first novel in the series, *The Pioneers* (1823), noted that Leatherstocking had been "modelled from the effigies of old Daniel Boone."[10] Both heroes wore buckskins, preferred the solitude of the wilderness, performed incredible feats of woodsmanship, and regarded their exploits with becoming modesty. In fact, the two characters became so completely identified in the public mind that they formed a composite stereotype. Even historians on occasion were unable to separate them. In attempting a factual description of one of Boone's extended periods in the wilderness, the historian Cecil B. Hartley said: "A reader of Mr. Cooper's *Last of the Mohicans* may comprehend, in some measure, the arts by which he was preserved."[11] When the reader is referred to a novel for historical information, fiction becomes history.

In the Boone legend there were thus assembled most of the ingredients for a great heroic tradition. There was the actual frontiersman, strong and fearless, who had in fact led American settlers westward. There were laudatory biographies in which the hero was given elegant speeches, noble sentiments, and epic

[9] Emerson Bennett, *Ella Barnwell: A Historical Romance of Border Life* (Cincinnati, U. P. James, 1853), 10.

[10] Quoted in Henry Nash Smith, *Virgin Land,* 268. On pages 59 and 60, Smith discusses the similarities between Boone and Leatherstocking.

[11] *Life and Times of Colonel Daniel Boone* (Philadelphia, G. G. Evans, 1860), 62.

achievements. There was a characteristic body of tall tales and blood-and-thunder stories in which the hero overcomes or outwits Indians, animals, and other perils of the frontier. There were novels, poems, and stories in which early experiments with literary representation of the frontiersman had been made. In short, a master-model had been created which subsequent writers eyed while sculpturing their own heroic figures.

Boone was joined in the late 1820's by Mike Fink and Davy Crockett, rip-roaring braggart heroes and jokesters both. Renowned for their exploits in drinking, gouging, and boasting, as well as the more conventional skills of shooting and Indian fighting, they were obviously in a different tradition from that of Daniel Boone and his successors. But although their legends had died out by 1860, they too made significant contributions to the composite portrait of the Western hero. Crockett in particular, during the height of his fame in the 1830's, came to rival Boone as the type-figure of the Old Southwest. Crockett's *Autobiography,* originally published in 1834, was a rich source of stories for later writers. Defeated for re-election to Congress from Tennessee, Crockett migrated to Texas in 1835. There his heroic death at the Alamo turned him into the prototype for another important Western character, the Texan.[12]

But Boone's natural heirs, in literature and legend as well as in history, were the mountain men of the Far West. Even while Boone was living out his declining years in Missouri, John Colter was tramping alone through the wilderness of the Yellowstone and Big Horn. Jedediah Smith in 1826 discovered a central route from the Rockies to the Pacific and became the first American to enter California from overland. In the Southwest, Ewing Young and the Patties, father and son, also blazed trails to the coast through deserts and mountains that were swarming with hostile Indians.

These mountain trappers were indeed fit subjects for romantic legend. As Washington Irving described them, they were "hardy, lithe, vigorous, and active; extravagant in word, in thought, and

[12] Joseph Leach, *The Typical Texan,* 37–38.

deed; heedless of hardship; daring of danger; prodigal of the present, and thoughtless of the future."[13] In dress and manners they copied the Indians whom they so often fought. They took scalps, had squaws, and wore the Indians' blankets and moccasins. Carrying the heavy steel traps on their shoulders, they scoured the Great West for beaver, and in so doing discovered the trails over which later and more celebrated "explorers" were to pass.

The earliest mountain-man narratives were edited by literary men. This was in fact the classic pattern in Western literature. The frontiersmen themselves either neglected to keep records of their exciting adventures or lacked the skill to dramatize the exploits which they had recorded. Consequently, their stories were told by professional writers from the East. And in the process, certain literary operations were performed upon the bodies of the original narratives.

Timothy Flint and Washington Irving were two of the earliest writers to sense the literary potentialities in the exploits of these Far Western heroes. Flint's *Shoshonee Valley* (1830) was the first novel about the mountain men. He also edited the first widely known account of a trapper-hero's adventures, James Ohio Pattie's *Personal Narrative* (1831). This semihistorical chronicle included enough tales of Indian fighting to satiate even the most bloodthirsty. Pattie's rescue of a beautiful Spanish maiden from the Indians bears comparison with John Smith's tales of Pocahontas. His escapades in and out of the prisons of Mexican California resemble the plot of a Hollywood adventure film. It is hard to tell at this distance just how much ornamentation Flint added to Pattie's basic story. In his preface, Flint denies that he had tampered with the facts, but this was simply a convention with him. The preface to his biography of Daniel Boone contains a similar claim, yet that book added more legends to Boone's name than any other narrative written about him.

Washington Irving's *Adventures of Captain Bonneville* was

[13] *The Adventures of Captain Bonneville.* 2d ed. rev. (New York, G. P. Putnam, 1850), 26–27.

originally published in 1837 under the more appropriate title of *The Rocky Mountains; or Scenes, Incidents, and Adventures in the Far West.* The book was a skillful reworking of the journals of an army officer who had heard from trappers so many "tales of wild scenes and wild adventures" that he had taken a leave of absence and gone into the Far West himself. Many of the famous names of the mountain fur trade, including those of Thomas Fitzpatrick and Jim Bridger, were here made known to Eastern readers for the first time. Irving's gift for characterization made the mountain trappers a memorable class.

It is significant that the name of Kit Carson is missing from the Bonneville account. In the 1830's no single individual had come to symbolize the trans-Missouri West the way Daniel Boone had typified the trans-Appalachian frontier. The representative figure might well have come from the men in Irving's book, but in fact he emerged from the narratives of John Charles Frémont a few years later. Kit Carson, though actually a minor actor in the fur trade of the 1830's, soon became the type-figure for that first great character of the Far West—the mountain man.

PART ONE

The Mountain Man:
Kit Carson

CHAPTER II

The Real Christopher Carson

THE ACTUAL KIT CARSON was not a likely candidate for heroic legend. He was short, plain featured, and walked with his toes turned in. Hero-worshipers who met him were skeptical. They could not believe that the small man before them was the hero of a hundred desperate encounters with Indians and wild animals.[1] Yet Carson became the best-known character among the whole brawny breed of mountain men.

Carson was born in Kentucky in 1809, but his family moved to the rugged Boone's Lick district of Missouri in 1811. Kit's early years follow the classic pattern for the frontier hero: much outdoor life and little formal schooling. He never learned to read or write, despite later narratives which have him doing both. After the accidental death of his father, Kit at age fifteen was apprenticed to a saddler, David Workman, of Franklin, Missouri. But mending leather had little appeal for a restless teen-ager of Kit's temperament. One is not surprised to find in the Fayette *Missouri Intelligencer* of October 12, 1826, an advertisement for the runaway apprentice, Christopher Carson.

Kit went to Santa Fe, then in Mexican territory, by joining a

---

[1] General William Tecumseh Sherman said of his meeting Carson in 1849: "I cannot express my surprise at beholding a small, stoop-shouldered man, with reddish hair, freckled face, soft blue eyes, and nothing to indicate extraordinary courage or daring."—*Memoirs,* I, 46–47. For another disappointed interviewer, see Edward S. Ellis, *The Life and Times of Christopher Carson, the Rocky Mountain Scout and Guide,* 82–83. In an interview, Jessie Benton Frémont described Carson as "perfectly Saxon, clear and fair . . . . He was very short, and unmistakably bandy-legged; long-bodied and short-limbed, a man of great strength and vitality."—*Land of Sunshine,* Vol. VI, (February, 1897), 98.

trading caravan in the lowly position of stock-tender. He was not the expedition's scout or hunter. Nor is it likely that he performed a celebrated amputation of the arm of one Broadus, a teamster who had accidentally set off a shotgun. Kit in his autobiography says merely that "one of the party" performed the operation,[2] and Kit probably held the hapless victim down.

Carson spent the winter of 1826–27 in Taos with an old mountaineer named Kincade. From him, Kit began learning the patois of the frontier. This was a hybrid of Spanish, Canadian-French, and Indian, mixed with ungrammatical English and seasoned with sign language. Kincade probably also gave him some rudimentary knowledge of the wilderness trading routes and fur trappers' trails.

But even a knowledge of mountain-man lingo and practical geography seemed to be of negligible value in the New Mexico country. So Kit, at this time a slender blond youth, had to drift from one menial job to another during the next two years. He worked as a cook for the fur trapper Ewing Young, as an interpreter for Colonel Tramell, and finally as a teamster for Bob Mc-Knight at the Santa Rita copper mines. Then his luck changed in August, 1829, when Ewing Young signed him up to go on a trapping expedition to California.

On this maiden trip as a mountain man and trapper, Carson proved his ability at tracking and killing Indians as well as wild game. Near San Rafael in California he pursued a party of recalcitrant "mission Indians," and after killing a large part of them, forced the survivors to return to the mission.[3] On the trip back to Taos, the trappers at one point split up, and Kit was left alone in camp with just a few men. Five hundred warriors rode up, but Kit says he bluffed them out of attacking the camp.[4] These are tremendous odds, and Kit may have been contributing a bit to his own legend here. It is perhaps fair to say that he was at this point

[2] Kit Carson MS "Autobiography," Newberry Library, Chicago, 1.
[3] *Ibid.*, 4.
[4] *Ibid.*, 5.

less adept at accurately estimating numbers of Indians than he was later.

When Carson and his companions got back to Taos in April, 1831, they "passed the time gloriously." It was normal procedure for the mountain men to spend their money in drinking and carousing at the end of a trip. Now a proved trapper, Kit was signed up for an expedition under Thomas "Broken Hand" Fitzpatrick of the Rocky Mountain Fur Company in the fall of 1831.

Carson's activities during the 1830's are somewhat obscure. The trappers moved from place to place, and fighting Indians or running trap lines gave them little time to keep records, even when they were inclined to do so. It it indeed remarkable that Carson and other mountain men were able to remember as much about their activities as they did. Then, too, just a few of them, such as Jed Smith and Old Bill Williams, could write. Only after explorers with classical or scientific educations had followed them into the West were their activities and discoveries made known to the world.

From the patchwork of available sources, it is clear that Carson spent most of these years in the Rockies as both a company and an independent trapper. His autobiography relates trapping expeditions with Fitzpatrick along the Laramie, Green, and Snake rivers. From 1834 he had his own group known as the "Carson Men." But he was not a historically important figure in the fur trade. Chittenden in his authoritative study reports: "It is a singular fact that so noted a character as Kit Carson should be so entirely unknown in the annals of the fur trade as he actually was. His name occurs only once in the correspondence or newspaper literature prior to 1843 so far as it has fallen under our observation."[5] The absence of his name from Washington Irving's books and other contemporary narratives is strong evidence in support of Chittenden's conclusion.

However, Carson did perform authenticated feats which found their way into history. He had sensational encounters with Indians,

[5] *The American Fur Trade of the Far West,* II, 539.

although these heroics were sometimes accidental. One day in the spring of 1833, explains Kit in his autobiography, "I saw in the distance, four Indians. I proposed to charge them. All were willing. We started for them, but, when near we found we had caught a tartar. There were upward of sixty Indians. They had us surrounded and our only chance to save our lives was a good run. We done so, the Indians firing on us from all directions."

But Kit was undeniably an eager warrior. He generally chose to fight the Indians rather than avoid them. One running fight with Blackfeet on the North Fork of the Missouri in 1837 he called "the prettiest fight I ever saw." This enthusiasm was maintained even though Kit had taken a Blackfoot bullet through his shoulder in February, 1835.[6]

In these years Carson also encountered other standard hazards of the frontier: wild animals and wild white men. In the spring of 1834, he was treed by two enraged grizzly bears,[7] an episode which he called his "worst difficult." At the trappers' summer rendezvous of 1835 in Wyoming, Carson in a hand-to-hand fight killed the French-Canadian bully Shunan. Shunan had ridden through the camp threatening to "take a switch to the Americans," and Carson had challenged him. He told the bully that "if he made use of any more such expressions, I would rip his guts"[8]—and we can be sure that his actual words were even stronger than this.

The Shunan episode may have involved the Arapaho girl Waa-Nibe ("Singing Grass") whom Carson in true mountain man style took as his wife shortly thereafter. Waa-Nibe died of "mountain fever" within three years, but not before giving Kit a daughter whose Christian name was Adaline. About 1840, Carson took a second wife, the Cheyenne woman "Making-Out-Road." But because of her violent temper, this union did not last. These Indian marriages were carefully ignored both by Carson in his dictated

[6] MS "Autobiography," 11–12.

[7] *Ibid.*, 10–11.

[8] *Ibid.*, 12; and Rev. Samuel Parker, *Journal of an Exploring Tour Beyond the Rocky Mountains,* 72.

autobiography and by most biographers in the nineteenth century.[9]

In 1838 the trapping brigades began to break up. Kit went down to Bent's Fort on the Arkansas River and became the post hunter. At this time he was not well known outside the trans-Missouri region. He was a competent leader of trapping expeditions, had proved himself in a requisite number of Indian fights, and had a fair local reputation as a hunter and trail guide. But there were many other mountaineers who were just as competent. Something else was needed to make him into the national hero that he became.

In April, 1842, Carson went to St. Louis to put his daughter in school. During a steamer ride on the Missouri he met John Charles Frémont, then a lieutenant in the Army Topographical Corps.[10] Kit says that the meeting was "luck," but it is highly probable that he got word that Frémont would be aboard the steamer and arranged the meeting. Frémont hired Carson as a guide, and Kit's service on the first two of Frémont's four expeditions into the Great West led to his becoming well known in the public prints. The meeting with Frémont was thus the magic elixir which changed Carson from a strictly local "character" into a national demigod.

Frémont's first expedition left Chouteau's Landing (western Missouri) on June 4, 1842, went as far as the South Pass in Wyoming, and returned on October 4.[11] Kit then took time off to go to Taos, where in February, 1843, he married María Josefa Jaramillo, sixteen-year-old daughter of a prominent Mexican family. Kit had to become a Roman Catholic to complete the marriage,

[9] The authenticity of these marriages has been questioned by filiopietistic writers. M. Morgan Estergreen says: "This could have been another piece of fiction made up by some ambitious writer, and carried on by the Indians themselves."—*The Real Kit Carson* (1955), iv. However, the marriages are substantiated in Cheyenne annals as recorded by George Bird Grinnell, a reliable informant. See his "Bent's Old Fort and Its Builders," *Kansas Historical Collections,* Vol. XV (1923), 37. Edwin L. Sabin also mentions letters from Carson descendants which refer to the brief existence of a child from the marriage to Making-Out-Road.—*Kit Carson Days,* II, 936.

[10] John Charles Frémont, *Memoirs of My Life,* 74.

[11] John Charles Frémont, *The Exploring Expedition to the Rocky Mountains in the Year 1842, and to Oregon and North California in the Years 1843–44,* 10, 174.

and he did so from convenience rather than conviction.[12] During 1843–44, he served as a hunter and guide with Frémont's second expedition, which went to California and back.

Carson became a national hero by means of Frémont's published *Report* on these first two trips. The reading public of the 1840's had become intensely interested in Western exploration, and the *Report* fed this hunger for information. It encouraged settlers by advertising the practicality of the Oregon Trail and the desirability of lands in California and the intermountain West. Brigham Young, for example, was one of those who acted on the basis of the book.[13] The report also fixed Carson in the national mind as a romantic and appealing character. Frémont's flair for dramatic writing publicized Carson in a factual report which still reads like an adventure story.

In the first expedition, Carson has a glorious role. "Mounted on a fine horse, without a saddle, and scouring bareheaded over the prairies, Kit was one of the finest pictures of a horseman I have ever seen." His hunting exploits are also admiringly recorded. In the second expedition, Frémont refers to him as "my true and reliable friend." He saves Frémont from an icy stream. He inspires and successfully guides the party in crossing the snowbound Sierras into California. Most important, he is featured in one of the most dramatic episodes in Western history. Carson and his fellow scout Alex Godey trail a band of thirty Indians who had murdered some Mexicans and stolen their horses. The two scouts attack the savages and recover the horses. Their return was described by Frémont in one of the classic passages in the literature of the West:

> In the afternoon a war-whoop was heard, such as Indians make when returning from a victorious enterprise; and soon Carson and Godey appeared, driving before them a band of horses, recognized by Fuentes

[12] Father Claudius Antony, "Kit Carson, Catholic," *New Mexico Historical Review,* Vol. X (October, 1935), 322–27. Carson later renounced Roman Catholicism to become a Mason.

[13] Sabin, *Kit Carson Days,* I, 374.

as part of those they had lost. Two bloody scalps, dangling from the end of Godey's gun, announced that they had overtaken the Indians as well as the horses. . . . The time, place, object, and numbers considered, this expedition of Carson and Godey may be considered among the boldest and most disinterested which the annals of western adventure, so full of daring deeds, can present. Two men, in a savage desert, pursue day and night an unknown body of Indians into the defiles of an unknown mountain—attack them on sight, without counting numbers—and defeat them in an instant—and for what? To punish the robbers of the desert, and to avenge the wrongs of Mexicans whom they did not know. I repeat: it was Carson and Godey who did this— the former an American, born in Boonslick County in Missouri; the latter a Frenchman, born in St. Louis—and both trained in western enterprise from early life.[14]

This exciting picture appealed to the public's imagination. Carson as a Western "character" became popular as a type-figure of the frontiersman in both fiction and nonfiction. Lewis Garrard, meeting Carson in April of 1847, said: "While at supper, a party of men rode up, the foremost of whom shook hands with Hatcher. It was the renowned Kit Carson, so celebrated as the companion and guide of Colonel Frémont."[15] William Tecumseh Sherman said of his meeting Carson in 1849: "His fame was then at its height, from the publication of Frémont's books, and I was very anxious to see the man who had achieved such feats of daring among the wild animals of the Rocky Mountains and the still wilder Indians of the Plains."[16]

While his fame was thus a-building in the East, Carson after a brief rest at his home in Taos, joined Frémont at Bent's Fort in August, 1845, for the third "exploring" expedition. Political motives and the looming struggle between Mexico and the United States for California dominated this trip. Frémont took sixty well-armed mountaineers and a canon with him; the party looked sus-

---

[14] Frémont, *Exploring Expedition,* 262–63.
[15] Lewis Garrard, *Wah-to-yah and the Taos Trail,* 238.
[16] Sherman, *Memoirs,* I, 46–47.

piciously like a filibustering expedition. When the group reached Sutter's Fort on December 9, the nervous Mexican authorities asked Frémont to leave California.

He did cross over the border into Oregon, where he had several scraps with the Klamath Indians. One of these was a surprise night attack in which two of Frémont's scouts were tomahawked. A Klamath chief was killed, and "hung to his wrist was an English half-axe. Carson seized this and knocked his head to pieces with it, and one of the Delawares, Sagundai, scalped him."[17] Frémont did not stay in Oregon very long. On secret orders from Washington, he moved back into California and began aggressive actions. In concert with the "Bear Flaggers," he seized Sonoma in June, 1846. That same month, Carson, acting under Frémont's orders, killed three unarmed Mexican prisoners at San Rafael. Although Carson does not mention this incident in his autobiography, it is reported by William Boggs, a respected pioneer in California and a reliable authority: "They held a short consultation and decided to kill the prisoners, and shot them dead. This I had from both Swift and Kit Carson himself, and I was inclined as well as many others who arrived a short time after this ocurrence to blame Kit Carson for what I thought to be a cold-hearted crime, having the men in their power."[18]

On September 5, 1846, Carson left for Washington as the bearer of dispatches announcing Frémont's bloodless conquest of California. He was stopped in New Mexico, however, by a west-bound army column under General Stephen Kearny and ordered to accompany this column to California. Thus he participated in the Battle of San Pascual, December 6, 1846, when the Americans were surrounded by Mexican troops. Carson, Lieutenant Edward Beale, and an Indian servant slipped through the enemy cordon

[17] Frémont, *Memoirs,* 492.

[18] "William Boggs Manuscript about Bent's Fort, Kit Carson, the Far West and Life Among the Indians," ed. by Leroy Hafen, *Colorado Magazine,* Vol. VII (March, 1930), 62.

and walked the thirty miles to San Diego barefoot to bring relief.[19]

In March, 1847, Carson again left for Washington as the bearer of dispatches to the War Department. In the capital he met President Polk and was commissioned a second lieutenant in the Mounted Riflemen. He was by now well known, and a newspaper interviewer found him to be "modest as he is brave, with the fire of enterprise in his eyes—with the bearing of an Indian, walking even with his toes turned in." Embarrassed by all this attention, Kit hurried west again and was back in California by December.[20]

Early in 1848, he again traveled east with government mail. He was accompanied by young Lieutenant George Brewerton, who wrote a magazine article on the trip which added to Carson's repute.[21] Brewerton's readers were enthralled by his descriptions of the scenery, the habits of the Mexican muleteers, the dress of the Indians, Carson's precautionary preparations for the night, and his tactics in dealing with a large war party. The magazines were also beginning to feature Carson as the hero of fictional adventure stories.[22]

While the fictional Carson was performing his improbable exploits in magazine stories and paperback novels, Kit Carson himself was making an unsuccessful attempt to rescue a white woman from the Apaches. Carson had declined to accompany Frémont's

[19] Carson's role in this episode has been deflated. According to the testimony of Commodore Stockton, who was in command at San Diego, it was the arrival of an earlier messenger from Kearny's command, one Lieutenant Godey, which set the relief column in motion. The appearance of Beale and the Indian speeded up the rescue operation, which had already been organized, and Carson arrived after the column had started. See Thomas Kearny, "Kearny and Kit Carson as interpreted by Stanley Vestal," *New Mexico Historical Review,* Vol. V (January, 1930), 1–16.

[20] San Francisco *Californian,* December 1, 1847.

[21] "A Ride with Kit Carson," *Harper's Magazine,* Vol. VIII (August, 1853), 307–45. Carson carried among his dispatches a California newspaper with an account of the gold discoveries. Whether or not this was the first news published in the New York papers about the strike is a matter of debate. See Leroy R. and Ann Hafen, *The Old Spanish Trail* (Glendale, Arthur H. Clark, 1954), 338–39.

[22] For example, "An Adventure of Kit Carson: A Tale of the Sacramento," *Holden's Dollar Magazine,* Vol. I, No. IV (April, 1848), 209–17.

ill-fated fourth expedition in 1848. Instead he established a cattle ranch at Rayado, about fifty miles east of Taos, in the spring of 1849. In November of that year, Kit rode out from the ranch with a party of Dragoons to rescue the Apache's captive, Mrs. J. M. White. When the soldiers came upon the Indian camp, Carson's companion guide Leroux counseled a parley, and because of this delay the Apaches killed Mrs. White and escaped. In their camp, Kit found a paperback novel, probably Charles Averill's *Kit Carson, Prince of Goldhunters,* depicting his theatrical rescue of a maiden from the Indians.[23]

However, Carson soon did get a chance to justify his adventure-story reputation. After spending the summer of 1850 uneventfully at Taos, in the fall of that year he helped arrest a bandit named Fox. Fox had joined the Elias Brevoort caravan with the intention of robbing it. Kit learned of the plot through an informer and with a party of soldiers intercepted the caravan and arrested the renegade.[24] Here was an accidental correspondence of authenticated adventure and legend.

From 1854 to 1861, Carson was a United States Indian agent. He has been regarded as one of the country's best.[25] Although as an army officer he was relentless in pursuing the Indians, he also understood their problems. This is evident from General Rusling's interview with him in 1867: "He declared that all our Indian troubles were caused originally by bad white men. . . . He pleaded for the Indians as 'pore ignorant creatures,' whom we were daily dispoiling of their hunting grounds and homes."[26]

In 1861 he resigned as agent to serve in the Union Army, being commissioned a colonel in the First New Mexico Volunteer Infantry Regiment. His principal job during the war was fighting Indians. In 1864 he drove the Navahos out of their "impregnable" stronghold at the Canyon de Chelly in Arizona. The same year, he

[23] MS "Autobiography," 37.

[24] Elias Brevoort MS, Bancroft Library, Berkeley, Calif.

[25] Marshall D. Moody, "Kit Carson, Agent to the Indians in New Mexico," *New Mexico Historical Review,* Vol. XXVIII (January, 1953), 20–31.

[26] James F. Rusling, *Across America,* 136.

managed to extricate his command from possible defeat by a large force of Indians at Adobe Walls, an abandoned trading post on the Canadian River in Texas. From 1865 until 1867, he was on plains and mountain service with the army, his principal command being Fort Garland in the Colorado Territory. He died of a hemorrhage on May 23, 1868, at Fort Lyons, Colorado.[27]

Kit Carson at his death was a hero not only to armchair frontiersmen back East, but also to thousands of dirty-faced youngsters west of the Mississippi. William F. "Buffalo Bill" Cody named his son Kit Carson Cody[28] and featured Kit in his (ghostwritten) *Story of the Wild West . . . A Full and Complete History of the Renowned Pioneer Quarette, Boone, Crockett, Carson and Buffalo Bill* (1888). Carson was also the boyhood idol of James Butler "Wild Bill" Hickok. There is a story that the two became friends and Kit introduced young Hickok to Santa Fe night life.[29] Carson's life and legend thus helped to form the next, and last, generation of frontiersmen.

[27] Sabin, *Kit Carson Days,* II, 803.

[28] W. F. Cody, *The Life of Hon. William F. Cody, Known as Buffalo Bill . . . An Autobiography,* 275.

[29] Richard O'Connor, *Wild Bill Hickok,* 53–55.

CHAPTER III

The Genteel Type

IF CARSON WAS TO BE THE HERO of a Victorian age, certain alterations in language, behavior, philosophy, and appearance were obviously necessary to convert the raw mountaineer into a figure attractive to genteel readers. The Indian wives, the coarse challenge to Shunan, the dangling scalps, would all have to be reported with circumspection rather than with accuracy. This purification was indeed accomplished by editing and interpretation of the facts. The operation is evident in the work of all of Carson's biographers, although the technique had been introduced even before the first biography was published.

Frémont was an accurate reporter, but he did some editing when he wrote about Carson. He was careful to omit incidents which might mar the idealized portrait of himself or his guide. Charles Preuss, Frémont's topographer, recorded arguments between the two men which naturally were not published in Frémont's *Report*.[1] Nor does Frémont allow Kit to speak in his natural mountain-man dialect, with its "thar" and "git." Kit speaks primly when he spots an important landmark in the Sierras: "There is the little mountain—it is 15 years ago since I saw it; but I am just as sure as if I had seen it yesterday."[2]

Carson's role as a type-figure for the whole class of frontiersmen also required that he be purified. The *Rough and Ready Annual* for 1848 included a sketch of him in its narratives of the Mexican War, and their reason for doing so is significant: "One of the most

---

[1] *Exploring with Frémont*, 40.
[2] *Exploring Expedition*, 232.

remarkable characters in Frémont's expedition is 'Kit Carson,' lately made a lieutenant by the President. The following description of him, though rather long, we insert, because it not only gives a very satisfactory view of the expedition itself, but may be considered a type of each of the hardy adventurers who conducted it."[3] And the *Annual,* in a typical development for a heroic legend, gave Kit all the virtues of his class and none of the vices. "In the school of men thus formed by hardship, exposure, peril, and temptation, our hero acquired all their virtues and escaped their vices." The authors seemed to overlook a logical inconsistency: if he lacked attributes of his class, how could he typify it?

Novelists who featured Carson in their adventure tales also had to bridge the gap between reality and the demands of polite literature. They knew that their readers could not quite accept the authentic Carson with his lack of refinement. Charles Averill resolved the problem quite neatly in his paperback novel, *Kit Carson, Prince of the Goldhunters* (1849). The narrator surmises that when Kit lapses into crude dialect, it is only a disguise:

> I have heard that of his character, which leads me to believe that the rough manner, the uncultivated speech, apparently peculiar to him, are in a degree assumed; that he in his youth received the benefits of a good education and good society, but that he ever loved the wild delights of a hunter's life, and with its freedoms and pleasures, determined to adopt its plain habits and plainer mode of speech.[4]

This was a popular revision, because a play, *Kit Carson* (1850), was adapted from Averill's novel.[5] In the play, Carson again hides his refinement under a pretense of ignorant dialect.

Thus even before a formal biography was published, writers had adopted various techniques for improving Carson's manners and erasing any suggestion of vice. Carson himself apparently conceived the idea of an autobiography when George Brewerton's

---

3 Page 153.
4 Page 82.
5 Blanche Davis, *The Hero in American Drama, 1787–1900,* 39.

article appeared in *Harper's Magazine* in 1853. After several desultory attempts with various collaborators, a biography was finally dictated to and written by DeWitt C. Peters.[6] It was published in 1858, although the dictated manuscript itself was not put into print until 1926. The dictation, says Edwin L. Sabin, "is as skinny as a hairless Chihuahua dog and as bald of details as a white egg. It is more a rapid diary than a romance of adventure."[7] Peters, or his collaborator, had the job of expanding this "diary" to exploit its values as a narrative.

Published under the title *The Life and Adventures of Kit Carson, the Nestor of the Rocky Mountains,*[8] the biography is edited with an eye for Victorian sensibilities. Carson is depicted as one of those true and noble characters which the frontier was thought to produce. Any facts which might mar the perfection of this image have either been removed or carefully edited. Carson's Indian wife Waa-Nibe is acknowledged in three short sentences, followed by a long and apologetic paragraph defending the propriety of such a marriage. Peters points out that Carson's "moral character may well be held up as an example to men whose pretensions to virtuous life are greater." Peters was uneasy about Carson's Indian wives, and apparently Kit was, too. As Mrs. Frémont said years later in recalling his visit to the Frémont home in St. Louis: "He had been afraid the ladies might not care to have him there if they knew he had married a Sioux wife."[9]

Actually, such a wife was an asset to a mountaineer, since she knew how to set up lodges, tan buffalo hides, and do all the other hard and unpleasant work required in primitive circumstances. But reality had to bow to moral conventions. In addition, Carson's role as a symbol of Anglo-Saxon racial superiority required that

[6] Milo M. Quaife believes that Jesse B. Turly took the dictation and that another writer collaborated with Peters on the published biography.—*Kit Carson's Autobiography,* ed. by Milo M. Quaife (Chicago, The Lakeside Press, 1935), xxviii.

[7] *Kit Carson Days,* II, 780.

[8] Nestor was a mythical king noted for his wisdom.

[9] *Land of Sunshine,* Vol. VI (February, 1897), 98.

his close relationships with the Indians be ignored. Any suggestion that he was on intimate terms with redskins was incompatible with the picture of the fearless Indian fighter, cleaning out Mexicans and Indians to clear a path for American civilization.

Peters inserts many eulogistic passages. One of these occurs in the description of Carson's return to Taos in 1831 from his trapping expedition with Ewing Young. Carson says that he "passed the time gloriously," and the statement leaves little doubt that he went on a terrific spree. Peters handles the incident in a moralizing manner, which makes one suspect that although Carson told him the truth, he felt obliged to "doctor" it:

> Young Kit, at this period of his life, imitated the example set by his elders, for he wished to be considered by them as an equal and a friend. He, however, passed through this terrible ordeal, which most frequently ruins its votary, and eventually came out brighter, clearer and more noble for the conscience-polish which he received. He contracted no bad habits, but learned the usefulness and happiness of resisting temptation, and became so well schooled that he was able, by the caution and advice of wisdom, founded on experience, to prevent many a promising and skillful hand from grasping ruin in the same vortex.[10]

This treatment of the episode became standard in biographies thereafter.[11]

Carson's speech is that of any literate gentleman in a New York drawing room. In the Shunan episode, Kit's actual words to the "big bully of the mountains" were that he would "rip his guts." But Peters has him saying:

[10] Pages 49–50.

[11] As late as 1889, Edward S. Ellis wrote of this incident: "Like so many sailors just ashore from a long voyage, most of the trappers went on a prolonged carousal, which caused their money to melt like snow in the sun. When their pockets were empty, they had aching heads, weak frames, and only the memory of their feverish pleasures. Kit Carson did not go through this trial unscathed. He drank and spreed with the rest, but he awoke to the folly and madness of his course sooner than they and the sad lesson learned at that time, lasted him through life."—*The Life of Kit Carson*, 26.

27

> Shunan, before you stands the humblest specimen of an American in this band of trappers, among whom, there are, to my certain knowledge, men who could easily chastise you; but being peaceably disposed, they keep aloof from you. At any rate, I assume the responsibility of ordering you to cease your threats, or I will be under the necessity of killing you.[12]

This editing also was repeated in biographies, dime novels, and anthologies.[13] It is a typical example of how literary and moral conventions were applied in all mountain-man biographies. Jim Beckwourth, for example, is given a similarly elegant speech in a crisis situation: "General . . . you have addressed language to me which I allow no man to use, and unless you retract that last epithet, you or I must surely die."[14] The coarseness of the mountain man's lingo, with its "hoss," "wuth it," and "wagh," which is accurately rendered in firsthand narratives like those by Lewis Garrard and George Frederick Ruxton,[15] is missing in the popular biographies. The language is always purified, and the barbarisms are replaced by refined expressions. From a technical literary viewpoint, it is difficult for an author to write a biography or a novel using dialect only. But the end result of this purification of language is an inaccurate record of actual frontier life.

Kit's exploits match his grandiose rhetoric. He "penetrated every part of the North American continent, wandered over a wild territory equal in its dimensions to nearly all the empires, kingdoms, and principalities of Europe combined." Here Peters is ascribing to Kit the accomplishments of the whole class of men

---

[12] Page 99.

[13] Lieutenant J. H. Randolph [Edward S. Ellis], *Carson the Guide; or, Perils of the Frontier* (1872), 49; J. W. Buel, *Heroes of the Plains,* 477: "I am an American, and no coward, but you are a vapid bully, and to show you how Americans can punish liars, I'll fight you in any manner your infamous heart may desire." Also William F. Cody, *Story of the Wild West and Camp-Fire Chats,* 327, where the speech is the same as in Buel, except that "vaporing" replaces "vapid."

[14] James P. Beckwourth, *The Life and Adventures of James P. Beckwourth,* ed. by T. D. Bonner (New York, Harper and Brothers, 1856), 29.

[15] Other authentic recorders of frontier speech are listed in Levette Davidson, "Old Trapper Talk," *American Speech,* Vol. XIII (April, 1938), 83–92.

which he represents. As Daniel Boone had been, he is also shown to be an instrument of Providence: "We regard, and we think a world will eventually regard, this extraordinary man as one raised up by Providence to fulfill a destiny of His all-wise decree." Since each adventure has taken him into regions where no white man has ever set foot, Peters concludes that

> He was, therefore, now an explorer in every sense of that distinguishing word, with the single exception that he had not produced the results which the early culture and advantages of a scientific and classical education might have brought about. But the history of the world furnished few examples, if indeed any, where the physical training, practical skill and knowledge of a country, as possessed by Kit Carson, have been united with scholastic lore.[16]

Peters here sees something of the significance of Kit's career. Carson was in many respects an appropriate symbol of the practical, unlettered mountain men who pioneered the wilderness trails. But Peters' scrupulous regard for the conventions of his day caused him to try to fit Carson into the conventional mold for a "hero": pure, literate, and cultured. The result was that he created an abstraction rather than an authentic frontiersman.

Peters and other biographers of frontier heroes assumed that life on the frontier developed nobility of character. It was thought that the fresh air and the contact with untouched nature produced virtuous men—"Nature's Noblemen." As one of Frémont's biographers said in speaking of Carson:

> His name is so intimately identified with that of Frémont, that these pages owe a special tribute to his manly and noble virtues. . . . The business of trapping was then in its more flourishing state, and formed a class of men of marked and striking traits. . . . This mode of life, in its perfect freedom and manly excitements and achievements, was favorable in many respects to the development of noble energies and sentiments.[17]

[16] Page 144.

[17] Charles Wentworth Upham, *The Life of J. C. Frémont* (Boston, Ticknor and Fields, 1856), 184–86. This was a campaign biography of Frémont, and thus Upham

Actually, life on the frontier produced both good men and bad, but the impact of the theory was important. Facts which did not square with it were simply ignored. The result was that many frontier heroes in many nineteenth-century biographies acquired a greater degree of nobility than the facts justified.

Peters set a precedent for eulogistic biography that was soon followed by others. In 1860, Charles Burdett published *The Life and Adventures of Christopher Carson, the Celebrated Rocky Mountain Hunter, Trapper and Guide.* This praises Carson as the "modern Nimrod," the "Monarch of the Plains," and fashions him into the same kind of dandified character that Peters had made of him. Burdett was a novelist and hence practiced in giving his imagination free rein. He invented stories, based upon nothing more substantial than a preconceived idea of what a frontiersman should be like. In one of these, Carson on his first trip to California visits a Spanish hacienda near Los Angeles and meets a beautiful *señorita* there. Carson talks to the owner of the haciendas as follows:

> Carson's youth commanded him to listen, rather than to advance his own sentiments; but he expressed his pleasure at hearing his host compliment the Americans, and said in reply: "I have not been an extensive traveler, and I have chosen the life of a mountaineer, for a time certainly; but since I came to California, I am half inclined to decide to make this my home when I get tired of trapping. I like the hunt, and have found game exceedingly plenty here, but there is no buffalo, and I want that. Give me buffalo, and I would settle in California.[18]

Youthful readers of this passage could be expected to draw lessons for their own deportment, since Kit was willing to listen rather

---

had particular reason to purify those associated with the candidate. The opposition had attempted to use Carson in attacking Frémont. The New York *Daily News* during the campaign reported on its front page: "Kit Carson says that Frémont, when a half-mile from camp, was always lost." This was of course a fabrication. See *New Yorker* magazine, November 6, 1956, p. 131.

[18] Pages 70–71.

than speak. Such were the moralistic purposes for which Carson's career was exploited.

Throughout the narrative, Burdett jealously guards the nobility of his hero. He handles the episode of Carson's return to Taos in the same moralizing manner as Peters.[19] He complains about Frémont's report on the first exploring expedition, because Frémont hogs the stage and "shows Carson so little like the bold, brave hunter we have known him hitherto." This seems rather unfair, since Frémont brought Carson to the public eye. Yet in this biography Carson overshadows Frémont, an interesting reversal of roles which testifies to the biographer's zeal.

In 1873, John S. C. Abbott published *Christopher Carson, Known as Kit Carson,* which displays evidence of considerable poaching from both Peters and Burdett. But Abbott's Carson is even more sensitive, more noble, more moral than he had been for the first two biographers. "Kit Carson was an extraordinary character. His widespread fame was not the result of accident. . . . He was a man of pure mind, of high morality, and intensely devoted to the life-work which he had chosen." Although the real Carson swore on occasion,[20] an oath never passes this Carson's lips. His true greatness can be attributed to the Christian manner in which he lives. Abbott says:

> Indeed Kit Carson was never a jolly man. He had no taste for revelry. As in every man of deep reflection and true greatness, the pensive element predominated in his character. . . . We can not doubt that Mr. Carson was in heart thoroughly a religious man. It is the element of religion alone, which, in the midst of such temptations, could form a character of such remarkable purity.[21]

[19] "The Party disbanded with several hundred dollars apiece, which most of them expended as sailors do their earnings when they come into port. Of course Carson was hail fellow well met with them for a time. He had not hitherto taken the lesson that all have to learn, viz., that the ways of pleasure are deceitful paths; and to resist temptation needs a large amount of courage."—page 77.

[20] "Personally he was mild. . . . sometimes when greatly excited he would swear, but not generally; he was not a dissipated man."—Elias Brevoort MS.

[21] Page 70.

This characterization bears no relation to the Kit Carson of history. But it was a popular distortion nevertheless. Abbott's book was republished in 1901 and in 1915, and is today the only Carson biography in many public libraries.

The idealized Carson was popular during the rest of the century. Edward S. Ellis wrote a biography in 1889 in which he made what must rank as the greatest overstatement of all: "He possessed in marked degree those mental and moral qualities which would have made him prominent in whatever pursuit or profession he engaged." Ellis in his dime novels had depicted Carson as a savage Indian fighter. He adheres to that formula in his biography, and Carson charges the Indians "with compressed lips and flashing eyes." Yet in attempting at the same time to endow his hero with sensitivity and depth of emotion, Ellis is forced into incongruous characterization. He says of Carson's return visit to Missouri in 1842: "His experience was touching. His parents were dead, the old building would ever linger in his memory, had tumbled down and nearly everyone whom he met was a stranger. The cheeks of the hardy mountaineer were wet with tears, and with a sigh, he turned his face away forever."[22]

The series of Carson biographies form a pattern. A rigid, artificial preconception of what the man should have been determined how he was represented. In this respect, the Carson legend is typical of all the nineteenth-century mountain-man biographies. The portraits are drawn less from actual research than from conventional literary formulas. They reveal less about frontier life than they do about the literary techniques and moral ideas of the period in which they were written.

The legend also required that the hero be of impressive physical stature and appearance. Thus, when Frémont neglected to include a physical description of Carson, the contemporary imagination built a giant. Herman Melville in 1851 described Hercules as "that antique Crockett and Kit Carson." Lieutenant Brewerton, reporting on tales he heard from Californians in 1848, said: "The Kit Carson of my *imagination* was over six feet high—a sort of modern

[22] *Life of Kit Carson*, 107.

Hercules in his build—with an enormous beard, and a voice like a roused lion." Novelists like Charles Averill were also describing Kit as a man of "powerful proportions and Herculean stature." These tales account for the disappointment of those, like General Sherman, who met the actual Carson. A man five feet, six inches tall by 135 pounds did not seem quite appropriate to the legend.

Carson's biographers also stressed his affinity with epic heroes. Comparisons with Old World heroes are essential if the actual frontiersman is to achieve epic stature in his own right. So in nineteenth-century narratives, Kit is compared not only with Hercules but also with Nestor (Peters, 1858), Nimrod (Burdett, 1860), Saladin (Ellis, 1861), Robinson Crusoe (Abbott, 1873), and Bayard (Frémont, 1883). Writers in the twentieth century maintained the tradition by comparing him with Hannibal and Odysseus.[23]

Thus Carson became a paragon. Did any writers in the nineteenth century question his reputation? Lewis Garrard said that among the mountain men themselves there were others whose abilities at least equaled Carson's.[24] David Meriwether, territorial governor of New Mexico in the 1850's, charged Kit with cowardice. In August of 1855, said the Governor, Carson hid under a riverbank when a large band of Utes threatened to get out of control. Meriwether concluded: "Poor Kit, he was a good trapper, hunter, and guide, and, in the latter capacity, while employed by Colonel Frémont, he had acquired a reputation which had spoiled him, and one which in after life and in a higher position, he failed to sustain."[25] And the California historian, Hubert Howe Bancroft, was not sure about Kit's accomplishments:

[23] George Creel, "Incredible Kit Carson," *Collier's,* Vol. LXXVIII (August 21, 1926), 11; Stanley Vestal, *Kit Carson, the Happy Warrior of the Old West, 3.*

[24] "Without a desire to detract from Carson's well-earned fame, I can say, in genuine good feeling and full belief, that there were numbers of mountain-men as fearless and as expert as he, though to the reading world little known, whose prowess in scalptaking and beaver trapping is the theme of many campfires, and the highest admiration of younger mountaineers."—*Wah-to-yah and the Taos Trail,* 278.

[25] An excerpt from Meriwether's memoirs, published in 1886, reprinted in the Santa Fe *New Mexico Sentinel,* October 9, 1938.

Somewhat less garrulous and boastful than many of the frontiersmen; yet the difference between him and others of his class in character and skill was by no means so marked as has been represented in eulogistic biographical sketches. No one, however, begrudged Kit the fame his biographers have given him. It is their custom, ignoring faults, to concentrate in one trapper all the virtues of his class for dramatic effect.[26]

This is exactly what happened in the Carson legend. The traits and exploits of an entire trade group came to be consolidated in the biography of a single mountain man. Kit became the symbol for a type of frontiersman because his biographers made him into one. To obtain a "dramatic effect," they built legends around the actual man.

[26] *History of California,* II (1802–24) (Vol. XIX of *Works* [San Francisco, History Company, 1886]), 747.

CHAPTER IV

A Blood-and-Thunder Hero

WHILE CARSON WAS BEING MADE OVER into a genteel character in biographies, a more savage Carson was appearing in magazine fiction and paperback novels. Of Herculean stature, this figure rescues swooning maidens and kills large numbers of Indians in a ritualistic series of hand-to-hand combats and hairbreadth escapes. The pseudobiographical format employed in many of these stories convinced readers that they were acquiring reliable information along with their entertainment. For many Americans, the Kit Carson of the adventure novels was the real article.

In April, 1848, *Holden's Dollar Magazine* of New York published "An Adventure of Kit Carson: A Tale of the Sacramento," by an anonymous author. This was the first in a series of fictional treatments which added to the Carson legend. Kit is described as a "tall and robust figure, of magnificent proportions" who dresses in a straw coat and a flashy red kerchief. His principal enemy is the Cheyenne chief Black Wolf, who is really the disguised white renegade Richard Inge (from "ingen"):

> "It's an out-and-out quarrel, then, is it?" said Kit, baring his brawny arm to give it fair scope—for although his rifle yet retained its charge, he scorned to take undue advantage of an adversary; "but mind, Richard Inge, should you be worsted in this affair, it was none of my seeking."[1]

Carson rescues a wagon train and saves the beautiful heroine from Inge and his ally, an evil Catholic priest. One recognizes here the

[1] *Holden's Dollar Magazine*, I, 210.

elements of the dime novel in embryonic form. Kit's large size, the preposterous language, and the white renegade are all standard fixtures in the dime-novel "westerns" which began to flourish after 1860.

The author of this story may have been Charles Averill, whose paperback novel of 1849, *Kit Carson, Prince of the Goldhunters,* was also subtitled "A Tale of the Sacramento." This story, too, suggested stereotypes for subsequent representations of Carson in popular literature. It exploited the current interest in the California gold rush by having Kit discover the gold fields. He also fights bandits, unearths hidden treasure, and kills no less than a dozen Indians in a single episode. He is young and handsome and has the physical proportions of a giant: "He had but time to see that his gallant preserver was a man of powerful proportions and Herculean stature, dressed in the rude deerskin suit of a western hunter."[2]

Averill had trouble with the speech of his hero. Should it be the elegant English of the conventional literary hero, marked by flowery sentences and flawless diction? Or should it be the crude dialect which passed for frontier speech among the novelists? Like many writers after him, Averill could not decide. So he used both: "See stranger, there the red devils come. Take another pull at the liquor, and keep a keen eye ahead—you'll need both soon. The critters are after us, there's no mistake. Hold my powder horn for me stranger, while I jest pick off a couple of these infarnal varmints, with *Old Sacramento!*"[3] As mentioned above, Averill also solved this problem by having his narrator explain that Kit's dialect is only assumed.

Carson appeared in another paperback novel in 1849, Emerson Bennett's *The Prairie Flower.* The complicated plot involves two chums from Harvard who set out for Oregon and become tangled in a web of mixed identities and lost lovers. Carson is characterized as an "incarnate devil in Indian fight," who had "killed and scalped more savages in the same number of years than any two hunters

2 Page 80.
3 *Ibid.*

36

west of the old Mississippi."[4] He justifies his Indian-fighter reputation in such episodes as the following:

> Discharging his rifle and pistols at the first he came to, Carson raised himself in his stirrups, and swinging the former weapon over his head, with as much apparent ease as if a mere whisp, he brought it down upon the skulls of the dusky horde around him with fatal effect. Not less than a dozen in the space of twice as many seconds bit the dust beneath its weight, while his horse, madly rearing and plunging, trod down some four or five more.[5]

Here is typical inflation of Indian-fighting episodes in popular narrative and one of the earliest uses of the phrase "bit the dust." It is hard to believe that Bennett was serious when he added this episode to the story. If they had accepted Bennett's stories, subsequent writers would have faced a shortage of Indians for their Carson to fight.

Many of the early tales were put into print by English travelers, men like Captain William Drummond Stewart[6] and George Frederick Ruxton. Ruxton in 1848 published a story in which Carson is more savage than his biographers were ever to make him. In a drunken riot during a dance at Taos, Kit and three companions kill several Mexicans:

> The odds began to tell against the mountaineers, when Kit Carson's eye caught sight of a heavy stool or stone, supported by three long heavy legs. In a moment he had cleared his way to this, and in an-

---

[4] *The Prairie Flower; or, Adventure in the Far West,* 56. This sketch might seem to have been drawn from firsthand experience, except that one finds the same phrasing in George F. Ruxton's article, "Life in the Far West," *Blackwood's Edinburgh Magazine,* Vol. LXIV (September, 1848), 442. "To look at Kit none would suppose that the mild-looking being before him was an incarnate devil in Indian fight, and had raised more hair from head of redskins than any two men in the western country."

[5] Page 62.

[6] In his novel *Edward Warren* (1854), Stewart established a formula for the handling of the Shunan duel in fiction. Carson intervenes to protect the narrator, in this case Edward Warren, from Shunan, and this becomes the cause of the historic duel.

other the three legs were broken off and in the hands of himself, Dick Wooton, and La Bonté. Sweeping them round their heads, down came the heavy weapons amongst the Mexicans with wonderful effect. . . .[7]

Historians regard Ruxton as a competent observer, and he stated when challenged that the story was *"true to the letter."*[8] Several considerations, however, lead one to question its authenticity. First, the book in which it was published, *Life in the Far West,* is a novel. Although this novel was based upon firsthand observation of the mountain man, its basic purpose was not to report facts but to tell a good story. Second, Ruxton himself did not witness the event. Since he visited the Southwest in 1846, long after this fight presumably took place,[9] he must have heard the tale secondhand. Probably one of Carson's associates told Ruxton the story, knowing that he was looking for material for a book. Third, Englishmen, even highly respected ones like Ruxton, were proverbial butts of frontier tall tales. Finally, Ruxton described other actual characters inaccurately.[10]

Dime novels began to be produced in large numbers after 1860, and Carson was a natural hero for these blood-and-thunder tales. The traits and exploits of the dime-novel Carson had been outlined by Averill, Bennett, and the author of "Kit Carson's Adventure" in *Holden's Dollar Magazine.* Carson's own reaction to these legendary stories is symbolized by an equally legendary anecdote. In 1866, so the story runs, Colonel Henry Inman showed him the cover of a periodical on which he is depicted as a huge figure embracing a conventional female, while dead Indians litter the ground

[7] The story originally appeared in the series of articles "Life in the Far West," *Blackwood's Edinburgh Magazine,* Vols. LXIII–LXIV (June–September, 1848), Vol. LXIV, 454. It was printed later in the book *Life in the Far West,* 2d ed. (1851), 242–43.

[8] *Life in the Far West,* x.

[9] Stanley Vestal places it in the fall of 1833. Vestal accepted the story, saying: "This adventure of Kit's has been ignored by earlier biographers, though vouched for by a gentleman and officer of H. M. 89th Regiment, and printed in Blackwood's Magazine, 1848, under the title *In the Far West."—Kit Carson,* 88.

[10] See Sabin, *Kit Carson Days,* II, 935, for a reference to his story on the death of Bill Williams.

about them. After studying the picture intently for a few seconds, Kit is said to have remarked "Gentlemen, that thar may be true, but I hain't got no recollection of it."[11]

One of the earliest dime novels in which Carson appeared was *The Fighting Trapper; or, Kit Carson to the Rescue,* by Edward S. Ellis. The story was originally printed as a newspaper serial in 1862 and then was republished as a dime novel under various titles and with various pseudonyms up to 1901.[12] Kit does not play a large part in the tale, but he is featured on the cover, and he does appear in time to rescue an entrapped party from an Indian attack in the Black Hills. His fighting techniques are interesting. He charges between two savages with a knife in each hand and is thus able to kill two at a time. He "slays two of his enemies at two different times by such devices."

Ellis used the pseudonym of "Lieutenant J. H. Randolph" in writing another novel, *Carson the Guide; or, Perils of the Frontier* (1870). He borrows much of his phraseology from Ruxton's *Life in the Far West,* characterizing Carson as a "devil incarnate in an Indian fight." He also borrows heavily from Peters, including an edited version of the Shunan duel. The cause of the duel is a Spanish beauty named Inez Alcado, whom Carson has rescued from the Apaches. It is staged in Santa Fe instead of Wyoming, and Kit replies to Shunan's insinuations: "Do you suppose I would retract to such a miserable coward as you? Do you think I am afraid of you? I despise you as I do the greatest loafer in New Mexico. If you don't like what I say, do what you think best about it."[13]

[11] Colonel Henry Inman, *The Old Santa Fé Trail,* 301.

[12] The story was published as a serial in the *Philadelphia Dollar Newspaper* for five issues beginning with Vol. XX, July 2, 1862, under the title of "Viola Vennond; or, Life on the Border," by Edward S. Ellis. It was rewritten as No. 1 of Beadle's Ten-Cent Novels, published on November 11, 1863, under the pseudonym of Latham C. Carleton and with the title *The Hunters; or Life on the Mountain and Prairie.* It was republished under its final title of *The Fighting Trapper; or, Kit Carson to the Rescue* by the American News Company in 1874, no author given; under pseudonym of Capt. J. F. C. Adams as Beadle's Dime Library No. 68 (1879); and again as Beadle's Dime Library No. 1045 in 1901.

[13] Page 49.

Kit is a rather effeminate character in the novel, despite the large numbers of Indians he kills. On one occasion when surrounded by Apaches, he "stamped the ground with vexation." When a poisonous snake drops into a boat he is piloting, he blandly announces, "I never fancied any kind of snake." Certainly this is a far cry from the authentic mountain-man speech reproduced in the narratives of Zenas Leonard, Washington Irving, or Albert Pike.

In Thomas Harbaugh's *Kiowa Charley, the White Mustanger, or Rocky Mountain Kit's Last Scalp Hunt* (1879), Carson is an old man. He is a much more earthy figure than Ellis makes him, and he speaks dialect ("durndest," "kentry"). He is introduced in a passage which proves his legendary stature:

> Tall and shaped like a Kiowa, he might have been mistaken for a warrior of that wily nation, but he was not.
>
> He was a white man, but the climate of many Indian lands had tanned his face; he was the best trailer, the grandest fighter, the greatest scout that ever crossed the Mississippi. . . . A keener eye was not to be found in the Indian lands of America; a deadlier rifle never rested upon a saddle.
>
> Need I name him now?
>
> The reader ere this has recognized that prince of pathfinders, the king of the plains, the hero of heroes—KIT CARSON![14]

Mixed with all the gore in the dime novels is the same kind of moral lessons that the biographers had been trying to inculcate. The editing of Carson's speech and behavior is especially noticeable when the dime novel is directed to young boys. Many "biographical" novels appeared in a Beadle and Adams series entitled "A Boy's Library of Sport, Story, and Adventure." In one novel of the series, Albert W. Aiken's *Kit Carson, King of Guides* (1882), Kit's language and respectful attitude are those of a model youngster. In petitioning the leader of a trapping expedition for permission to go along, Kit makes a speech that is typical of many hundreds delivered by young dime-novel heroes:

[14] Page 2.

My name is Christopher Carson, sir, Kit Carson for short. I was born in Madison County, Kentucky, but when I was only a baby my folks emigrated to Upper Louisiana and I was taught by my father, who was as good a woodman as all Kentucky could boast, how to read the signs of the forest and on the prairie, how to handle weapons and take care of myself in any situation, and from the time I was a little boy I have always wanted to be a trapper and a prairie-guide, and so with my father's permission I have set out to make my own way in the world.[15]

Carson's father died years before Kit ran away to the West, but young readers could still be instructed in the necessity of asking their parents' permission on all occasions.

Like other proper boys of the contemporary literature, Kit puts his faith in Providence. When the Mexicans at Santa Fe plan to lynch Carson, Big Foot Wallace, and Bill Williams, Kit says: "It is a fiendish plan! . . . . but a just Providence will not, surely, permit such a scheme to be successfully carried out." Sure enough, Josefa Jaramilla slips the boys a file in a loaf of bread, and they make their Providential escape.

In this novel, Kit is given a greater range of exploits than usual. Fifteen years old at the time of the story, he performs the celebrated Broadus amputation while more experienced men stand paralyzed. "I say, boys, this is the cock-sparrow w'ot sawed a feller's leg [*sic*] off on the train only a while back; I hearn'd on it up to Albuquerque t'other day." He vanquishes Mangas Coloradas, "the best fighting man in the Apache tribe," in a knife duel. (This would have been 1824; Mangas was not well known as a chief until the late 1830's.) In a pistol duel over a beautiful *señorita,* who turns out to be Josefa Jaramilla, Kit defeats the principal Mexican bully by creasing his skull. He saves Silver Bell, lovely daughter of the Comanche chieftain White Buffalo, from a charging bison. When the ungrateful White Buffalo forces Kit to run the gantlet, Silver Bell saves him in Pocahontas-like fashion. With General Kearny at the Battle of San Pascual, Carson *alone* carries the

[15] Page 2.

41

S O S to San Diego after overpowering a guard and riding the captured horse to headquarters.

So dime-novel readers, young and old alike, learned about Kit Carson. Kit was known to be an actual character, and the dime novelists generally described their narratives as "true" or "authentic" accounts. Thus these subliterary tales were the sources of a good deal of historical misinformation. They also created a generic character who appeared in later magazine stories, popular novels, and other dime novels.[16]

Dime-novel writing techniques are apparent in much of the other Carson material in the later nineteenth century. A popular method of dealing with frontier characters was the multiple biography treating several heroes in one volume. Such anthologies as Charles McKnight's *Our Western Border* (1876), E. G. Cattermole's *Famous Frontiersmen, Pioneers, and Scouts* (1883), J. W. Buel's *Heroes of the Plains* (1883), and Cody's *Story of the Wild West* (1888) are filled with old legends and newly invented tales. Buel, for example, contributes several animal-encounter stories to the Carson mythology. One of these has Kit in a hand-to-claw fight with a "Mexican lion." This was a standard frontier anecdote which originally appeared in the Davy Crockett *Autobiography*.[17] Buel simply transferred it to Carson, and it was later copied by other writers including Cody and William F. Drannan.[18] Buel's own tall-tale masterpiece is that of Carson and the wounded buffalo, here reproduced as a choice example of the rhetorical flourishes which embroider frontier legends:

The bullet struck the buffalo low under the shoulder, which only

[16] The stereotype is used in various ways. In Major Sam Hall's *Kit Carson, Jr., the Crack Shot of the West* (Beadle & Adams New York Dime Library, No. 3 [N.Y., 1873]), young Kit performs the same exploits as his more noted father. In Joseph Badger's *Old Kit and His Comrades* (Beadle's Boy's Library, No. 178 [N.Y., 1887]), the nominal hero, Christopher Duncan, follows the Carson prototype in a series of standard frontier adventures.

[17] *Life of David Crockett* (Philadelphia, John E. Potter, 1865), 355–57.

[18] Cody, *Story of the Wild West*, 331; William F. Drannan, *Thirty-One Years on the Plains and in the Mountains*, 82.

served to so enrage him that the next moment the infuriated animal was pursuing Kit, who, fortunately, not much hurt, was able to run toward the river. It was a race for life now, Carson using his nimble heels to the utmost of their capacity, accelerated very much by the thundering, bellowing bull bringing up the rear. For several minutes it was nip and tuck which should reach the Platte river first, but Kit got there by a scratch a little in advance. It was a big stream, and deep water under the bank, but heavens! it was paradise indeed compared with the hades plunging at his back, so Kit leaped into the water trusting to Providence that the bull would not follow. The trust was well placed for the bull did not follow, but stood on the bank and shook his fists—head—vehemently at the struggling hunter, who preferred deep water to the horns of a dilemma on shore.[19]

Other stories were assigned to the famed hero because they seemed appropriate to his legend. During a night attack by Indians near Pawnee Rock in Oklahoma, a nervous young Carson shoots what he thinks is a prowling savage. In the morning, however, his companions make fun of him when they find that he has killed his own mule.[20] This story is a generic anecdote known all over the West under various names. In Amador County, California, for example, it is called "Daugherty's Mule." While the episode may have happened to a frontiersman at some time, its assignment to Kit Carson is not historically justified.

A similar judgment must be made about a story which was published in the biography of Joe Meek (1870).[21] In May of 1834, Meek, Carson, and four others are hunting somewhere in the Arkansas-Cimarron River country when they are attacked by two hundred Comanches. The men construct a "mule fort" by slitting the throats of their mounts. From behind these barriers, they kill forty-two Indians and wound several more, "for the charge had been repeated fifteen or twenty times." This makes a good story, and it is frequently included in Carson essays;[22] but the Indian

---

[19] *Heroes of the Plains,* 489–90.
[20] Inman, *The Old Santa Fé Trail,* 408–409.
[21] Mrs. Frances Fuller Victor, *River of the West,* 154–57.
[22] Gene Caesar, "Kit Carson Country," *Holiday,* Vol. XXXII (July, 1962), 118.

behavior is not characteristic here, and the story bears evidence of frontier exaggeration. Meek, of course, was a flamboyant story-teller in the Jim Bridger tradition. Furthermore, Carson does not mention the incident in his autobiography, as he would certainly have done for an event of this magnitude.

Another popular narrative in the dime-novel tradition was Leon Lewis' (Julius Warren Lewis) *Kit Carson's Last Trail* (1891). The similarities of this tale to the 1848 story in *Holden's Dollar Magazine* indicate that the rules of Carson portraiture did not change substantially during this forty-three-year period. The frontier is idealized, the evil Indian Red Knife is actually a disguised white man, and Kit is a noble and sensitive philosopher as well as a brutal Indian killer. "A noble son of the New World, honest, good and brave, a chief among heroes, he was one of those men of the Great West who have achieved universal renown." This language echoes that of the eulogistic biographers like Peters and Burdett, obvious sources for Lewis's manipulation of the legend.

The depth of Carson's nature is revealed by the "mist in his eyes" when he gazes at the gracious heroine, Miriam Dane. He is a moralizer: "That's right, child. We must act always as if everything were right or coming out so. Do our best, and hope for the best, this is the real watchword of life." On discovering Red Knife's camp, he reveals also that he is religious: "My heart is full of gratitude to Heaven." This moral depth, however, does not prevent him from creeping up on the surrounding Indians with his rifle barrel in his teeth [*sic*], and killing five of the besiegers.

Lewis inherits the confusion of earlier writers on what speech to give his hero. So many models had become available by 1891 that Kit's diction is a patchwork of various traditions. There is straight dime-novel lingo: "But keep cool, child. Old Kit's between you and the yellow [*sic*] devils, and they won't easily climb over his scalp-lock—not if he knows it!" There are lines from stage melodrama: "He knows of course that you abominate him, and that no earthly combination of circumstances could induce you to marry him, unless the lives of your parents were to depend upon the acceptance of his hand." There are even lines betraying Shake-spearean influence: " 'Twere madness to set you free, if we are all going to be detected the minute thereafter. Hark! I hear foot-steps approaching."

Such fancy language does not prevent Kit from fulfilling his standard functions. He thwarts a road agent, rescues the heroine's parents from the Indians, and finally kills Red Knife in a hand-to-hand duel. His symbolic role in literature is well summed up by one of the characters: "Oh George, we are saved. The very presence of Kit Carson is safety."

Thus the line between fact and fiction became obscured. It was an easy step from using Carson's name in fictional stories to using him in fictional stories disguised as fact. William Thomson's article of 1896, "On the War-path with Kit Carson,"[23] is a case in point. It describes a journey to California in the summer of 1850, amidst "prowling swarms of hostile savages," although the best evidence indicates that Carson spent that summer at his home in Taos.[24] In an episode obviously borrowed from fictional treat-ments, Carson rescues Kate and Mrs. Ellis, two handsome white women, from the Indians. During the trip he kills ten Indians; one of these he shoots off a cliff at four hundred yards. The "four-hundred-yard shot" is a traditional badge of prowess that Thomson probably copied from a Buffalo Bill story.[25] The article demon-strates the value of Kit's name to popular writers. It also indicates how the legend had grown.

During the nineteenth century Kit Carson was celebrated in a wide variety of legends. His character and actions were misrepre-sented in what were essentially idealized versions of his life. The Kit Carson of history rarely moralized and never spoke elegantly. He spoke a frontier patois, rather than the polite language which his biographers felt they had to give him. He could neither read nor write. He had moments of savagery and revelry. Thus he

[23] *Lippincott's Magazine*, Vol. LVII (April, 1896), 555–64.
[24] Sabin, *Kit Carson Days*, II, 625.
[25] *Story of the Wild West*, 589.

was quite at variance with the reflective and gentlemanly figure sketched in biographies.

Furthermore, he appeared in a contradictory role which was unrelated either to the genteel hero or to the historical personage. In dime novels and magazine fiction he was a savage and vindictive figure, performing superhuman exploits in a staggering variety of combats with Indians, animals, and renegade whites. In these tales, he lost most of his genteel qualities but gained the physical dimensions of a Hercules.

In the legend, the actual historical significance of Kit Carson was exaggerated. Writers who ranked him with Hercules, Nestor, or Napoleon were not making defensible comparisons. Although it was conventional to say that Carson, like Daniel Boone and Bill Cody, had "made the settlement of the West possible," his actual role in the fur trade and in Western exploration was small. Episodes clustered about his name because he was a well-publicized hero. The workings of legend explain the gap between actual significance and popular reputation.

CHAPTER V

The Carson Legend in Perspective

IN TWENTIETH-CENTURY NARRATIVES, the romanticized image of Kit Carson has endured. A dependable source of legend is the recollections of "old-timers." William F. Drannan in his subscription book of 1900, *Thirty-One Years on the Plains and in the Mountains,* tells of a youth spent with "Uncle Kit." When Carson first appears, he lays down the newspaper he is reading [*sic*] and saves "Willie" from humiliation by a hotel clerk. Carson fights the bully "Shewman" in 1852 (actual date 1835), fights a "Mexican lion" (copied from Buel's fabrication), speaks flawless English, and in general follows the ritual now expected of him.

Despite its fictions, this book was immensely popular and was read by millions in the early years of the century.[1] It is in many libraries today, the copies worn with use. Drannan was able to imagine his life with Carson so vividly that his dream took on the shape of reality. Yet he was also shrewd enough to combine classic elements of frontier narrative: tall tales, dime-novel episodes, and a genteel hero, with the result that his book had wide appeal.

Other old-timers drew their picture of Carson not from actual experience but from books they had read. Thus William E. Goodyear remembered Carson as follows:

He was about 5 feet 9 inches high, and weighed some 260 pounds [*sic*].

[1] Walter Bate, *Frontier Legend, the Texas Finale of Capt. William F. Drannan, Pseudo Frontier Comrade of Kit Carson,* 11. Bate says that a hundred editions were published, many of the books being sold on trains by "newsbutchers." See also Homer Croy, "They Built the Saga," *This is the West,* ed., by Robert West Howard (New York, New American Library, 1957), 180.

He had a round, jolly-looking face, dark, piercing eyes, that looked straight through you, and seemed to read your every thought. His long brown hair hung around his shoulders. His dress consisted of buckskin coat and pants, with leggings coming up to his knees, in which he carried, in true Mexican style, his machete, a long, two-edged knife. His coat and pants were heavily fringed, and there the quills of the porcupine bore a conspicuous part. A cap of fox-skin surmounted his head, with four coon's tails sticking out around the edges of the cap. . . . Around his waist was a heavy belt, fastened by a large, highly polished silver buckle. Attached to the belt were a pair of revolvers and a hunting knife.[2]

The idea of Kit Carson walking around with a three-foot machete as well as a knife and two revolvers is straight from some dime novel or border anthology.

One also finds an idealized Carson in juvenile literature. In Everett McNeil's *With Kit Carson in the Rockies* (1909), the author dresses Carson in the bold colors of a medieval knight transplanted to the American West. The foils for Carson are two adolescents, Rex Holt and Dill Conroyal, who enjoy the "wild freedom and romantic delights of a hunter's life in the Rocky Mountains." Carson rescues these two delinquents on several occasions, the most sensational being the encounter with Shunan. The bully threatens to thrash one of the boys, but Carson appears opportunely. In impeccable English drawn straight from Peters' biography, Kit warns the bully that he will be chastised unless he desists.

Everett Tomlinson's novel of 1916, *Scouting with Kit Carson*, was part of the "American Scouting Series," and the Carson of the story represents the appropriate ideals. In fact, it is almost an allegory, with Carson as Virtue and the bully Shunan (appearing here under the name of "Rat True") as Evil. Exaggerated feats of Indian fighting and editorializing about American virtues form the substance of the novel. One would not expect the reality of

[2] Reprinted in Perry Worden, "Kit Carson," *Pasadena Star-News,* May 30, 1938.

mountaineer life to be reported in such literature, but Tomlinson has created a sterile hero and then attached Kit Carson's name to him.

The tradition of genteel biography lives on also in magazine articles and books whose common characteristic is uncritical hero-worship. George Creel called Carson a "Hannibal of the plains," and his eulogy incorporates an antisocial theory which reminds one of the legends about Daniel Boone: "A strange, wild race, hating the civilization they had fled from, yet bringing civilization nearer with every path they found, every trail they blazed; conquering the great sweep of the Golden West."[3] There is an epic tone here. Stanley Vestal, a well-known popularizer, confessed frankly that his biography was designed as an epic. To him, Carson's exploits suggest those of the heroes of antiquity. Vestal claims that "Kit Carson's endless journeys throug the wilderness make the fabled Mediterranean wanderings of Odysseus seem week-end excursions of a stay-at-home; his humanity rivals Robin Hood's; in readiness to fight and in chivalry to women he rates a *siege* at the Round Table; his courage and coolness against hopeless odds may be matched but not surpassed by the Old Norse heroes; while his prowess in innumerable battles . . . makes Achilles look like a wash-out."[4]

This poetic approach led Vestal to stray from the path of history.[5] And other biographers have been more eager to praise Carson than to investigate his career. M. Morgan Estergreen's *The Real Kit Carson* (1955) is in the eulogistic tradition of the nineteenth century. In discussing the Mexican War, she makes this claim for Carson: "Because of his skill to outwit [*sic*] the savages and his

[3] "Incredible Kit Carson," *Collier's,* Vol. LXXVIII, (August 26, 1926), 12.

[4] *Kit Carson,* 3–4.

[5] Kearny, "Kearny and Kit Carson as Interpreted by Stanley Vestal," *New Mexico Historical Review,* Vol. V (January, 1930), 1–16; review by Charles Camp in *California Historical Society Quarterly,* Vol. VIII (June, 1928), 194–95. "The author proceeds with his tale, an alluring, colorful mingling of strict fact and highly imaginative fancy. . . . whatever is 'new' in this book may be taken *cum grano salis.*"

49

loyalty to duty and his intelligence as a guide, his service was invaluable, and without it the war might well have been lost."

Carson also entered frontier legendry by becoming a model for mountain-man novels. In Harvey Fergusson's *Wolf Song* (1927), the travels of the hero Sam Lash resemble those of Carson. Lash takes part in a riot at a Taos dance, his first wife is an Indian woman named Mountain Flower (who resembles Kit's Waa-Nibe), and his second wife is a Mexican woman. Carson is the hero of Courtney Ryley Cooper's *The Pioneers* (1938). In this one he leads an emigrant train to Oregon in the summer of 1842, though historically he had been with Frémont's first expedition that summer. Kit's semihistorical, semifictional status is well exemplified by Claude Gentry's *Kit Carson* (1956). This is a fictionalized biography, part novel and part chronicle. Thus Carson's actual career has been an invitation to literary myth-making and exploitation.

Carson also figures in a variety of other legends, local and national. Just as Kentucky is dotted with trees on which Daniel Boone carved his name, so the Southwest is marked by Kit Carson inscriptions on various rocks.[6] His name has been given to lakes, passes, and mountains—often with legendary stories attached. Near Halstead, Kansas, there is a "Kit Carson Tree" where Kit was camping when attacked by Comanches under Black Kettle (who was actually a Cheyenne) and was saved by a platoon of the Seventh Cavalry under General Custer![7] Kit Carson Peak near Raton, New Mexico, is said to have gotten its name when Kit was attacked there by Comanches while on his way back to Taos from a visit with Dick Wootton:

> He made for this peak, tied the reins of his horse to the saddle pommel, and whipped it off in the direction of Taos by way of Red River Canyon. Then he scrambled on foot up the sides of the peak to the top

[6] The Gallup (N.M.) *Gazette*, November 16, 1939, reports three such inscriptions, two of them being at El Morro and at Kit Carson's Cave east of Gallup.

[7] *Wichita Eagle Magazine*, July 22, 1956 (files of the Kansas State Historical Society). The tale was originally put into print by Mart Ingals in a souvenir edition of the Halstead *Independent* in 1937.

From M. Morgan Estergreen: Kit Carson

KIT CARSON AND JOHN C. FRÉMONT
"Carson became a hero by means of Frémont's published
Report of his first two journeys."

From Albert Johannsen: The House of Beadle and Adams
and Its Dime and Nickel Novels

KIT CARSON AND THE INDIANS

"He generally chose to fight the Indians rather than avoid them."

where there is a natural fortification of rock. Here he held off the Indian band for two or three days. The horse went on to Taos, pawed at the corral gate and roused Carson's family. A party was made up and went to Carson's relief.[8]

On the national level, Kit is often the subject of articles in glossy magazines. There is also a television program which claims to dramatize his adventures.

Yet students of Carson's life have given us a clearer picture of the man behind the legend. Edwin L. Sabin wrote an honest biography based upon original sources.[9] Several historians of the West have given Carson a less grandiose role, but have placed him in the mainstream of western development.[10] And Carson himself has been allowed to tell his own story in two printed versions of the *Autobiography*.

Even at the cost of his subject's purity and heroism, Sabin dispelled many of the legends. His Carson has vices as well as virtues, an admission which would have shocked the genteel biographers. Not until this biography appeared was the general reader informed that Carson spoke a frontier patois rather than flawless English, that he had shot down unarmed prisoners, or that historically his exploits were probably of minor significance.

One may also find honest representations of Carson in fiction. Willa Cather's novel *Death Comes for the Archbishop* depicts a Carson whose appearance and character reflect the actual man:

This Carson was not so tall as the Bishop himself, was very slight in frame, modest in manner, and he spoke English with a soft Southern

[8] Manville Chapman MS (1938), New Mexico Writers' Program, WPA, Santa Fe
[9] The original one-volume edition was published in 1914 by Doubleday, Doran, while the two-volume edition appeared in 1935 under the Press of the Pioneers imprint.
[10] LeRoy Hafen and W. J. Ghent, *Broken Hand: The Life of Thomas Fitzpatrick, Chief of Mountain Men* (Denver, Old West Publishing Company, 1931), 264; Bernard DeVoto, *Across the Wide Missouri* (Boston, Houghton Mifflin, 1947), 226; Allan Nevins, "Kit Carson—Bayard of the Plains," *American Scholar,* Vol. VIII (July, 1939), 333–39; Henry Nash Smith, "Kit Carson in Books," *Southwest Review,* Vol. XXVIII (Winter, 1943), 164–90.

drawl. His face was both thoughtful and alert; anxiety had drawn a permanent ridge between his blue eyes. . . . The Bishop felt a quick glow of pleasure in looking at the man. As he stood there in his buckskin clothes one felt in him standards, loyalties, a code which is not easily put into words but which is instantly felt when two men who live by it come together by chance.[11]

Miss Cather brings the actual and the fictional Carson closer together because she is not afraid to write about the controversial aspects of his career. She regards Kit's conversion to Catholicism as a matter of form rather than conviction. She views his Navaho campaign of 1864 from the Indian side: "It was his own misguided friend, Kit Carson, who finally subdued the last unconquered remnant of that people. Carson was a soldier under orders, and he did a soldier's brutal work."

In juvenile literature, Sabra Conner's *On Sweetwater Trail* (1928) features a Carson who is close to the historical model. Events are telescoped (Frémont's second and third expeditions being combined), but the characters—Frémont, Edward M. Kern, and Oliver Wiggins, as well as Carson—seem true to the individuals we know in historical documents. Authentic mountain-man dialect replaces the usual dandified diction.

Kit did not see the dramatic values in his own career. He was, in Bancroft's words, "less garrulous and boastful than many frontiersmen." As James F. Meline testified: "He has to be drawn out. I had many questions to ask and his answers were all marked by great distinctness of memory, simplicity, candor, and a desire to make some one else, rather than himself, the hero of his story."[12] Basically, Carson was a practical but unimaginative man.

However, the story values were there, and they were exploited by Eastern writers who built a legend. They saw that Carson's life had elements of drama: an interesting plot, fascinating characters, and picturesque setting. And Kit, as Allan Nevins pointed out, did a number of things well. His encounters with grizzlies,

[11] Page 76.
[12] *Two Thousand Miles on Horseback,* 272.

Indians, and bad men and his activities as a guide were authentic exploits subject to infinite elaboration.

For Kit Carson, then, less of a gap exists between history and the legend than is the case with other Western characters, particularly the outlaws and gunfighters. He did perform some notable exploits, although he had no great historical significance. He was virtuous, although somewhat less so than the legend claims. He spoke of his exploits with becoming modesty, and he was respected by most of his contemporaries. Thus he could become a model for his group, and he did. The prominence of the mountain man as a type in the literature and legend of the West is linked with the popular representations of Kit Carson.

PART TWO

The Outlaw:
Billy the Kid

CHAPTER VI

The William Bonney of History

THERE ARE TWO Billy the Kids in legend. The first is a tough little thug, a coward, a thief, and a cold-blooded murderer. The second is a romantic and sentimental hero, the brave and likable leader of an outnumbered band fighting for justice. The dominance of the second legend in our day marks his significance as the personification of a general type, the outlaw-hero. But what of the actual Billy, the Kid?

The Kid's early years are known to legend but not to history. In the absence of facts, the audience to a heroic legend agrees upon certain conventions. One of these is the Kid's birth at New York City on November 23, 1859. This place and date depend upon nothing more substantial than one newspaperman's statement. Ash Upson, who wrote a biography of Billy, purportedly acquired this information while boarding with the Kid's mother in Silver City, New Mexico.[1] The earliest printed reference is in the Santa Fe *Rocky Mountain Sentinel*, April 30, 1879. A "Special Correspondent," probably Upson, wrote the *Sentinel:* "From a trustworthy source I have learned that Wm. Bonny, who has figured so conspicuously in the Lincoln County troubles in this Territory, was once a resident of your city. When quite a youth he came from New York State. His stepfather's name is reported to be Antrim. Bonny is known here by the name of 'The Kid.' "

Despite the vagueness about his birth and early life, diligent researchers have recovered some fragments of this period. The

---

[1] Pat F. Garrett, *The Authentic Life of Billy, the Kid* (Norman, University of Oklahoma Press, 1954), 4. This edition, with an introduction by J. C. Dykes, is a reprint of the book originally published in April, 1882.

Sentinel's correspondent was right about the Kid's early residence in Santa Fe. He was there at the second marriage of his mother, who had resumed her maiden name of Catherine McCarty upon the death of her first husband, William H. Bonney. On March 1, 1873, she married William Antrim.[2] Antrim was a miner, and when he moved to the boom town of Silver City later in the year, he took with him his two stepsons, Joseph and Henry Mc-Carty. Mrs. Antrim kept a boardinghouse, and the heavy work involved overtaxed her frail health. She died on September 16, 1874,[3] leaving young William H. Bonney, later Henry McCarty, later Henry Antrim, and still later William Bonney once again, to shift largely for himself in early adolescence.

The oft-broken home is a classic seedbed for criminals, and the motherless boy is a prime prospect. William Antrim was respected in the community and did his best for the boys. But young Henry soon teamed up with other delinquents and learned the wrong things in bars and gambling halls. The result was reported in the Grant County *Herald,* September 26, 1875.

> Henry McCarty, who was arrested on Thursday and committed to the jail to await the action of the Grand Jury upon the charge of stealing clothes from Charley Sun and Sam Chung, celestials, sans cues, sans Joss sticks, escaped from prison yesterday through the chimney. It's believed that Henry was the simple tool of "Sombrero Jack," who done the stealing whilst Henry done the hiding. Jack has skinned out.

Although it is a big step from petty thievery to manslaughter, the Kid soon made it. The Tuscon *Arizona Citizen* of August 25, 1877, reported the Kid's first known killing. The victim was F. P. Cahill, a blacksmith known locally as "Windy." On August 17, the two exchanged hard words at Fort Grant, Arizona Territory, and their feud was abruptly terminated by the Kid's bullet. The coroner's jury confirmed that the murderer was Henry Antrim, alias Kid, and decided that the shooting was unjustifiable.

[2] Santa Fe County Book of Marriages, "A," 37–38.
[3] Silver City *Mining Life,* September 19, 1874.

The fugitive headed east into New Mexico and loitered near Mesilla. Needing money, he tried the only job he had ever learned, thievery. He probably worked with a rustling gang under Jesse Evans. The Mesilla *Independent*, October 13, 1877, identified Henry Antrim as one of a gang of thieves who had run off three horses. The reporter hoped for the arrest of the rustlers and the recovery of the stock. But the Kid was by this time riding toward Lincoln County.

Up to this point, the fall of 1877, his recorded career had not been very promising. There had been one jail break from a clothes-stealing charge, one murder, and at least one rustling episode. But the Kid's exploits in the Lincoln County War, which was the historical prototype for the "range wars" of Western fiction and films, explain much of the subsequent interest in his career. The war came to be viewed as an epic drama, with the Kid the hero of the play.

Billy appeared at the cabin of George Coe, on the Río Ruidoso about ten miles below Lincoln. The two men hunted together and became friends. Through Coe's cousin Frank, the Kid met the English rancher John Tunstall, who hired him as a cattle hand. Tunstall owned a large ranch on the Río Feliz, about forty miles southeast of Lincoln, as well as a large store in town. His partner was Alexander McSween, an ambitious but erratic lawyer who lived in Lincoln. The partners' financial backbone was John S. Chisum, cattle baron of the upper Pecos and a cautious nonpartici-pant in the Lincoln County War.

Ranged against Tunstall and McSween was the well-entrenched Murphy-Dolan-Riley ranching and trading combine. This group had the backing of powerful territorial officials, the notorious "Santa Fe Ring," in their attempt to monopolize trading activity in Lincoln County. They were creditors to many of the small rancher-farmers of the Bonito and Ruidoso valleys. And when com-petition threatened, they were prepared to meet force with force.

Thus McSween and Tunstall in opposing this powerful firm could claim to be representing the small farmers of the area. Tes-timony in many books seems to support this view of the war, and certainly the McSween side has been the most popular and the most vocal. McSween in an affidavit stated his case:

> For instance, the farmers would buy merchandise of them at exorbitant prices, and were compelled to turn in their produce in payment thereof at prices that suited L. G. Murphy & Co., and if a farmer refused to do so, they were subject to litigation and the whole judicial machinery was used unwittingly to accomplish that object. The results of these proceedings were that L. G. Murphy & Co. were absolute monarchs of Lincoln County and ruled their subjects, the farmers and others, with an oppressive iron heel.[4]

The removal of this iron heel became the "cause" for which the Lincoln County War ostensibly was fought. And the Kid's identification with this cause has been used to justify his killings. As Mrs. McSween said years later, "Most of those he did kill deserved what they got."[5]

However, the Kid's role as the champion of the "right side" must be viewed more critically. Certainly the Murphy-Dolan faction was selfish and violent, but this does not automatically make Mc-Sween and Tunstall the defenders of the Mexicans or the protectors of the oppressed rancher-farmers. Their motives appear to have been almost as sordid. In fact, the war was essentially a struggle for power between two rival gangs.

John H. Tunstall, for example, was rather different from the refined and sensitive idealist depicted in most histories. In a letter home, April 27, 1877, Tunstall revealed the true motivations for his ventures in Lincoln County: *"Everything* in New Mexico that pays at *all* . . . is worked by a 'ring.' . . . I am at work at present making such a ring & I have succeeded admirably so far. . . . I propose to confine my operations to Lincoln County, but I intend to handle it in such a way as to get the half of every dollar that is made in the county by any one. . . ." He also revealed something of his character in a letter of November 29, 1877: "I never

---

[4] Affidavit of June 1, 1878, to Special Investigator Frank Angel. Reprinted in William A. Keleher, *Violence in Lincoln County,* 267.

[5] Miguel Otero, *The Real Billy the Kid,* 179.

was notorious for 'rubbing the right way' & the people here know that I usually say about what I think and take chances on how it suits the audience.'"[6]

The extent of the Kid's personal devotion to Tunstall must also be examined more carefully, since the assassination of the Englishman is usually given as the motivation for the Kid's subsequent killings. It is true that George Coe recalled Tunstall's saying that Billy was "the finest lad I ever met."[7] But Tunstall does not mention the Kid in his letters except as one member of a work party or posse. In addition, the Kid's shrewd and cool appraisal of men and events in Lincoln County[8] and his cold-eyed behavior when his comrades were killed indicate that his ties with one party or the other were more accidental or practical than personal. Some old-timers have in fact testified that he was with the Murphy crowd before he joined Tunstall.[9] Undoubtedly the Kid was willing to assassinate Tunstall's killers—so long as he was on McSween's payroll.

Billy and the McSween-Tunstall faction have also been identified as champions of the native Mexican population. The Kid became a culture-hero in the Mexican folklore, and the testimony of the native New Mexicans is overwhelmingly favorable to him.[10] But actually there were many Mexicans on the Murphy-Dolan side; Pantaleon Gallegos, José Cháves y Baca, Lucio Montoya, and others were among them. The significant fact is that the Mexi-

---

[6] Philip J. Rasch, "Prelude to the Lincoln County War: The Murder of John Henry Tunstall," Los Angeles *Westerners Brand Book,* Vol. VII (1957), 80; "A Document of the Lincoln County War: John H. Tunstall's 'Letter to His Parents,'" *New Mexico Folklore Record,* Vol. X (1955–56), 5.

[7] *Frontier Fighter: The Autobiography of George W. Coe,* 35.

[8] His letters to Governor Wallace and to the newspapers are quite knowledgeable. See his statements to Governor Wallace, March 23, 1879, reprinted in Frazier Hunt, *The Tragic Days of Billy the Kid,* 173.

[9] Francisco Trujillo MS, New Mexico Writers' Program, WPA, Santa Fe; Coe, *Frontier Fighter,* 38.

[10] See the following unpublished MSS in the New Mexico Writers' Program, WPA, Santa Fe: Ismael Valdez, Josh Brent, Mrs. Carlota Brent; also the testimony of Mrs. José Jaramillo and Martin Chávez in Otero, *The Real Billy the Kid,* 179.

cans who took up arms on either side were usually forced to do so. The Las Vegas *Gazette* of June 15, 1878, reported: "When one party or the other gets in close quarters in Lincoln County, they send out couriers to warn the people to come in, and aid in the fight. These riders are kind of press officers, and make them turn out, whether they want to or not." The "armies" of both sides were indeed strange combinations: hired gunmen, impressed Mexicans, and ordinarily peaceful farmers.[11]

Legal maneuvers by the two factions preceded the outbreak of violence. Then on the afternoon of February 18, 1878, a large Murphy-Dolan posse under Billy Morton caught up with Tunstall near the Ruidoso. Tunstall's four companions, including the Kid, rode for their lives. But Tunstall, courageous and foolhardy to the end, attempted to face the posse. They killed him on the spot and initiated the Lincoln County War.

Warrants for the arrest of the posse were issued to Dick Brewer, Tunstall's foreman. Brewer and his men captured Morton and Frank Baker, a free-lance gunman who had ridden with the Murphy posse. On March 9, the two captives were killed "attempting to escape." Whether the Kid shot both of them is not known. The statement of Frank McNab, one of Brewer's men, is the only first-hand account of what happened. It appeared in the Mesilla *Independent* of March 12, 1878:

> When he had ridden some 20 miles and had reached a point about 5 or 6 miles from Black Water, Morton was riding side by side with one of the posse, when he suddenly snatched McClosky's pistol from his scabbard and shot him dead.
>
> Although mounted on a slow horse, he put him to his best speed,

[11] George Coe on the McSween side and Marian Turner of the Dolan faction would be good examples of the latter. Both were strong-minded farmers, used to handling weapons, but not in any sense professional gunfighters. Coe explains how brutal treatment at the hands of Sheriff Brady made him a bitter enemy of the Murphy-Dolan faction.—*Frontier Fighter,* chap. X. Turner was a rancher from the Seven Rivers district. He became a deputy sheriff because he hated John S. Chisum and believed that Chisum was behind McSween. See his letter to the Las Vegas *Gazette,* May 14, 1878, reproduced in Keleher, *Violence in Lincoln County,* 23.

closely followed by Frank Baker. They were speedily overtaken and killed.

This report reads like a hundred other shot-while-escaping tales. Did Morton shoot McClosky, his one friend on the posse? It does not seem likely.

McSween's enemies soon got control of the machinery of the law. Brewer's warrant was revoked, and Governor Samuel B. Axtell urged that U.S. troops be assigned to assist William Brady, the Dolan-backed sheriff of Lincoln County. In desperation the McSween partisans turned to assassination. On April 1, 1878, Sheriff Brady walked down the center of Lincoln's only street accompanied by Deputy Sheriff George Hindman and two other men. From behind a plank gate next to the Tunstall store, Billy the Kid and five other gunmen opened fire. Brady and Hindman were killed almost instantly. These two murders were often credited to the Kid alone, but historians now describe them as gang killings. In some narratives, the Kid confronts Brady before the shooting begins, an act of chivalry which the history of the Lincoln County War does not validate.

Later the same week, on April 4, the Kid was present at the killing of a Murphy-Dolan gunfighter named "Buckshot" Roberts at Blazer's Mill. Legend has added Roberts to the Kid's famous list of twenty-one men. But the testimony of George and Frank Coe, as well as that of Justice of the Peace David M. Easton, indicates that Charlie Bowdre rather than the Kid fired the fatal bullet.[12] In fact, the Kid was on the other side of the building when Roberts was shot. Before he died, the redoubtable Roberts killed Dick Brewer and shot off one of George Coe's thumbs. The coroner's jury declared that Roberts had been killed by Richard Brewer and ten other men, among whom was "W. H. Antrim, alias 'The Kid.'" The Kid's name was also appearing regularly in New Mex-

---

[12] Coe, *Frontier Fighter*, 59; Frederick Bechdolt, *Tales of the Old Timers* (New York, Century, 1924), 17–18 (testimony of Frank Coe); Philip J. Rasch, "The Twenty-One Men He Put Bullets Through," *New Mexico Folklore Record*, Vol. IX (1954–55), 13.

ico newspapers reporting on Lincoln County affairs. James J. Dolan, in a letter to the Santa Fe *New Mexican,* May 25, described him as "a renegade from Arizona, where he killed a man in cold blood." In truth, the Kid was usually there when someone was shot.

The McSween gang hid out in the Ruidoso and Feliz valleys, but there were skirmishes and ambushes throughout April, May, and June. Governor Axtell had appointed George "Dad" Peppin as county sheriff. And Peppin's hand was strengthened by the availability of troops under Colonel Nathan Dudley at Fort Stanton, eight miles west of Lincoln.

On July 15, the war neared its climax. McSween and his men rode in and attempted to seize the town. When this move failed, they holed up in his fortress-like home. A party of native New Mexicans under Martin Chávez also entered Lincoln to aid McSween. Dolan and Peppin deployed their fighters in the Murphy store to the west. There followed a five-day, long-range shooting match. On the nineteenth, Colonel Dudley bivouacked in Lincoln with a detachment of troops, for the purpose of offering protection to the women and children in town. He also forced Martin Chávez and his men to vacate their positions in the Montano House and leave Lincoln. That afternoon the Dolan men managed to set fire to the west wing of the McSween home.[13]

Billy the Kid is often said to have directed the last defense of the house and the escape of the survivors from it. But he was among the first of the defenders who, silhouetted by the burning building, raced through the night amidst a hail of bullets to gain the safety of the Bonito River. However, Alexander McSween and three of his men were killed. On the Murphy-Dolan side, Bob Beckwith was shot down, and the Kid has traditionally been named as the killer. But the Kid was already across the Bonito when Beckwith was shot, according to the testimony of Dolan gunfighter Andrew Boyle, before the Dudley Court of Inquiry in June, 1879.[14]

[13] Philip J. Rasch, "Five Days of Battle," Denver *Westerners Brand Book,* Vol. XI (1955), 293–323.

[14] "Proceedings of a Court of Inquiry in the Case of Lt. Col. N. A. M. Dudley,"

The death of McSween virtually ended the Lincoln County War, and the Kid no longer had either a cause or a job. Now the inexorable laws of early experience began to work themselves out. With a handful of other fugitives, the Kid rode the outlaw trail. The ambiguity of established "law" during the war had prevented Billy from being definitely labeled an outlaw, but this he now became.

The former McSween fighters needed horses; therefore, on August 5, they helped themselves to the herd at the government Indian reservation near Mesilla. The agency clerk, Morris Bernstein, came out to stop them and got killed for his trouble. Legend has added this killing to the Kid's list, but reliable testimony again places the credit elsewhere.[15] With their fresh horses, the gang rode up to Fort Sumner. Here some of the men left for parts far removed from the "bloody ground" of south central New Mexico. And here Billy the Kid met his future nemesis, Pat Garrett, who was tending bar in Beaver Smith's saloon.

The Kid and half a dozen friends now turned to stealing horses, running them east to be sold at Tascosa in the Texas Panhandle. It was at this time, in the fall of 1878, that he resumed use of the name Bonney. Dr. Henry Hoyt bought a (stolen) horse from the Kid, and the bill of sale is signed by "W. H. Bonney."[16] Hoyt had a favorable opinion of the Kid and described him as a natural leader, which does not seem to be far off the mark. The gang also rustled steers from John S. Chisum, on the theory that Chisum owed them wages for their part in the Lincoln County War.[17]

Records of the War Department, Office of the Adjutant General (National Archives), 641–42. Reproduced in Rasch, *New Mexico Folklore Record*, Vol. IX, 11.

[15] Coe, *Frontier Fighter*, 77–78; Otero, *The Real Billy the Kid*, 140.

[16] Henry F. Hoyt, *A Frontier Doctor* (Boston, Houghton Mifflin, 1929), Chap. XIII. Hoyt reported: "Billy was an expert at most Western sports and dissipations with the exception of drinking. Much has been published of his exploits during drinking bouts, but it is my opinion that they are mostly fiction. I never knew of his taking a drink of liquor all the time he was in the Panhandle."

[17] "Billy never denied that he was in the habit of stealing cattle from John Chisum, of Roswell, against whom he professed to have a claim, for wages I believe which Chisum refused to pay, and hence he was determined to secure himself."— Godfrey Gauss MS, New Mexico Writers' Program, WPA, Santa Fe.

In September, General Lew Wallace replaced Axtell as governor of New Mexico. He issued an amnesty proclamation for those who had been in the war. But it did not apply to the Kid, who was under indictment for the murder of Sheriff Brady. Billy was also short of money. He appealed to Mrs. McSween and her lawyer, Huston I. Chapman, for back wages. Then Chapman was killed by a Dolan gunman. The Kid was an eyewitness to the murder, and Wallace concluded that he had been involved in it. He instructed his army commander to send "a detachment after the two men [the Kid and Tom O'Folliard]; and if they are caught, send them to Fort Stanton for trial as accessories to the murder of Chapman." He also offered a $1,000 reward for the Kid's arrest.

Billy soon wrote a letter to Wallace, offering to surrender if the murder charges against him could be erased. At a secret meeting with Wallace, March 17, 1879, the Kid agreed to surrender himself in order to testify against Chapman's murderers. Two days later he carried out his word and was lodged in the jail at Lincoln. His popularity among the local Mexicans is revealed by the Governor's sour comment: "A precious specimen named 'the Kid' whom the sheriff is holding here in the Plaza, as it is called, is an object of tender regard. I heard singing and music the other night; going to the door I found the residents of the village actually serenading the fellow in his prison."[18]

Wallace's efforts to solve the knotty problem of justice in Lincoln County came to nothing. All his moves were blocked by Colonel Rynerson and other of the Kid's enemies in the "Santa Fe Ring." The Kid was not pardoned, because he did not stand trial. Many believe that Wallace's failure to secure the pardon frustrated Billy's last chance for a better life within the law, but Wallace could not pardon him until he had stood trial. When the Kid and O'Folliard broke their arrest and headed for Roswell, they prevented the Governor from carrying out his end of the bargain.

On January 10, 1880, Bonney killed a Texan named Joe Grant at Fort Sumner. Grant may well have been hired by Chisum or

18 Reprinted in Keleher, *Violence in Lincoln County,* 216.

MURDER OF THE TWO GUARDS IN THE LINCOLN COUNTY JAIL
"The most plausible account of the Kid's escape is that friends of his
hid a six-shooter in the privy back of the jail."

THE KILLING OF BILLY THE KID BY SHERIFF PAT GARRETT
"In all these stories the Kid is dressed in outrageous clothing, speaks incredibly elegant English, and performs exploits which obviously originated as the 'gauziest fabrics of a whiskied brain.'"

another cattleman to remove the troublesome Kid. But the Santa Fe *New Mexican,* in reporting the incident (January 17), could only say that "the origin of the difficulty was not learned." The extent of the Kid's commitment to a life outside the law is revealed by his alliance sometime in the spring with the notorious Dave Rudabaugh of the Las Vegas Toughs.

In the middle of November, 1880, the Kid's gang sold some stolen cattle to a perhaps unwilling "fence," Jim Greathouse. At the Greathouse ranch they were surrounded by a posse from White Oaks led by Jim Carlyle, who surrendered himself as a hostage to the outlaws. He was killed trying to escape from the house.[19] The event turned local sentiment strongly against the Kid, blameless or not. The press howled for his scalp, but without effect. The Las Vegas *Gazette* of November 30 reported that the Kid's "gang of horse thieves" were continuing to commit "depredations." The Kid read the report and wrote a letter to Governor Wallace which reveals a shrewd defense of his own actions. He denied that he was the "Captain of a Band of Outlaws who hold forth at the Portales," called Carlyle's posse a "mob," and blamed most of his troubles on "the impression put out by Chisum and his tools."[20] In truth, the Kid was stealing cattle in the Panhandle and selling them to Pat Coughlan near Fort Stanton and to men in Arizona.[21]

Meanwhile Pat Garrett had been elected sheriff of Lincoln County with the backing of the local cattle barons. They wanted the stock thievery ended and felt Garrett could do the job. Many Bonney sympathizers then and since have tagged Garrett a Judas for selling out his onetime friend.[22] The sheriff and a posse of Texas

[19] The standard version of the affair is that by Joe Steck in the Lincoln County *Leader,* December 7, 1889. The Kid's version is embodied in a letter to Governor Wallace, printed in the Las Vegas *Gazette,* and cited below.

[20] The full text of the letter, which was dated December 12, 1880, is reprinted in M. G. Fulton, "Billy the Kid in Life and Books," *New Mexico Folklore Record,* Vol. IV (1949–50), 2–3.

[21] Charles A. Siringo, *A Texas Cowboy; or, Fifteen Years on the Hurricane Deck of a Spanish Pony,* 198; Thomas Cruse, *Apache Days and After* (Caldwell, Idaho, Caxton Printers, 1941), 40.

[22] "We all felt that it was a dirty, cowardly trick for Pat Garrett to pull when

cattle detectives laid an ambush for the Kid's gang at Fort Sumner. On December 18 the outlaws rode into the trap. Tom O'Folliard was killed, but the rest of the gang wheeled about and escaped. Garrett trailed them to Stinking Springs, east of Sumner. Surrounded in a small cabin, they were forced to surrender.[23] Garrett took his prisoners back to Las Vegas on the twenty-sixth.

Las Vegas newspapers had a field day reporting the incarceration of the outlaws. A *Gazette* reporter interviewed the Kid:

> He did look human, indeed, but there was nothing very mannish about him in appearance, for he looked and acted a mere boy. He is about five feet eight or nine inches tall, slightly built and lithe, weighing about 140; a frank open countenance, looking like a school boy, with the traditional silky fuzz on his upper lip; clear blue eyes, with a rougish snap about them; light hair and complexion. He is, in all, quite a handsome looking fellow, the only imperfection being two prominent front teeth slightly protruding like squirrel's teeth, and he has agreeable and winning ways.

The *Optic* also interviewed him and said that he was "about 24 years of age, and has a bold yet pleasant countenance." Perhaps the Kid was twenty-four or twenty-five instead of twenty-one. In the absence of reliable information on his birth, the experienced reporter from the *Optic* may have been right.

Billy was held in Santa Fe for several months after his capture and then was tried in Mesilla for the murder of Sheriff Brady. The deck was stacked against him. He had already been tried and found guilty by the New Mexico newspapers, which printed all

---

he killed the boy. Billie had been a friend to Pat Garrett when he first came to Lincoln County, even furnishing the man with a horse, then after the war was over and the government wanted a man to capture the boy, Garrett was willing to take the job of capturing the man that had been his friend, the man that he knew all of his friends and hide-outs."—John Allred MS, New Mexico Writers' Program, WPA, Santa Fe.

23 A standard account of the episode is that given to Siringo by Lon Chambers, one of Garrett's possemen.—*A Texas Cowboy*, 218–22. A more detailed statement may be found in J. Evetts Haley, "Jim East—Trail Hand and Cowboy," *Panhandle-Plains Historical Review*, Vol. IV (1931), 39–61.

kinds of rumors about him. Typical of these was a letter in the Las Vegas *Gazette* of April 5, 1881, from W. S. Fecher, of Mesilla, who said, "I think that twenty murders can be charged against him." With the old Murphy-Dolan associates like Colonel Rynerson backing the prosecution, the Kid was certain to be found guilty. As has been pointed out, he was the only fighter in the Lincoln County War to be tried, convicted, and sentenced to death. However, the court clerk reported that the Kid took little interest in his trial and said nothing at all when sentenced.[24]

Billy was taken to the Lincoln County Courthouse (the old Murphy-Dolan store) to await hanging on May 13. On Thursday, April 28, while Garrett was away, the Kid escaped from the jail after shooting his two guards, J. W. Bell and Bob Olinger. The most plausible account of the Kid's escape is that friends of his hid a six-shooter in the privy in back of the jail.[25] Billy got the drop on Bell, but had to shoot when Bell tried to break away. The Kid then grabbed Olinger's loaded shotgun from the armory. When Olinger approached the courthouse, the Kid greeted him from the second-floor window and then killed him, using both barrels.

The reaction of the contemporary newspapers was one of horror. The editor of the Las Vegas *Optic* on May 2 remarked that "the men, Bell and Olinger, are well known in Las Vegas and have friends all over the territory who should see that their horrible deaths are avenged." In a follow-up story on May 4, he said that "this picture of ruthless murder in a stronghold dedicated to justice, is sad beyond portrayal by our weak words. To this young demon . . . the drooping forms of widows and the tearstained eyes of orphans, give no token of the anguish within." The White Oaks

[24] The clerk was I. M. Bond, whose recollection of the trial was published in the Denver *Post*, February 22, 1903. The Kid "took no more interest in the trial than I would in a hand organ and a monkey."

[25] This explanation was advanced by Leslie Traylor, "Facts Regarding the Escape of Billy the Kid," *Frontier Times*, Vol. XIII (July, 1936), 506–13. For a similar explanation by Maurice G. Fulton, see Hunt, *Tragic Days of Billy the Kid*, 288. The closest thing to an account of the escape is the story of Godfrey Gauss in the Lincoln County *Leader*, January 15, 1890, reproduced in the Godfrey Gauss MS.

Golden Era of May 5, under the title "Reign of Terror," said that "Mr. Robert Olinger was a Deputy United States Marshal, and we understand was admired for his efficiency as an officer and his bravery and geniality as a man."

After his escape, Billy hid out in the Fort Sumner area. Apparently he lacked either the money or the inclination to escape to Old Mexico. Some writers have said that he stayed for the love of a sweetheart, and the names mentioned include Celsa Gutiérrez, Paulita Maxwell, and the pseudononymous "Dulcinea del Toboso." A love affair at this point has somehow seemed appropriate to the story, but there is no solid historical evidence to support it.

The end came on July 14, 1881. The brave, implacable, and ambitious Pat Garrett caught up with the Kid at the old fort. In Pete Maxwell's darkened bedroom, a well-placed bullet ended the Kid's life at what tradition says was twenty-one years, seven months.[26] The general reaction of the press was one of relief. Said the White Oaks *Golden Era* for July 21: "To those who are not familiar with the deceased criminal record cannot comprehend the gladness that pervades the whole of New Mexico and especially this county. He was the worst of criminals." According to the Silver City *New Southwest and Grant County Herald* of July 23, "the vulgar murderer and desperado known as 'Billy the Kid' has met his just deserts at last. . . . Despite the glamor of romance thrown about his dare-devil life by sensation writers, the fact is he was a low down vulgar cut-throat, with probably not one redeeming quality."[27]

Many people in New Mexico could not believe that the desperado was dead, so strong was the legend of his invincibility. A notice posted at Las Vegas on March 24, 1882, eight months after his death, is addressed to "thieves, thugs, fakirs, and bunco steerers," and among the undesirables listed is Billy the Kid. The good citizens sought to banish him even in death.

[26] Readily available accounts of the Kid's death are in Garrett's *Authentic Life of Billy, the Kid* and in John W. Poe's *The Death of Billy the Kid*.
[27] Rasch Collection, Old Lincoln County Memorial Commission, Lincoln, N. M.

CHAPTER VII

The Satanic Billy

THE KID'S DEATH was national news. He had already been introduced to Eastern audiences through several stories in the *National Police Gazette*.[1] But newspaper reports of his lurid career inspired a batch of dime novels and dime "biographies." In these narratives, the Kid is an out-and-out villain; a cold-hearted wretch who giggles while his victims writhe in their death agonies. It was a quarter of a century before a saintly Billy began to elbow out this satanic killer.

His story was first told in a complex network of borrowings among the newspapers. The Eastern papers borrowed heavily from those in New Mexico, the territorial papers reprinted legendary stories from the Eastern press, and the dime novelists copied indiscriminately from both. In all these stories, the Kid is dressed in outrageous clothing, speaks incredibly elegant English, and performs exploits which obviously originated as the "gauziest fabrics of a whiskied brain."

A prime source at this time was a story printed in the Philadelphia *Times* of July 20. Based upon reports from a Mr. Duncan, identified as "a successful trader at Alamosa, New Mexico," the story is essentially dime-novel fiction. Duncan stumbles upon the Kid's impregnable adobe castle, located on the Staked Plains and staffed by handsome women and carefree desperadoes. The Kid dresses in drawers of fine scarlet broadcloth, a blue dragoon's jacket, black buckskin pants decorated with silver bells, and a beaver hat covered with gold and jewels. He is extremely cruel in appearance: "His lips were thin and his upper lip very short; two

[1] These are described in J. C. Dykes, *Billy the Kid, the Bibliography of a Legend*, 11–12.

71

sharp, fierce-looking teeth, much longer than any others in his head, grew out from under that upper lip in an extremely cruel and vicious manner. He was exceedingly vain, not only of his position as leader of a band of between two and three hundred desperadoes [*sic*], but of his personal appearance and his skill with the rifle." Duncan also learned something of the Kid's early history, including the information that he had been born in Ireland.

Duncan's story was "The Wildest Bosh" according to one P. Donan, who published his own account of the Kid's career in the *Chicago Tribune* of August 7, 1881. His history, says Donan, "eclipses all Beadle's dime romances of ruffianism and crime, and dims by comparison the luster of Missouri's pet heroes and exemplars, the dashing Jameses. He needs no bogus silver spurs stuck on his heels by a Philadelphia scribbler to send him galloping down to A BLOODY AND DARE-DEVILISH IMMORTALITY." Donan claims that the Kid exemplified "civilization" in New Mexico at the time, which was the law of the pistol and the knife. There follows a garbled and inflated version of the Lincoln County War. The Kid delights in murder, and Donan paints him in darkest hue, although conceding at the end of his story that "he was calculated to make friends, and strange as it may seem, left many who sincerely mourned his death." Donan's phraseology indicates that he drew on other newspapers for much of his information. He reports that "as many regions clamor for the honor of his birth as for that of ancient Homer." This phrase was borrowed from a story in the Las Vegas *Optic* of July 30, a story which had in turn been borrowed from the Kansas City *Journal* of July 22.

The legend of Billy's killing twenty-one men also passed swiftly from paper to paper. The Santa Fe *Weekly Democrat* in its obituary of July 21 said the Kid had *boasted* of killing twenty-one: "Billy Bonny, alias Antrim, alias Billy the Kid, the twenty-one year old desperado, who is known to have killed sixteen men, and who boasted that he killed a man for every year of his life, will no longer take deliberate aim at his fellow man and kill him, just to keep in practice." The Denver *Republican* of July 22 was more definite. It listed all the twenty-one men, including Brady and Hindman, Morton and Baker, Bernstein and Buckshot Roberts, and Bob Beckwith. The New York *Sun* was also positive that "Bonney, who was born in Brooklyn, had slain twenty-one men and was twenty-one years old when Garrett's shot ended his fiendish career." The New York *Mail* said: "At the time of his death there were twenty-one 'notches' on his gun."[2] Thus the 21–21 formula became fixed in the legend by means of that polite system of plagiarism known to the newspapers of the day as "exchanges."

When dime novelists exploited the Kid's career, they drew most of their material from the garbled newspaper accounts. Two of these novels, both published in 1881, are simply expanded copies of Donan's article in the Chicago *Tribune*. They are *The True Life of Billy the Kid* by Don Jenardo (John Woodruff Lewis) and *The Cowboy's Career, or the Dare Devil Deeds of "Billy, the Kid," the Noted New Mexico Desperado*, by "One of the Kids." Only three chapters of the latter have been recovered, but these fragments reveal shoddy paraphrasing of Donan.[3]

In all three of the accounts, Billy is a young monster. He is the

[2] A collection of obituaries from the New York newspapers has been reprinted in Edwin Corle, *Billy the Kid*, 285–87.

[3] Chapters V, VI, and VII of *The Cowboy's Career* are reprinted in B. A. Botkin, ed., *A Treasury of American Folklore* (New York, Crown Publishers, 1944), 97–104. The novel was originally published in Chicago by Belford, Clark. Donan says in his article:

> Early in 1879 Chisum had "The Kid" appointed Deputy Constable, and armed with a warrant for the arrest, on some trivial charge, of William Morton, and Frank Baker, herdsmen in the employ of Tom Catron, formerly of Lafayette County, Missouri, and the partner of the Hon. Stephen B. Elkins, also a Missouri boy, but long the New Mexican delegate in Congress, and now one of the "solid men" of New York.

The *Cowboy's Career* says:

> Early in 1879 Chisum had arranged for the appointment of the Kid as deputy constable and clothed with this authority he was given a warrant for the arrest, on a trivial charge, of Billy Morton and Frank Baker, two herders employed by Tom Catron. This Catron, by the way, used to live in Lafayette County, Missouri, and was the partner of Hon. Stephen B. Elkins, himself a Missouri boy, later delegated to Congress from New Mexico and now one of the moneyed men of New York.

tool of his evil employers, Chisum and McSwain [*sic*], who are attempting to crush the small ranchers. He is credited with most of the fatalities in the Lincoln County War, and he alone kills Morton and Baker as well as Brady and Hindman. After his escape from the burning McSwain house, he even plans to kill Colonel Dudley, but is dissuaded from doing so. Says Donan: "How many men he killed, how many cattle he stole, how many deeds of daring deviltry and cruelty he perpetrated will probably never be known until the record books of damnation are opened and cowboys and Congressmen, law-makers and law-breakers, Presidents, pirates, Governors, and thugs are summoned to Judgment." Says "Don Jenardo": "How many murders he committed, how many cattle he stole, how many daring deeds of deviltry he performed, will never be known until the dark deeds of cowboys, congressmen, governors, thieves, law-makers, law-breakers, are laid bare to the world."

The Kid's character is hardly credible in these "true" accounts because the authors strain too hard to make him into a villain. Jenardo has the Kid's criminal career originate in the murder of a rival for the hand of the jailer's daughter, Nettie Jones. This villainy is compounded when the Kid later kidnaps Nettie and she dies of ill treatment and exposure. The actual Billy the Kid was, of course, respectful of women and popular with them. The kind of characterization found in the novels is exemplified by Lewis' description of the Kid's behavior after murdering Morton and Baker:

> Dismounting, he dipped his finger in the blood, and made two cross marks on his writ; then, mounting his horse, rode to the office of the magistrate.
>
> "Where are your prisoners?" asked the justice.
>
> "I left 'em," replied the Kid, with the grin of a devil.
>
> "You did not arrest them, eh? Well, what return to you make on the writ?"
>
> "I have already made my mark on the writ, you can fill it out," he said, coolly, drawing forth the paper, and showing the two crosses made with the blood of his victims.

"Great God!" cried the justice, "you have killed them. Where is McCluskey?"

"Ah! I forgot to make one for him," replied the Kid, with a hideous leer.

"Murderer!" shrieked the magistrate, "get out of my presence!" and the frightened justice fled through the rear door of his office.

With the laugh of a demon, Billy the Kid went out to his horse, vaulted into the saddle, and rode away.

Other pseudobiographical dime novels followed, and they too depicted the Kid as a fiendish killer. Edmund Fable, Jr., wrote one, published at Denver in September, entitled *Billy the Kid, The New Mexican Outlaw; or the Bold Bandit of the West! A True and Impartial History of the Greatest of American Outlaws . . . Who Killed A Man For Every Year In His Life.* Borrowing from Donan, Fable claims in his preface that he is writing "the life of an outlaw who was the very incarnation of border civilization, at a period when it was the civilization of the knife and rifle."

The Kid turns to crime, not because he is innately evil, but because of extreme provocation, a view which foreshadows later biographical interpretation. In Silver City, a "syren" robs him, and he is unjustly accused of a store robbery and thrown into jail. "I have tried to do right. . . . Since I came to this country I have molested no man, and see where I am? Robbed of all my hard earnings, passing my time in this dingy prison, why should I strive any longer for that which in this country seems impossible? I'm done with it." He then escapes through the chimney and is launched on his infamous career.

Billy joins the Englishman Tonstill [*sic*], "whose mild and gentle disposition made him the prey to the cattle thieves that swarmed the border." He builds a hide-out on the Staked Plains, a passage lifted from Duncan's tale in the Philadelphia *Times,* and wears the same black buckskin trousers and jeweled hat. Fable also borrows heavily from the Denver *Republican,* and his account of the Kid's twenty-one killings is drawn from that paper's issue of July 22.

Fable threw in another story which had originated in the newspapers. The Santa Fe *New Mexican* of May 1 reported that the Kid had ridden into one of Chisum's camps and shot down three of the four cowboys there. By the survivor he sent word to Chisum that he would continue to "collect" in this manner until Chisum paid him his back wages. The Las Vegas *Optic* of June 10 picked up the story, and Duncan's tale in the Philadelphia paper contains a similar version. After Fable printed the story, it became embedded in the legend and can be traced in a number of publications.[4]

In John E. Morrison's *Life of Billy the Kid, A Juvenile Outlaw*, also published in September, the Kid has a heart "only for anatomical purposes." In this one, even the semihistory of the other novels is abandoned for an imaginary tale of mail robbery in Chicago and stage holdups in Colorado. Later dime novels did not claim to be authentic history, but they featured the Kid as a familiar symbol of the bloodthirsty outlaw. In J. C. Cowdrick's *Silver Mask, the Man of Mystery* (1884), the Kid is cast as a "common cut-throat." He unsuccessfully attempts to force the hero to take a drink, appears with a false beard, escapes from jail on two occasions, and persistently tries to kidnap the heroine. Cowdrick insists on dressing Billy in "a rich Mexican suit, that was ornamented with gold lace and bright buttons. On his head he wore a sombrero, around which was a gold cord with two heavy tassels that dropped over the brim at the left side."[5] In Francis W. Doughty's *Old King Brady and Billy the Kid; or, the Great Detective's Chase* (1890), the Kid remains a contemptible coward and villain. From Billy's infamous career, Doughty draws a moral for the reader: "There is no pleasure or profit—in an outlaw's life."

The first softening of the image, the first tentative step toward

---

[4] Frank Hall, *History of the State of Colorado*, III, 258; Arthur Chapman, "Billy the Kid, A Man All 'Bad,' " *Outing Magazine*, Vol. XLVI (April, 1905), 73–77; William MacLeod Raine, "Billy-the-Kid," *Pacific Monthly*, Vol. XX (July, 1908), 40; George Griggs, *History of Mesilla Valley or the Gadsden Purchase* (Las Cruces, Bronson, 1930), 121; E. C. Abbott ("Teddy Blue") and Helena Huntington Smith, *We Pointed Them North*, 56.

[5] (4th ed., New York, Beadle & Adams, 1884), 6.

a heroic interpretation, occurred when newspaperman Ash Upson in 1882 wrote a biography of the Kid under Pat Garrett's name.[6] Upson specifically states in his preface to *The Authentic Life of Billy, the Kid* that he wishes "to correct the thousand false statements which have appeared in the public newspapers and in yellow-covered, cheap novels." Hence the William Bonney of the book is closer to being a hero. He has virtues which exhibit him "the peer of any fabled brigand on record, unequalled in desperate courage, presence of mind in danger, devotion to his allies, generosity to his foes, gallantry, and all the elements which appeal to the holier emotions."

The necessity of proving this estimation valid explains why Upson included so much fictional material in the book. Although he claims to be writing history, Upson's problem was more literary and commercial than historical: how to make a hero out of a criminal. So he employs time-tested literary techniques to achieve this purpose. There are melodramatic episodes of the dime-novel variety, elegant speeches by the hero, and a vividly imagined act of provocation which drives Billy to his career in crime. If he is to be a hero, his outlawry must result from social injustice rather than from any defect of character.

Take Upson's story of the Kid's first killing. The victim is not F. P. Cahill, the Arizona blacksmith known to history, but an unnamed "filthy loafer" who insults the Kid's mother and whom twelve-year-old Billy subsequently stabs to death. When the Kid's adult friend Ed Moulton is attacked by this loafer in a saloon brawl, the Kid springs into action with fatal results. The loafer still appears in biographical essays, even though the story has been proved false.[7] But of greater interest is why Ash Upson put the episode into his book. Of course, youthful exploits of this nature

[6] Upson discusses his authorship of the biography in a letter to a relative, reprinted in William A. Keleher, *The Fabulous Frontier* (Santa Fe, Rydal Press, 1945), 125. Siringo described Upson as a "jovial old soul" who "drank too much Tom and Jerry." *A Texas Cowboy*, 260, 265.

[7] Newspaper feature articles and popular magazine stories are the chief media for perpetuating the legend. Delos Avery, "The Life and Death of Billy the Kid,"

are part of most heroic narratives.[8] Since little authentic information is available to biographers, they usually invent precocious episodes for their heroes. Upson also needed some sentimental justification for the crimes of his hero. Such an incident had to be found or created. What could be more appealing or justifiable in Victorian America than punishment of an insult to motherhood?

There are other generous acts which redeem much of the Kid's nominal villainy. He and another "young knight" named Jesse Evans rescue a wagon train from the Apaches. This is one of the familiar feats by which we identify the hero in Western stories, and later writers interested in fashioning a heroic Billy borrow this episode.[9] Similarly, the Kid's loyalty is proved by his rescue of an old comrade, Melquiades Segura, from a prison cell at San Elizario, Texas. This legendary story seemed to fit the picture of Billy that Upson was trying to create.

Upson throws in other escapades for literary effect. Billy kills a "soldier blacksmith" at Fort Bowie, Arizona. This is a distant echo of the authenticated Cahill shooting. Cahill was a blacksmith, but he was not a soldier, nor was he a Negro as later versions

---

Chicago Sunday Tribune, August 27, 1944; Norman Wiltsey, "Killer Kid," *True West,* Vol. IV (April, 1957), 5; W. Thetford LeViness, "Tourists Take Up the Trail of Billy the Kid," New York *Sunday Times,* June 3, 1962. For refutations of the legend, see Jim Blair MS, New Mexico Writers' Program, WPA, Santa Fe; statement by Ed Moulton, Old Lincoln County Memorial Commission, Lincoln, N. M.; Philip J. Rasch and Robert N. Mullin, "New Light on the Legend of Billy the Kid," *New Mexico Folklore Record,* Vol. VII (1952–53), 1–6. Blair, who was Moulton's son-in-law, said in part: "Billie the Kid never did kill anyone in Silver City. That story is all false. The story of him killing a man over Ed Moulton is positively not true. Mr. Moulton never would read an article about Billie because he would get angry for he said, 'They write so many lies about the boy, and I know the ones are false about his killings in Grant Co.'"

[8] Thus, Buffalo Bill Cody at the age of nine captures an outlaw band.—Prentiss Ingraham, *The Adventures of Buffalo Bill from Boyhood to Manhood* (Beadle's Boy's Library, No. 1) (New York, Beadle & Adams, 1881), 2.

[9] Harvey Fergusson, "Billy the Kid," *American Mercury,* Vol. V (May, 1925), 224; E. B. Mann, *Gamblin' Man* (1934), 30.

would have us believe.[10] In fact the "loafer" at Silver City and the "blacksmith" at Fort Bowie became fused into one episode in the legend. Even competent historians had a hard time separating the two.[11]

Lacking substantial information on the Lincoln County War, Garrett and Upson credit the Kid with most of the killings by the McSween faction. According to the authors, his victims total twelve, although history now records only four "positives" (Cahill, Grant, Bell, and Olinger) and three "possibles" (Brady or Hindman; Morton or Baker; Carlyle).[12] But these killings are not the senseless sadism of the dime-novel psychopath. Rather they are revenge for the assassination of Tunstall, for whom the Kid entertained "a strong friendship and deep respect, which was fully reciprocated by Tunstall." The reader of the Garrett-Upson biography could, if he chose, find some excuse for the Kid's murderous propensities.

The *Authentic Life* was not a commercial success. Upson in a letter to a relative blames the publisher, which happened to be the Santa Fe *New Mexican,* for improperly marketing the book.[13] But the volume was the source from which later writers drew their facts about the Kid. The loafer, the blacksmith, the Apache–wagon train episode, even the same dialogue, appear over and over again in a hundred succeeding narratives. This is proof positive that the *Life* makes good reading, even though it is only semi-history.

One who borrowed the sentimental approach from Upson was Charlie Siringo, the cowboy-author of *A Texas Cowboy* (1885).

---

[10] Siringo, *A Texas Cowboy,* 270; Walter Noble Burns, *The Saga of Billy the Kid,* 78; Edwin Corle, "Billy the Kid in Arizona," *Arizona Highways,* Vol. XXX (February, 1954), 34.

[11] Eugene Cunningham, *Triggernometry,* 135; Ramon Adams, *A Fitting Death for Billy the Kid,* 19, 146–47.

[12] Rasch, *New Mexico Folklore Record,* Vol. IX, 8–14; J. C. Dykes, "Introduction" to Garrett, *Authentic Life of Billy the Kid,* xxiv.

[13] Keleher, *Fabulous Frontier,* 125.

Siringo adds touches of his own to the basic narrative. He reports that the Kid's first killing was "a Negro soldier at Fort Union"; his second, a "young blacksmith at Silver City." He chooses the newspaper-dime-novel version of the battle at Lincoln and includes an episode in which Billy the Kid plays battle songs on the Mc-Sween piano.

Billy emerges as a likable, if not heroic, character in the book. There are plenty of tears shed in Chapter XXVII, which is entitled "A True Sketch of 'Billy the Kid's' Life." One of the anecdotes relates how Billy cares for a sick man and pays his bills. When the invalid tells Siringo about the episode, "tears chased one another down his manly cheeks." When the Kid leaves home, we are given this word picture: "It was a cold stormy night when he, after kissing his mother's pale cheeks for the last time on this earth, rode out into the darkness." And when the Kid dies, more tears are shed: "The remains of what was once a fond mother's darling were buried next day in the old dilapidated Military Cemetary, without a murmur, except from one, a pretty young half-breed mexican damsel, whose tears, no doubt, has dampened the lonely grave more than once." The key statement in Siringo's sketch is this: "Let it be said right here that the Kid was not the cruel hearted wretch that he was pictured out to be in scores of yellow-back novels, written about him. He was an outlaw and maybe a very wicked youth, but then he had some good qualities which, now that he is no more, he should be credited with."[14]

It is somewhat surprising to find a cowboy publicizing this basically sentimental version of the Kid. To the average Southwestern cowboy of the 1880's, Billy the Kid was a murderous cow thief.[15] Siringo's book was more expertly marketed than the Garrett-Upson

---

[14] *A Texas Cowboy,* 279.

[15] Abbott, *We Pointed Them North,* 56; N. Howard "Jack" Thorp (in collaboration with Neil M. Clark), *Pardner of the Wind* (Caldwell, Idaho, Caxton Printers, 1945), 168–93. Thorp said: "Actually, Billy the Kid was just a little, small-sized cow-and-horse thief who lived grubbily and missed legal hanging by only a few days. . . . his killings were more often on the order of safe butchery than stand-up-and-fight-it-out gun battles."

biography. It sold many thousands of copies and went into several editions, being constantly in print up to 1926. Here then was the nucleus of a heroic interpretation.

It was many years, however, before the public changed its view of the Kid. Writers continued to describe him as did Frank Hall in his *History of the State of Colorado* (1891) as "the most desperate and bloody-minded civilized white man that ever cursed the border with his crimes. . . . The earth was well rid of him."[16] Similarly, James Cox in *The Historical and Biographical Record of the Cattle Industry* (1895) referred to Billy as a "cur" who shot men in the back.

Emerson Hough was a popular writer of Western history who also viewed the Kid as an archfiend. Hough practiced law at White Oaks in the early 1880's, and this community was virulently anti-Bonney because of the Kid's role in the Carlyle shooting. Hough was also a close friend of Pat Garrett, who was being criticized for his "betrayal" of the Kid and who was eager to build up Billy's reputation as a bad man. Hough reflects such views in *The Story of the Cowboy* (1897):

> The whole region was full of horse thieves and outlaws, the worst of these being under the leadership of the notorious cut-throat, Billy the Kid, a name famous even yet along the border. Billy the Kid died at the ripe age of twenty-three, and at that time had killed twenty-three men, committing his first murder when he was but fourteen years of age. He and his men inaugurated a reign of terror, which made his name a dread one from one end of the country to the other.[17]

Hough added several legends to the Kid's biography, since they seemed appropriate to the figure he imagined the Kid to be. The young fiend and his gang shoot down seven Mexicans at a water hole, "just to see them kick." The gang also raids various towns; on one occasion, they shoot out the windows of a house at White Oaks where some women are staying, and this enrages the entire

[16] III, 258.
[17] Page 304.

community. When Billy is just about to leave for Old Mexico, he tarries to say good-by to his Mexican sweetheart, and Pat Garrett kills him.

Hough also publicized his views of the Kid in an article appearing in *Everybody's Magazine* in 1901.[18] This piece is a moral rather than a historical study of the Kid. Billy was doomed after "he first found the brand of Cain upon his brow." The Kid is characterized by a series of animal metaphors: "an animal born with a cat soul"; "the little tiger"; "the little wild beast." All the Kid's twenty-one killings (Hough changes the 23–23 ratio of his book to 21–21 in the article.) are unjustified. In particular, the Kid's murder of J. W. Bell and Bob Orrendorf (Olinger) is inexcusable, since they "treated their prisoner kindly and with a certain good fellowship." Hough was careless as a historian, but as a contributor to the legend of a satanic Billy, he has an important role.

Other magazine writers borrowed their episodes and interpretations from Hough. One of these was Arthur Chapman, whose article in *Outing Magazine* in 1905 had the title, "Billy the Kid— A Man All 'Bad.'" Chapman reports that the Kid killed out of pure wantonness, one example being the slaughter of three Mexicans at a water hole "just to see them kick." In the Lincoln County War, Billy sides with the rustlers who are making life miserable for the honest men. Chapman's greatest contribution to the legend, however, was his version of the Kid's court trial at Mesilla. Judge Bristol sentences the Kid to be "hanged by the neck until you are dead, dead, dead. . . . Whereupon the boyish prisoner laughed in the judge's face and chanted in mockery; 'And you can go to h——l, h——l, h——l!'" Since this defiance of society seemed appropriate to the villainous Billy, later writers copied the story even though it was historically incorrect.[19]

Thus an antihero tradition had been created by 1905. Origi-

[18] "Billy the Kid, The True Story of a Western 'Bad Man,'" Vol. V (September, 1901), 302–10.

[19] Raine, *Pacific Monthly,* Vol. XX (1908), 44; Lorenzo Walters, *Tombstone's Yesterdays* (1928), 118, 231; Marshall Fishwick, *The American Hero: Myth and Reality,* 97.

nating in early newspaper accounts, dime novels, and popular magazine articles, the tradition was drawn upon by later historians, magazine writers, and novelists who were skeptical of any glorification of the outlaw.[20] But as time softened memories of the Kid's crimes, the legend changed. The seeds of a heroic saga were embedded in the apologetic sections of the Garrett-Upson biography and Charlie Siringo's book. It was only necessary that new interpreters exploit the sentimental potentialities of the Kid's biography to create a new and saintly Billy.

[20] E. Douglas Branch, *The Cowboy and His Interpreters* (New York, D. Appleton, 1926), 176; Burton Rascoe, *Belle Starr* (New York, Random House, 1941), 3–12; Nelson Nye, *Pistols for Hire* (novel); Thorp, *Pardner of the Wind* (1945); Adams, *A Fitting Death for Billy the Kid* (1960).

CHAPTER VIII

The Saintly Billy

IN 1903, Walter Woods wrote a play called *Billy the Kid*. It was a four-act melodrama in which Billy, though nominally an outlaw, is actually the hero. He is betrayed into outlawry by his father, who is the real villain of the story. The father murders Billy's mother, seizes her ranch, and frames the Kid for the crime. Billy organizes an outlaw band which steals from the rich and helps the poor. He finally catches up with his father, but in a generous mood he gives the villain some of his clothing and a chance to escape. The father is killed by the sheriff's posse, who think they have gotten Billy the Kid. But the real Billy happily leaves with his beautiful sweetheart to start a new life: "To the law I am dead. Today my life begins anew. Come Nellie—we'll wander down life's pathway together, where the sun shines always. . . ."[1]

This sentimental version of the Kid's career became popular in subsequent literary interpretations. In particular, the device of allowing the Kid to escape to Old Mexico at the end of the story identifies him as the real hero. Novelists and motion picture script writers have been especially attached to this happy ending. In their versions, as in Woods' play, the Kid usually rides off with his lady love while someone else is buried at Fort Sumner.[2] Thus Woods's treatment signifies an important shift in the psychology of the

1 The play is reprinted in Garrett H. Leverton, ed., *The Great Diamond Robbery and Other Recent Melodramas*, Vol. VIII of *America's Lost Plays*, 199–255.

2 *Billy the Kid* (*Metro-Goldwyn-Mayer*, 1930); Mann, *Gamblin' Man* (1934); *The Outlaw* (Howard Hughes, 1943); *Son of Billy the Kid* (Adventure Productions, 1949). The publisher's prologue to Mann's novel reads in part: "History says that the bullets of the law got Billy the Kid in the end. But legend, in the fifty years since then, has insisted that the Kid escaped. E. B. Mann has chosen to follow the

Bonney saga. From being a symbol of malicious criminality, the Kid now is viewed as a victim of circumstances who deserved a better life.

Billy the Kid opened on Broadway in 1906 and then played in theaters across the country for the next dozen years. It helped to create a new and sympathetic Billy the Kid in the public mind. But despite the play, the Bonney legend did not flourish. The absence of any biographies was striking evidence that it was languishing. By 1925, Harvey Fergusson was asking in a magazine article, "Who remembers Billy the Kid?"[3] Some new effort that would exploit the heroic potentialities of the Kid's career was needed to rekindle public interest in him.

Fergusson himself took a step toward reviving the legend. He characterized Billy as a "quixotic romantic, who cared nothing for money. He lived and died an idealist." This was getting pretty far from the facts, but Fergusson cited episodes which he thought proved the Kid's idealism. These include the murder of the loafer who had insulted his mother, the rescue of the wagon train from the Apaches, and the manner of his death. As a true romantic, he had preferred to die rather than leave his Mexican sweetheart. Furthermore, "like Robin Hood, he befriended the poor." The comparison with the prototypical English bandit indicated the direction that the legend was soon to take.

The writer who really initiated the modern revival of the legend was a Chicago newspaperman, Walter Noble Burns. His *Saga of Billy the Kid,* first published in 1926, is neither an objective narrative of the Lincoln County War nor a reliable account of the Kid's career. It is rather a magnificent classic of American folklore and mythology. Burns was a superlative writer rather than an objective reporter, and the virtues of the book are those of novelistic fiction.

The defects of the *Saga* as history have been sufficiently noted

legend, and has shown us the Kid's spectacular get-away so vividly that it seems it must have happened so."

[3] "Billy the Kid," *American Mercury,* Vol. V (May, 1925), 224–31.

by critics.[4] Burns does not cite a single historical source, refers to specific dates only three times, and makes glaring factual errors. He relies heavily on imaginary conversations and "reconstructed" conversations—devices which historians generally eye with suspicion. He repeats most of the dime-novel and Garrett-Upson legends about the Kid's early years, explaining that though they are not authenticated, "they have at least always gone with the legend and have such authority as long-established currency may confer."[5] Among these traditional tales are those of the loafer at Silver City and the rescue of Melquiades Segura. Other serious charges are that the book is a partisan defense of the McSween faction and a sentimental apologia for Billy the Kid.

Certainly when Burns was collecting material for his saga, he talked only with the McSween side or with the Kid's friends. George and Frank Coe, Mrs. McSween, Ygenio (Higinio) Salazar, and other native New Mexicans all testified that the Kid was a likable and grossly wronged youth. (Frank Coe remembered Billy as a generous lad who'd give a friend the shirt off his back, while Mrs. Paulita Jaramillo said that he had been courteous, gallant, and respectful.) The ambiguous nature of the war itself was obscured by a one-sided presentation, which, however useful for literary purposes, was historically unjustified. McSween and the Kid emerge as the symbols of true justice, and Billy in particular becomes another Robin Hood fighting for the oppressed farmers and Mexicans. He fights out of a selfless belief in the right and as retribution for the death of Tunstall. "Others fought for hire. Billy the Kid's inspiration was the loyalty of friendship."

[4] Eugene Manlove Rhodes, "In Defense of Pat Garrett," *Sunset Magazine,* Vol. LIX (September, 1927), 26–27, 85–91; Burton Rascoe, *Belle Starr* (New York, Random House, 1941), 3–42; Ramon Adams, "With Our Rocking Chair Historians," Denver *Westerners Brand Book* (1952), 17–35. As an example of Burns's carelessness, he reported that Lucio Montoya of the Murphy faction was seriously wounded during the battle in Lincoln (p. 121). The statement has been vigorously denied by Montoya's relatives, among others. See interview with Mrs. Rufina Maes, Montoya's daughter, in Alamagordo *News,* April 6, 1960 (Rasch Collection); also Otero, *The Real Billy the Kid,* 163.

[5] Page 83.

Burns was the first writer to exploit the richly romantic Mexican background with its connotations of strumming guitars and beautiful *señoritas*. Some of his Mexican storytellers are fabrications,[6] but he did make effective use of genuine Mexican characters and of lovely names like San Patricio, Puerto de Luna, and Río Bonito. The net effect was the creation of just the right atmosphere for a folk legend and added sympathy for the Kid as a friend of the simple and gentle natives.

Burns's rhetorical ability produced some of the classic passages in the literature of the West. His description of the Kid's escape from the burning McSween house has been the model for many other accounts of the episode.[7] It is a splendid example of vivid writing, even though its historical accuracy must be questioned:

> A yell of triumph went up from his enemies. This was the man they wanted. "Here comes the Kid!" They rose behind the wall. They threw their rifles to a level on the flying figure. "Get him, boys!" "Kill him!" A salvo of twenty guns welcomed him into that crimson square of death.
>
> The Kid's trigger fingers worked with machine-gun rapidity. Fire poured from the muzzles of his forty-fours in continuous streaks. Bob Beckwith, slayer of McSween, fell dead across the wall, his rifle clattering to the ground. . . . On he ran like a darting, elusive shadow as if under mystic protection. He cleared the back wall at a leap. He bounded out of the flare of the conflagration. Darkness swallowed him at a gulp. Splashing across the Bonito, he gained the safety of the hills.[8]

The best tribute to Burns's literary skill is the extent to which novelists have adopted not only his general point of view but also much of his specific phraseology.[9] In fact, Burns established cer-

[6] Page 65.

[7] Compare Burns's description with that of E. B. Mann in *Gamblin' Man*, 190:

> A yell went up outside the wall. "There he comes! Get him! *Get the Kid*." This was the man they waited for; the man they wanted most of all.

[8] Pages 139–40.

[9] Compare Burns's description of the shooting of the Kid (p. 284) with the same episode in Charles Neider's *The Authentic Death of Hendry Jones*, 191.

tain conventions for novelistic treatment of character and events. For example, the antagonism between the Kid and Bob Olinger is steadily built up, and we get an inside view of the thoughts of J. W. Bell and Olinger just before the Kid kills them.[10]

Olinger is expertly portrayed as a snarling, foulmouthed bully. The reversal of roles for Olinger is required by the legend of a saintly Billy. A quarter of a century before, Emerson Hough in his article in *Everybody's* had described Bell and Olinger as "worthy deputy sheriffs," who "treated their prisoner kindly and with a certain good fellowship." But in the *Saga*, Olinger "never ceased to revile the Kid in tirades of scurrility and billingsgate." He taunts the Kid to escape so that he can be potted like a rabbit. " 'Eighteen buckshot, Kid,' he snarled. 'Don't forget what I said. Make a break and you get 'em right between your shoulder blades.' " This dramatic writing enlists sympathy for the helpless Kid, and when Billy greets Olinger from over the sights of the bully's own shotgun, one exults to see the tables turned. All the contemporary newspapers were horrified at Olinger's murder, but for latter-day enthusiasts it has been one of the most satisfying episodes in the legend, thanks to Burns's revision.

Burns also brings his rhetorical artillery to bear upon Pat Garrett. Garrett and his "man-hunters" unmercifully hound the Kid, and the sheriff even employs "savage trackers" from the Apache reservation to pick up the Kid's trail. When Billy and his band of merry men ride into Fort Sumner to enjoy Christmas Eve, Garrett uncharitably ambushes them and kills Tom O'Folliard. Burns sketches a poignant description of the episode: "Good cheer and happiness in the air. Latch strings hanging out. Warm-hearted hospitality in every home." Actually the event took place on December 18; the use of "Christmas Eve" for sentimental imagery is what Eugene Manlove Rhodes called a "jury trap."[11]

[10] Compare Burns, 245; Corle, *Billy the Kid*, 242; Neider, *Authentic Death of Hendry Jones*, 78–79.

[11] "In Defense of Pat Garrett," *Sunset Magazine*, Vol. LIX (September, 1927), 87.

The theme of betrayal runs through the narrative. Governor Wallace betrays the Kid by reneging on a promise to pardon him for the Brady murder. Garrett becomes a Judas when he agrees to hunt down his onetime friend. He finally traps the Kid at Fort Sumner only because "the Kid was betrayed for a silver dollar by a rum-soaked bum of the boozing-kens." Thus Billy's tragedy is caused not by any defect in his own character, since he genuinely wanted to reform, but by the persecution he suffered. The graphic and convincing way in which Burns developed this thesis made his book a classic and persuaded millions that Bonney was indeed the "idol of the Southwest." Even in New Mexico itself, the testimony collected from old-time residents ten years after the book was published simply echoed Burns's interpretation.[12]

Burns served an important function in reviving a great Southwestern legend that was in danger of dying out. He rewrote and consolidated the old tales and legends, making them suitable for further elaboration by a host of subsequent popularizers. He was obviously working from a pre-set literary formula rather than from any plan of objective research. In fact, he used exactly the same formula in *The Robin Hood of El Dorado* (1932) to resuscitate the Joaquín Murieta legend. One finds there the same Mexican characters, the same "reconstructed" conversations, and the same sentimental sympathy for the doomed young hero. While Burns's book must be criticized for its defects as a work of history, one has to admit that he was sensitive to what the American people wanted in their legends. He capitalized on the age-old appeal of outlaw biographies. He realized that men admire, however covertly, the rebel against authority.

The *Saga of Billy the Kid* was written like a movie script, and when Metro-Goldwyn-Mayer adapted it in producing the first Billy the Kid movie in 1930, they used Burns's basic plot structure. Johnny Mack Brown, former All-American football player, portrayed a clean-cut Billy the Kid. Reviewer Creighton Peet re-

[12] John Allred MS.

marked that the Kid is shown as "sort of a philanthropic Robin Hood who shot only to avenge a wrong done to a friend."[13] There was a further revision of history when the Kid was permitted to escape at the end of the story. This doctoring annoyed Mr. Peet, who said that "Billy has been whitewashed—at the end he rides off into the night with the sweet little gal, contrary to all history." However, *Billy the Kid* popularized themes which were utilized in subsequent films—the Kid as a defender of the weak, as an avenging justice for the honest and upright (Tunstall), in short, as an outlaw in name only.

The same themes were also popularized by E. B. Mann in his 1934 novel, *Gamblin' Man*. Mann draws on Burns for interpretation and some phraseology. The Kid fights on the side of right and justice in the Lincoln County War. To the heroine, Kathie, he appears as "just a youngster; just a friendly, clear-eyed boy with a smile that was sometimes gay and sometimes wistful." The Kid fights because of Tunstall's murder: "a swift deep friendship had sprung up between him and the Englishman that was based upon mutual respect." Even in the war, the Kid retains his sense of fair play. He confronts Sheriff Brady on the street before Brady and Hindman are slain. Such small but significant revisions of history are in the nature of apologetics, because the Kid's actual behavior was quite different.

Billy and other characters are given speeches in defense of his reputation. The Kid comments upon the ambiguity of "law" and "justice" in New Mexico during his time:

> The law's a great thing, ain't it Pat? I killed Morton and Baker and they made me an outlaw. You killed O'Folliard and Bowdre and you're the most famous fightin' Sheriff in New Mexico! I killed Bob Beckwith, Ollinger's side-kick, in open fight—me, alone, against not less than twenty killers churnin' lead at me. Ollinger, with twenty killers helpin' him, murdered Tunstall who never fired a shot! I must stand

[13] Review of *Billy the Kid, Outlook*, Vol. CLVI (October 29, 1930), 353.

trial for my life, with Ollinger standin' guard over me with a gun! . . .
It's sure a funny world![14]

If the reader has any doubts concerning where Mann's sympathies
lie, they are clearly revealed by his adoption of a device first used
by Walter Woods twenty-eight years previously. A look-alike is
killed by Pat Garrett, and the Kid and Kathie are permitted to
leave for a new life in Old Mexico.

In his book *The Real Billy the Kid* (1936), Miguel Otero
worked the same vein that Burns had. Otero talked to the same
people, and their testimony became even more enthusiastic. Martin Chávez reported that "Billy was one of the kindest and best
boys I ever knew, and far superior in many respects to his pursuers. He was not blood-thirsty, he was forced into killing in defense of his own life. . . . a perfect gentleman and a man with a
noble heart."[15] Higinio Salazar also expressed a popular view
among the Mexicans when he said: "Pat Garrett, who took up the
pursuit of the Kid for them was a cow thief himself, as everybody
in Fort Sumner knew. He went back on Billy the Kid for money
and for the promise of office. He was not the brave man many think
he was."[16] Otero himself endorsed these opinions. In contrast to
the Kid, he thought that Garrett was of a "mercenary and grasping
nature." He pointed out that the Kid "was loyal to his friends and
above all, loved his mother devotedly. He was unfortunate in
starting life, and became a victim of circumstances." In legend,
most outlaws love their mothers and suffer from "circumstances"
rather than from defects of character.[17]

Otero's account of the Kid's early life is drawn from legend

[14] Page 267.

[15] Pages 167, 172.

[16] Page 128.

[17] The motivation for Jesse James's outlawry was a brutal attack by Pinkerton
detectives on his mother's house, in which she was seriously injured. Joaquín Murieta
was driven to crime by oppression at the hands of the Americans, who also ravished
his sweetheart. See Mody G. Boatright, "The Western Bad Man as Hero," *Publications of the Texas Folklore Society,* Vol. XXVII (Dallas, 1957), 96–105.

rather than from history. The dialogue in many of the stories betrays their dime-novel origins. In one encounter between the Kid and John Long at Fort Sumner, there is the following:

> Long hailed them. "Where do you think you're going, you damned little bastard?"
>
> The Kid wheeled quickly, walked up to him, his eyes ablaze, and said quietly: "Who did you address that remark to, sir?"
>
> "Oh! I was just joking with that other fellow," said Long.
>
> "Be very careful how you joke fellows in whose company I happen to be. You'll notice that I'm the littlest of the two. I am too stupid to understand your jokes. If you ever drop another one that hits the ground as close to me as that last one did, I'll crack your crust. Do you understand?
>
> Long made no reply. He was completely cowed.[18]

In another episode, the Kid outwits Joe Grant by examining Grant's gun and setting the hammer on an empty chamber. When Grant draws on the Kid, Billy kills him and then remarks with grand oratory: "Unfortunate fool! I've been there too often to let a man of his calibre overhaul my baggage. I wonder if he's a specimen of the Texas desperadoes?"[19]

The contemporary newspaper reports say nothing of how the Kid shot Grant. Otero used his imagination in reconstructing the event, and in so doing he unconsciously drew upon a classic device from folklore. The "Clever Hero" of folklore always outwits his opponent by such smart moves.[20]

The conversion of the Kid into a knight-errant is also evident in folklore. Oral tales feature the Kid's generosity or justify his actions by linking him with a "cause." In one tale told by the native New Mexicans, the Kid saves a girl from the unwelcome attentions of a "bad" outlaw. In another story, clearly descended

[18] Otero, *The Real Billy the Kid,* 76–77.

[19] *Ibid.,* 87.

[20] Orrin Klapp, "The Clever Hero," *Journal of American Folklore,* Vol. LXVII (January–March, 1954), 21–34.

from the original anecdote introduced by Charlie Siringo in 1885, the Kid nurses an old-timer back to health. In a third story of this type, he save a prospective victim from being robbed of his gold.[21]

Testimony collected by the New Mexico Writers Project in the mid-1930's reflects the justification of the Kid's actions popularized by Burns and Otero. Josh Brent said that "Billie the Kid was not a killer but was fighting for a cause and father told us that he was an unusually nice boy." John Allred said that his family "always felt that the McSweens were fighting for a cause," and there were echoes of Burns in his comment that "it was a dirty, cowardly trick for Pat Garrett to pull when he killed the boy." These views from Lincoln County itself are measures of the growing legend of a saintly Billy.

The lore also incorporates resurrection or Billy-the-Kid-still-lives tales. Albuquerque and El Paso newspapers printed such stories in 1926.[22] In the mid-1930's, a railroad conductor told one writer that the Kid was still alive in Texas, and an old Mexican in Santa Fe gave another scribe the same information.[23] The WPA guide to New Mexico in 1940 took note of such legends by saying that "a number of people in remote parts of the state believe the Kid is still alive, despite the fact that the circumstances of his death are well authenticated."[24] As recently as 1955, a book published in New Mexico was entirely devoted to a resurrection tale.[25] Such legends, of course, surround Jesse James, Joaquín Murieta,

[21] Frank G. Applegate, "New Mexico Legends," *Southwest Review,* Vol. XVII (Winter, 1932), 201–208; Paul Wesley, "Bandit Samaritan," *New Mexico Magazine,* Vol. XVII (October, 1939), 57; Mrs. Flora Miller in El Paso *Times,* July 10, 1955 (clipping in Rasch Collection).

[22] Owen P. White, *Trigger Fingers,* 261–67.

[23] Frank M. King, *Mavericks* (Pasadena, Trail's End Publishing Company, 1947), 51; Eugene Cunningham, "The Kid Still Rides," *New Mexico Magazine,* Vol. XIII (March, 1935), 13–15.

[24] *New Mexico: A Guide to the Colorful State* (New York, Hastings House, 1940), 104.

[25] C. L. Sonnichsen and William V. Morrison, *Alias Billy the Kid.*

and other outlaw-heroes.[26] Their existence indicates a sentimental sympathy for the hero involved.

When the hero has been featured in a sufficient number of biographies, novels, plays, and folk tales, his legend can be said to have reached maturity. That point came for the Bonney legend in 1938, when Aaron Copland created a ballet about him. Far removed in space and time from the Kid's misdeeds, Copland and his sophisticated metropolitan audiences could sentimentalize about the tragic fate of the boy outlaw. The ballet has been quite popular and is periodically restaged. Here was a further step in the deification of the Kid, the only American outlaw to be immortalized in this art form.

To Harvey Fergusson's query of 1925, "Who remembers Billy the Kid?" anyone surveying the legend in 1940 could reply that he had become the Robin Hood of the Southwest and of the nation. But there were still many Southwesterners who were not convinced by the contemporary glorification of the Kid. Frank King's wry comment is perhaps typical of these: "I see where them movie people are figgerin' on makin' another picture of 'Billy the Kid.' This time they are goin' to represent the Kid as a bold 'Robin Hood' robbing the rich an' givin' the loot to the poor. This is the first time I ever heard that the Kid was that sort of a feller."[27]

[26] Homer Croy, *Jesse James Was My Neighbor* (New York, Dell Publishing Company, 1949), 205–10; J. C. Cunningham, *The Truth About Murieta* (Los Angeles, Wetzel Publishing Company, 1939), 32, 278.

[27] *Mavericks*, 58.

CHAPTER IX

The American Robin Hood

By the 1940's the tradition of a saintly Billy, anchored firmly in the Garrett-Burns-Otero line of interpretation, had become the standard version of his life. This tradition incorporated the betrayal motif so expertly formulated by Burns, the redeeming personality traits emphasized by Otero, and the Kid's association with a "cause" which was the theme of so many of the folk tales and legends. The result has been the creation of a national hero, and indeed the popularity of the Bonney saga indicates that it will become an American version of the Robin Hood legend.

In biography, the sentimental tradition has continued to flourish. Frazier Hunt, in his *Tragic Days of Billy the Kid* (1956), views the Kid as a romantic idealist. Hunt utilized materials collected over many years by the late Maurice Garland Fulton, a leading authority on the Kid's life. But while Hunt's biography is more factually reliable than Burns's, the interpretation is basically the same. The Kid is a likable boy betrayed by powerful and ambitious men such as Garrett and Wallace.

Emphasis is placed upon the Kid's diminutive size and pathetic situation. "The slight figure of the homeless, motherless boy, cast in his desperate role, must have appealed to this romantic girl with the compassionate heart." Everything about the Kid is "little"; he has a little bay mare, and all he wants to do is sing a little, dance a little, and live out his own little adventurous life. But there are always the big, bad men who will not leave him alone. Chief among these is Pat Garrett, who was mercenary where the Kid was idealistic. Garrett "hired out his pistols to the highest bidder," and he is compared to the "bought Indian scouts" who helped exterminate their fellow Apaches.[1] One's sympathies are all with Billy in his final moments after reading rhetoric like this (italics mine): "The break was Pat's—the priceless second of hesitation, the *decent* second the Kid gave this *man-hunter* rather than kill him without giving him a chance to draw his gun." The implication is that only the Kid played fair, but this is an injustice to Pat Garrett. Even the Kid's friends were willing to admit that Garrett had to shoot first if he wanted to survive.

Hunt also dramatizes other features of the legend as it is currently interpreted. After the defeat of the McSween faction at Lincoln, the Kid and his friends are not really outlaws but fighters for a cause. "They had been on the right side, but unfortunately the right side was the side that had lost." This assumption somehow makes the Kid's outlawry more excusable, although as a historical conclusion it is subject to debate. This "cause" and this idealism, presumably passed on to the Kid by John Tunstall, keep him in Lincoln County even when he has a chance to escape to Old Mexico. He simply could not abandon "his own projected vision of himself as a valiant boy on horse-back, fighting his lone battles seemingly against insurmountable odds." Judging from his letters to the newspapers, the Kid did not see himself as this kind of an idealist, but Hunt states here how the legend sees him. In retrospect, he appears as a hero because he fights for the "right" and not for himself alone.

Novelists have tended to be less sentimental about the Kid than biographers. Nelson Nye's *Pistols for Hire* (1941) is one of the most critical portraits of the Kid which can be found in literature. The point of view is the Murphy side, as seen by the gunfighter-hero Flick Farson, and the Kid appears as a vicious hired killer lacking any human qualities. He tries to shoot Farson in the back, his usual method of operation in the novel. In Edwin Corle's *Billy the Kid* (1953), a love story is woven into the fic-

[1] Hunt, *Tragic Days of Billy the Kid,* 303, 215–16.

tionalized biography. But the Kid is again an inhuman killer. The historically unverified story of his killing the clerk Bernstein at the Mescalero reservation is reintroduced to point up his amoral qualities: "Casually the Kid drew his six-shooter and without giving it any thought he sent a bullet through the clerk's heart, and his irritating voice bothered them no more. The Kid returned the gun to its holster. He had merely swatted a fly. He never thought about it again."

Another novelist to manipulate the myth is Charles Neider in his *Authentic Death of Hendry Jones* (1956). The scene is shifted from New Mexico to California, but the classic story remains the same. Names like Dedrick, Zamora, Longworth, and Carlyle are borrowed from Lincoln County chronicles. The inspiration for many of the episodes comes from Walter Noble Burns's interpretation of the legend. This is particularly noticeable in the Kid's (Hendry Jones) escape from jail, in the handling of the tension between him and Olinger (who appears here as "Lon Dedrick") and in the description of his death. The Mexican theme is also utilized by means of a love affair with the girl Nika Machado—a theme which was elaborated in a movie made from this book.[2] The appeal of the Bonney legend for novelists proves that an important reason for its vitality is its story values.

Motion picture producers, ever alert to popular themes of a semihistorical nature, have periodically exploited the legend also. At least twenty-five films based on the Kid's career have been produced in the last twenty years. Their plots differ little from that of the first Billy the Kid movie in 1930. The Kid is clean-cut and likable, champions the poor people, and in many of the pictures is allowed to ride off at the end. The title of one recent production, *The Left Handed Gun* (1958), reveals a small but characteristic

[2] The film was entitled *The One-Eyed Jacks* (1961), with Marlon Brando playing Rio, "the Kid." The sheriff, Dad Longworth, is the villain. He had betrayed the Kid five years before the action takes place, another example of the reversal of roles in outlaw legends. At the end, the Kid rides off into the sunset after having disposed of Longworth.

97

error in these Hollywood interpretations. The Kid was always right-handed. The "left-handed" myth stems from the manner of producing tintypes, in which the sides become transposed. The one surviving tintype of the Kid is often but erroneously printed showing him as left-handed.[3]

The television industry has also gotten quite literally into the act. In 1961, it initiated a series called "The Tall Man." in which the Kid shared billing with Pat Garrett. But Billy was usually the hero of the episodes, and the series added to his deification. Linking the Kid to Pat Garrett and stressing his appealing character has helped to rivet the Robin Hood legend even more firmly into the public imagination. This development has not pleased all critics, one of whom called "the metamorphosis of the snivelling juvenile delinquent, Billy the Kid, into a mischievous but good-hearted Casanova on the current television series, as the neatest trick of the year."[4]

There is a mountain of periodical literature on the subject of Billy the Kid. Stories appear in such diverse publications as *The Journal of American Folklore, Life,* and *Real Men.* Popular magazines not only keep the old legends alive, but they also make new contributions by exploiting gaps in the historical record. *True Magazine* in June of 1959 published an old-timer's narrative by Peter Jerome Atkins entitled "I Rode and Robbed with Billy the Kid." The action takes place during the seventy-one-day period between the Kid's escape from the Lincoln courthouse and his death. Since there are no authentic records of what happened in these days, it is a convenient place for an elaborate tale of stage holdups and other feats of derring-do performed by the Kid and the narrator in tandem.

[3] Frank M. King, *Pioneer Western Empire Builders* (Pasadena, Trail's End Publishing Company, 1946), 300. Garrett, George Coe, John Poe, and King himself all remembered the Kid as being right-handed. The left-handed myth was also dispelled by Herbert Cody Blake in a letter to the *Tombstone Epitaph,* March 2, 1933 (clipping in Rasch Collection).

[4] John Greenway in "Notes and Queries," *Western Folklore,* Vol. XX (October, 1961), 275.

The extent of the legend has prompted scholars to study it, and this scholarly attention symbolizes the stature of the legend as an American epic. Folklorists have compared it with such classic legends as those of Hercules, Ulysses, and Faust.[5] They have found that the Kid's exploits in outwitting stronger opponents mark him as the kind of "Clever Hero" found in all cultures. The Kid shares characteristics of folk heroes in all ages; his exploits and legendary exploits taken together "represent a constellation of symptoms indicative for heroes in the widest distribution."[6]

Thus the Bonney story has penetrated every level of American culture. The Southwest in general and the state of New Mexico in particular have had to acknowledge that this criminal is one of their leading tourist attractions. The "Billy the Kid country" draws thousands of hero-worshipers each year and is the subject of articles in national travel magazines.[7] Authorities at Lincoln itself have been busy turning the little town into a Southwestern equivalent of colonial Williamsburg. Buildings have been restored, markers erected, and an annual Billy the Kid pageant is staged in August.

Thus the career of Billy the Kid is more than a classic narrative of the plains and cattle country. It is also one of the great All-American legends. People who have been taught to condemn outlaws can find redeeming features in the Kid's biography which transform him into a heroic figure. In fact the reversal of roles in which the Kid becomes a hero and Garrett the villain is one of the more startling features of this legend. What are the reasons for the Kid's appeal?

[5] Alfred Adler, "Billy the Kid: A Case Study in Epic Origins," *Western Folklore*, Vol. X (April, 1951), 143–52; Marshall Fishwick, "Billy the Kid: Faust in America," *Saturday Review*, Vol. XXXV (October 11, 1952), 11–12, 34–36; Klapp, "The Clever Hero," *Journal of American Folklore*, Vol. LXVII (January–March, 1954), 21–34.

[6] Adler, "Billy the Kid: A Case Study in Epic Origins," *Western Folklore*, Vol. X (April, 1951), 151.

[7] John Meigs, "Billy the Kid Country," *Ford Times*, Vol. XLVII (March, 1955), 51–53.

The villains in the Bonney saga are the powerful, the ambitious, and the ruthless. The heroes are the poor and the persecuted. Murphy and Dolan, Pat Garrett, and the Santa Fe Ring relentlessly crush the "small men" who oppose them. The Kid, as the idealized defender of the weak against the strong, has the same kind of appeal as other champions of "the people" such as Robin Hood and Jesse James. His nickname and his diminutive stature aid in this identification. And the fact that his side lost endows his career with the same fascination that surrounds the Confederates at Gettysburg, the Texans at the Alamo, and Custer's troopers at the Little Big Horn.

The Kid's outlawry is not self-centered but is identified with a cause. Originally driven to crime by unfortunate circumstances, he acquires for his career a broader purpose of vengeance because of the death of the idealistic Tunstall. It seems fitting that injustice should be punished, and so the Kid's pursuit of Tunstall's killers gives his biography the aura of a holy Crusade. There appears to be an acceptable motive for his crimes.

The theme of "betrayal" has been carefully pointed up by Bonney's biographers and has gripped the folk imagination. Time and again we are told that the Kid would have settled down and become a law-abiding citizen if only the man hunters had given him half a chance. But Governor Wallace "double-crossed" the Kid by reneging on a promise of an amnesty.[8] Garrett was a Judas who tracked down his friend for a few silver dollars. The story unfolds like a classical Greek drama, with the tragic hero moving inexorably toward death by treachery.

The Kid's appealing personality is at the center of the legend. He had a sense of humor, was popular with women and Mexicans and loyal to all his friends. His generous and selfless acts are legion. There is a large body of supporting anecdotes for all these traits, many of the tales being typical of outlaw-heroes in the folklore of all times and places.

[8] "How the West Was Won" (Part IV), *Life,* Vol. XLVI (May 4, 1959), 87.

The Kid's technical skill is also admirable. His daring escapes from impossible situations are the stuff from which folk tales and movie thrillers are made. His ability to survive while his associates are picked off one by one helps to sustain dramatic interest. His gun-fighting skill is closely tied to the themes of vengeance and defense of the "right" which are involved in the legend, because his victims and reputed victims like Beckwith and Olinger are villains who got "just what was coming to them." And his ability to outwit the law despite the heavy odds against him always enlists the sympathy of young and old alike.

Finally, the Mexican background helps to put a picture frame of romance around the Kid's exploits. As in the Joaquín Murieta legend in California, the beautifully poetic Spanish names help to elevate a sordid cow-country melodrama into ageless allegory. Writers like Burns and Neider have made expert use of the Spanish names and characters to create an appropriate atmosphere for a folk legend.

Is there any historical truth in these legends? The Kid may have been fighting for the right cause during the war, although objectively considered neither cause was particularly admirable. After the war, however, he was fighting society's legal and moral laws; he was a dangerous killer as well as a cow-and-horse thief. Nor does the view that the Kid was betrayed stand historical examination. Betrayal implies promises, and no promises were made him. He had several chances to leave the territory, and he did not take them. That Billy had a pleasing personality is proved by the independent testimony of the Las Vegas newspaper reporters, Dr. Hoyt, and others. But his enemies and the supporters of law and order in New Mexico did not feel that an engaging personality excused murder and thievery. There seemed only one possible solution to the Kid's obnoxiousness, and that was death at the hands of the law.

The question of the historical validity of various aspects of the legend will continue to be debated. A hundred years from now people will still be asking, "Was Billy the Kid a real person?" But it is the legend and not the history which has gripped the American imagination. The laughing and likable Billy will continue to gallop through biographies and ballets, fiction and films, just as long as this nation needs a Robin Hood figure. Indeed, it does seem that Walter Noble Burns was right when he claimed that the Bonney saga was "destined to a mellow and genial immortality."

PART THREE

The Gunfighter:
Wild Bill Hickok

CHAPTER X

The History of a Reputation

THE GUNFIGHTER is another classic figure in our great Western myth. Of commanding presence, wearing black mustache and string tie, he moves with lionlike grace down the main street of a dusty cow town. His job is to seek the lawless and vanquish them in armed combat. His courage and his deadly proficiency with weapons are part of both the history and the legend of a violent American past.

There were many notorious gunfighters who worked on both sides of the law. But none typifies the class better than Wild Bill Hickok, who overshadows such latecomers to legendary fame as Wyatt Earp and Bat Masterson. The air of fiction and romance that surrounds Wild Bill is so rich that even the authenticated facts about him do not seem credible. A frontiersman who wore starched collars, Zouave jacket, and a scarlet vest would seem to be more the creature of dime novelists or Hollywood script writers than of history. Yet this is what Hickok, in self-conscious enactment of his role, actually wore on occasion.

Historians have found out little about the early life of James Butler Hickok. It is usually asserted that he was born in Troy Grove, Illinois, on May 27, 1837.[1] He came from a large family of pronounced abolitionist views. Beyond this, the details of his youth must be filled in by historical probability. He was taught how to read and write, probably by his Bible-loving parents, and

[1] It is difficult to confirm this date. Charles N. Hickok's *Hickok Genealogy* (Rutland, Vt., Tuttle Publishing Company, 1938), 166, states merely that he was born in 1837, but no day or month is cited. The page from the Hickok family Bible which records his birth is missing, and the state of Illinois did not keep official birth records prior to 1877.

also learned to speak "respectable Anglo-Saxon vernacular."[2] He undoubtedly worked as a teamster and at the other odd jobs that were the lot of a frontier youth. Since the Illinois and Michigan Canal ran through LaSalle County, it is likely that he also worked on the towpath at various times. The youthful Hickok was quiet and lawabiding, and there is no record of any trouble with either the law or his fellow townsmen.

Hickok left home and emigrated to "Bleeding Kansas" in 1855.[3] The territory was then acquiring its sobriquet because of the battles between Free State men and Southern sympathizers. Some writers have suggested that Hickok went west to fight for Free Soil, but he seems to have been more interested in becoming a farmer. He filed land claims in Johnson County, and his letters home are filled with details of hunting and hay cutting rather than politics.[4] However, Hickok undoubtedly rode with Jim Lane's Free State band on several occasions during 1856 and 1857 when the Border Ruffians from Missouri were a particular threat. The earliest documentary record of his activities is Governor Denver's commission to him, April 21, 1858, as constable of Monticello township, Johnson County.[5] Even at the age of twenty, Hickok's potentialities as a lawman were being recognized.

Later the same year, Hickok began a period of service with the freighting firm of Russell, Majors and Waddell, for whom he worked as a teamster and station attendant. There are few reliable records of his service until the spring of 1861, when the company sent him to their stage station near Rock Creek, Nebraska, as an assistant stock-tender. And at Rock Creek occurred one of the

[2] Mrs. Annie Tallent, *The Black Hills; or, Last Hunting Ground of the Dakotahs,* 100.

[3] Archives, Kansas Territorial Census of 1859, Johnson County, Monticello Township (Kansas State Historical Society, hereafter cited as KSHS).

[4] Some of these letters are reprinted in William E. Connelley, *Wild Bill and His Era: The Life and Adventures of James Butler Hickok,* 19–21.

[5] Nyle H. Miller and Joseph W. Snell, "Some Notes on Kansas Cowtown Police Officers and Gun Fighters," *Kansas Historical Quarterly,* Vol. XXVI (Winter, 1960), 410.

pivotal events of the Wild Bill saga. The facts are by now well known, but the interpretation of these facts has varied with the sympathies of those writing about them. Hickok on July 12, 1861, shot and killed one David McCanles and wounded two of Mc-Canles' associates, who were then finished off by Hickok's friends at the station.

The basic cause of the shootings lay in the strained relations between McCanles and the stage company. In April, the company had purchased the Rock Creek property but had been unable to meet their payments because of financial difficulties. McCanles continually pressed the station agent, Horace Wellman, for the unpaid money, and this led to friction between the two men. There may also have been some antagonism with Hickok, whom McCanles is said to have called "Duck Bill" because of his prominent nose. Some writers have asserted that the two men were rivals for the affections of one Kate Shell (born Sarah Shull), an attractive young woman whom McCanles had brought out from North Carolina. However, there is no convincing evidence to support this claim.

On July 12, the aggressive McCanles appeared at the station, determined to gain some satisfaction from Wellman. He apparently felt that the stage company had gone bankrupt or that Wellman had been pocketing the payments himself. McCanles was accompanied by his cousin James Woods, a hired hand named James Gordon, and his twelve-year-old son, W. Monroe McCanles. That the three men were unarmed was confirmed by the testimony of Frank Helvey, who buried the bodies the next day.[6] As McCanles stood outside the station demanding Wellman's appearance, Hickok fired from behind a curtain in the station and killed him with a single rifle bullet in the heart. When Woods and Gordon ran up to the cabin, Hickok again fired and wounded both of them. Woods fell near the station, where Wellman came out and crushed his skull with a hoe. Gordon ran along the creek until "Doc" Brink, the station stock-tender, caught up with him and ended his misery

[6] George W. Hansen, "The Rock Creek Ranch Events and the Trial of Wild Bill," *Nebraska History Magazine,* Vol. X (April–June, 1927), 86.

with a shotgun blast. Young Monroe McCanles raced back to the McCanles ranch three miles away and sobbed out his story.

Hickok, Wellman, and Brink were arraigned for murder before T. M. Coulter, justice of the peace for Gage County, Nebraska. They were all acquitted on pleas of self-defense during a trial in which Monroe McCanles was not permitted to testify. Coulter was perhaps not the best-qualified official to try this case. He was politically ambitious and would naturally hesitate to alienate the great Overland Stage Company by jailing their employees. Later, as county treasurer, he was arrested for embezzlement of public funds. But the real reason why justice was not served was that the costs of a long trial and of holding the defendants in prison were prohibitive in a newly organized and scarcely settled county. There simply was not enough money to carry this, the first criminal case in Gage County, to its natural conclusion.

It is little to Hickok's credit that he spread fictional stories about the Rock Creek affair by attempting to make McCanles into a Confederate conspirator.[7] The earliest printed account of the episode, in the Brownville (Nebraska) *Advertiser* of July 25, incorporates this interpretation:

> Three wagon loads of arms and ammunition passed through the neighborhood below here last week, going westward. On Friday three men were killed at Rock Creek on the Military Road about 30 or 35 miles west of this. All we know is that the difficulty originated in the distribution or division of a wagon load of stuff from the Missouri

[7] For Hickok's own contribution to the legend of the Rock Creek affair, see *ibid.*, 92–93, and the letter from Cyrus Edwards to J. B. Edwards, April 8, 1926, in the KSHS. Edwards remembered that Hickok had related to him an inflated version of the affair, involving a desperate attack by seven or eight men. There is abundant evidence, often overlooked, that Wild Bill enjoyed puffing up his exploits. The Cheyenne *Leader* of August 16, 1876, reported that "Bill delighted in joining a crowd of 'tender feet' at the bar and soaking himself with whiskey at their expense, while he stuffed them in return with Münchhausenish tales of thrilling adventures and hair-breadth escapes from red fiends and white desperadoes. In such moments he was the very personification of happiness."

river, and it is supposed it was one of the three wagons mentioned above. During the difficulty some secessionists put a rope around a Union Man's neck, and dragged him some distance toward a tree with the avowed purpose of hanging him. He managed to escape. They then gave him notice to leave in a certain time or be hung. At the end of the time five of them went to his house to see if he had gone, when he commenced firing upon them and killed three out of the five; the other two making a hasty retreat.[8]

The Rock Creek affair was soon forgotten in the greater excitement of the Civil War, but it was later resurrected by Hickok biographers to become one of the most celebrated exploits in Western legend.

Hickok soon left the area to become an army wagon master in Missouri. During the latter part of the war, he also served as a government scout. Records from the provost marshal's office contain references to his services, and William F. Cody in his *Autobiography* told of meeting Hickok dressed as a Confederate officer for a spying mission.[9] Wild Bill did some valuable scouting along the Missouri border during the war, but unfortunately his services were exaggerated by biographers until they bore little relation to the facts.

Immediately after the war, Hickok made his living as a gambler. This was a hazardous occupation in these tense years when men experienced in handling weapons still nursed political grievances. One result was reported in the Springfield *Missouri Weekly Patriot* of July 27, 1865: "David Tutt, of Yellville, Ark., was shot on the public square, at 6 o'clock P.M., on Friday last, by James B. Hickok, better known in Southwest Missouri as 'Wild Bill.' The difficulty occurred from a game of cards." Tutt was also a former Confederate, which may have added bitterness to the gambling dispute. Other writers were to suggest that the two men were rivals for the same woman. These are all classic explanations for

[8] Reprinted in Hansen, *Nebraska History Magazine*, Vol. X, 93.
[9] *The Life of Hon. William F. Cody . . . An Autobiography*, 136.

gunfire in the Hickok saga: poker, politics, and prostitutes. The *Patriot* in later issues deplored this violence in the center of the city and regretted that Hickok had been acquitted of murder. But this authentic, man-to-man gunfight in the public square became the historical prototype for many similar encounters in fiction and films.

That same summer of 1865, an Eastern writer named George Ward Nichols was in Springfield looking for a local-color story. He selected "William Hitchcock" as his subject, because Wild Bill had acquired a reputation as a scout during the war, had just killed a man in a pistol duel, and was an impressive physical specimen whose long hair and deerskin suit would remind Eastern readers of Cooper's Leatherstocking. Nichols wrote a highly colored story, whose chief contribution to the Hickok legend was an inflated account of the McCanles affair. When the story was published in the February, 1867, issue of *Harper's Magazine,* it made Wild Bill a national hero. Eastern writers henceforth had a name around which to build stories of frontier derring-do.

Early in 1866, Hickok left Springfield and went to Kansas. There he worked as a deputy U.S. marshal out of Fort Riley and as a scout for various military expeditions out of Fort Harker. He spent his free time at the gaming tables in Junction City, and the *Rocky Mountain News* of February 18, 1867, reported that he was employed as a gambler there. In the spring of 1867, he scouted for General W. S. Hancock's Indian expedition. Wild Bill was enough of a hero after the *Harper's* article that he appears prominently in newspaper dispatches on this campaign. The literary classic of the expedition was an interview published by the later-famous Henry M. Stanley, correspondent for the New York *Tribune* and the St. Louis *Missouri Democrat*. In a *Democrat* article date-lined April 4, Stanley made Hickok's archetypal role quite clear: "James Butler Hickok, commonly called 'Wild Bill,' is one of the finest examples of that peculiar class known as frontiersman, ranger, hunter, and Indian scout." In his book, Stanley appended a description of Wild Bill in his prime:

He is now thirty-eight [actually twenty-nine] years old, and since he was thirteen the prairie has been his home. He stands six feet one inch in his moccasins, and is as handsome a specimen of a man as could be found. We were prepared, on hearing of "Wild Bill's " presence in the camp, to see a person who might prove to be a coarse and illiterate bully. We were agreeably disappointed, however. He was dressed in fancy shirt and leathern leggings. He held himself straight, and had broad, compact shoulders, was large chested, with small waist, and well-formed muscular limbs. A fine, handsome face, free from blemish, a light mustache, a thin pointed nose, bluish-grey eyes, with a calm look, a magnificent forehead, hair parted from the centre of the forehead, and hanging down behind the ears in wavy, silken curls, made up the most picturesque figure. He is more inclined to be sociable than otherwise; is enthusiastic in his love for his country and Illinois, his native State; and is endowed with extraordinary power and agility, whose match in these respects it would be difficult to find. Having left his home and native State when young, he is a thorough child of the prairie, and inured to fatigue. He has none of the swaggering gait, or the barbaric jargon ascribed to the pioneer by the *Beadle* penny-liners. On the contrary, his language is as good as many a one that boasts "college larning."[10]

Occasionally the press commented upon Wild Bill's fondness for the liquor bottle. The editor of the Manhattan (Kansas) *Independent* said in his issue of October 26, 1867: "All the party [army scouts] were more or less affected by frequent potations from their bottles, and Wild Bill himself was tipsy enough to be quite belligerent." The Leavenworth *Times and Conservative* of July 17, 1869, reprinting a story from the St. Joseph *Union*, said: "If the enthusiastic admirers of this old [*sic*] plainsman could see him on one of his periodical drunks, they would have considerable romance knocked out of them." However, the dominant emphasis in the periodical literature of this period is on Hickok's genteel qualities.

During the early part of 1868, Hickok was again a deputy U.S. marshal and was charged with recovering deserters from the Kansas army posts. He did not impress Theodore Davis, correspondent

[10] *My Early Travels and Adventures in America and Asia*, I, 5–6.

for *Harper's Weekly*, who disliked Bill's boiled shirts, scarlet jackets, and perfumed hair. "The man was by nature a dandy, sufficiently vain of his personal appearance, physique and constitution."[11] Despite the eye-catching apparel, Hickok did get results. The Topeka *Weekly Leader* of April 2 reported Wild Bill's capture of eleven deserters on the Solomon River.

In the fall of 1868, Hickok was a scout for General W. H. Penrose in the Colorado Territory. In September he rescued thirty-four men besieged on a mesa near Gomerville, about fifty miles south of Denver. The Central City *Daily Register* of September 8 carried the details:

> Our boys concluded it was the intention of the redskins to keep them hemmed in until this morning, or until their ammunition was exhausted, selecting a daring man called "Wild Bill," put him on their fleetest horse and started him for the Basin for relief. He ran the gantlet through the enemy's line, receiving only a slight wound in the foot, and reached the Basin at 8 o'clock.

Bill spent the winter of 1868–69 campaigning through northern New Mexico and western Oklahoma. He and Buffalo Bill Cody did some heavy drinking on this expedition and also provoked a full-scale brawl with their Mexican fellow scouts.[12] On one mission as a courier, Wild Bill was attacked by Indians and received a spear wound in the thigh. He went back to Troy Grove to visit his ailing mother in the spring of 1869, and an operation was performed for the removal of the spearhead.[13]

One of the jobs open to the "picturesque" frontiersmen of the period was that of guiding parties of Easterners or foreign dignitaries around the plains. Like Buffalo Bill and General Custer, Hickok dutifully performed this representative function of the

---

[11] Theodore Davis MS, "Stanley's Indian Campaign," printed in Chicago *Westerners Brand Book*, Vol. II (1946), 97–106.

[12] Cody, *Autobiography*, 226.

[13] A report on the operation written by Hickok's sister appeared in the Chicago *Inter-Ocean*, October 26, 1896, and is reprinted in Frank Wilstach, *Wild Bill Hickok, the Prince of Pistoleers*, 146.

plains hero. United States Senator Henry Wilson, of Massachusetts, wrote Wild Bill that his party, having "heard much concerning your wonderful exploits in the West," desired to hire him as a guide.[14] Hickok took the group on a month-long tour through Kansas and Colorado during May and June. Senator Wilson was so pleased with Wild Bill's services that he presented the scout with two ivory-handled .44 pistols.

Hickok soon had use for this armament. In August of 1869, he was elected sheriff of Ellis County, Kansas, and went to Hays City to assume the post. Hays was a wide-open town noted for its rowdyism. It seemed an appropriate setting for gunfights, and writers have printed many anecdotes about Wild Bill's encounters there. But it is now known that Hickok killed only two men in Hays during his four-month tenure as sheriff. One victim was Sam Strawhim, a teamster who was shot when Hickok stopped a drunken brawl in a saloon.[15] The other unfortunate was one Jack Mulrey, but the manner of his departure from this earth was not recorded. The Leavenworth *Times and Conservative* of August 26 said simply that "J. B. Hickok (Wild Bill) shot one Mulrey at Hays Tuesday. Mulrey died yesterday morning. Bill has been elected sheriff of Ellis county."

Hickok was defeated for re-election by his deputy, Peter Lanihan, and went back to Topeka. The *Commonwealth* of that city reported on February 8, 1870, that "Wild Bill was up before Judge Holmes yesterday, and fined five dollars for striking straight out from the shoulder and consequently hitting a man."

In July, Hickok was back at his old stamping grounds in Hays City, this time without his sheriff's badge. There he managed to get into a shooting scrape with several Seventh Cavalry troopers from nearby Fort Hays. The Topeka *Kansas Daily Commonwealth* of July 22, 1870, reported: "On Monday last 'Wild Bill' killed a soldier and seriously wounded another, at Hays City. Five soldiers

---

[14] Letter reproduced in Connelley, *Wild Bill and His Era,* 123.

[15] Miller and Snell, "Some Notes on Kansas Cowtown Police Officers and Gun Fighters," *Kansas Historical Quarterly,* Vol. XXVI, (Winter, 1960), 423–24.

attacked Bill, and two got used up as mentioned above. The sentiment of the community is with 'Bill,' as it is claimed he but acted in self-defense." There are other printed versions of this episode[16] and an oral tradition concerning it, but the immediate effect of the encounter was to send Hickok traveling rapidly to parts unknown.

On April 15, 1871, Wild Bill was appointed city marshal at Abilene, replacing the late and greatly admired Tom Smith. Where Smith had used his fists to keep order in the railhead town, Hickok used weapons and the threat of weapons. Where Smith had kept his headquarters in the mayor's office, Hickok operated out of the Alamo Saloon, where he spent much of his time playing poker. This combination of law enforcement and gambling has been the basis for criticism of many frontier peace officers. Some of the citizens compared Tom Smith's strictly moral behavior with Hickok's "life in the bosom of Abilene's criminal population as one of its steady gamblers."[17] Hickok permitted lawlessness, they said, as long as it did not interfere with his own interests.

But Wild Bill undeniably performed the job for which he had been hired—keeping a lid on the town during the peak of the cattle season. Reported A. T. Andreas, in the quaint language of 1883:

[16] The Junction City *Union* of July 23 gave the names of the soldiers as Langan and Kelly and stated that "the citizens were out *en masse* looking for Bill so that he might be summarily dealt with." This does not seem likely, because Hickok always had many friends in Hays. There is confirmation of the episode in the "Register of Sick and Wounded at Fort Hays, Kansas, During the Month of July, 1870," Records of the War Department, Office of the Adjutant General, National Archives records group 94 (microfilm copy at KSHS). This lists the soldiers as Kelly (who died of gunshot wounds) and Lanigan (who recovered). Also the Muster Roll of the Seventh Cavalry for July and August, which stated that "Private John Kile, Co. I, 7th U.S. Cavalry, died July 18, 1870 at Fort Hays of a pistol shot wound received July 17th, 1870 at Hays City, Kansas, in a drunken row and not in the line of duty" (letter from National Archives to Joseph G. Rosa, Ruislip, England, April 15, 1963, a copy of which is in the files of the KSHS). There is an oral tradition about this episode, recorded in the "Dickinson County Biographical Sketches," Vol. I, 79, files of the KSHS. It is in the form of an anecdote told by A. D. Gilkeson to H. L. Humphrey. Gilkeson was a judge in northern Kansas and seems a reliable source. He said that three soldiers were killed and that General Custer held a court of inquiry which exonerated Wild Bill.

[17] Stuart Henry, *Conquering Our Great American Plains,* 286.

"He was a terror to the cow-boys, he having caused several of them to bite the dust on short notice."[18] Early settlers remembered that their mothers used to make them behave by invoking the dread name, "Wild Bill."[19] And the old cowboy Pascal Brown remembered Hickok as follows: "When I came along the street, he was standing there with his back to the wall and his thumbs hooked in his red sash. He stood there and rolled his head from side to side looking at everything and everybody from under his eyebrows— just like a mad old bull. I decided then and there I didn't want any part of him."[20]

Hickok used both pistols and persuasion to accomplish his ends. Much of the resentment at his iron-handed control of the town was generated at the bar of the Bull's Head saloon, run by the Texas gamblers Phil Coe and Ben Thompson. The Texans in Abilene always regarded Hickok as a grafter. Thompson's biographer said that with Hickok "were associated and congregated the worst set of men that ever lived. . . . top and bottom scoundrels . . . Dollar store thieves."[21] When the young desperado John Wesley Hardin came up the trail from Texas in June, Thompson tried to persuade him to kill the obnoxious marshal. In dealing with Hardin, Hickok used diplomacy rather than bullets. Over a bottle of champagne, he arranged a truce with the untamed youngster. Hardin later claimed that he had humbled the great lawman when Hickok had tried to disarm him. Holding out the butts of his pistols, Hardin suddenly reversed them in the "road agent's spin" and got the drop. This episode was recorded in Hardin's *Life* a quarter of a century after it presumably took place.[22] The years may have dimmed Hardin's memory of his exploits in Abilene, and there are inac-

[18] *History of the State of Kansas,* 688.

[19] Henry, *Conquering Our Great American Plains,* 277.

[20] Cunningham, *Triggernometry,* 249.

[21] William M. Walton, *Life and Adventures of Ben Thompson* (Austin, privately published, 1884), 151.

[22] *The Life of John Wesley Hardin, As Written by Himself* (Norman, University of Oklahoma Press, 1961), 45. The *Life* was originally published at Seguin, Texas, in 1896.

115

curacies in other parts of his narrative.[23] More important, there were no printed versions of this encounter prior to the *Life;* the oral traditions in Texas postdate the book.[24] But the whole Hardin adventure does prove that Wild Bill occasionally recognized discretion to be the better part of valor.

At one point, however, gunfire became the only solution to the Texas-Hickok feud. On October 5, 1871, Phil Coe joined Mc-Canles, Tutt, Strawhim, and Mulrey on the list of Wild Bill's victims. The Abilene *Chronicle* reported the episode on October 12:

> On last Thursday evening a number of men got on a "spree," and compelled several citizens and others to "stand treat," catching them on the street and carrying them upon their shoulders into the saloons. The crowd served the Marshal, commonly called "Wild Bill," in this manner. He treated, but told them that they must keep within the bounds of order or he would stop them. They kept on, until finally one of the crowd, named Phil Coe, fired a revolver. The Marshal heard the report and knew at once the leading spirits in the crowd, numbering probably fifty men, intended to get up a "fight." He immediately started to quell the affair and when he reached the Alamo saloon, in front of which the crowd had gathered, he was confronted by Coe, who said that he had fired the shot at a dog. Coe had his revolver in his hand, as had also other parties in the crowd. As quick as thought the Marshal drew two revolvers and both men fired almost simultaneously. Several shots were fired, during which Mike Williams, a policeman, came around the corner for the purpose of assisting the Marshal, and rushing between him and Coe received two of the shots intended for Coe. The whole affair was the work of an instant. The Marshal, surrounded by the crowd, and standing in the light, did not recognize Williams whose death he deeply regrets. Coe was shot through the stomach, the ball coming out through his back; he lived in great agony until Sunday evening; he was a gambler, but a man of natural good impulses in his better moments.

The *Chronicle* also reported that Coe "had a spite at Wild Bill

[23] Thomas Ripley, *They Died With Their Boots On,* 164.

[24] *Ibid.,* 94; and Robert Dykstra, "Exit John Wesley Hardin," Los Angeles *Westerners Brand Book,* Vol. VI (1956), 123–29.

and had threatened to kill him—which Bill believed he would do if he gave him the opportunity." Exactly what the "spite" was again involves the classic elements of the Hickok saga—politics, poker, and women. Coe, like Dave Tutt, was a Southerner as well as a gambling rival. In addition, Wild Bill kept quite a harem in Abilene,[25] and rivalry over the affections of one of these Cyprians may have caused antagonism. Among the leading candidates were Susanna Moore, Jesse Hazel, and Mattie Silks, a famous bordello operator. Whatever the cause, the Kansas press supported Wild Bill. As the Junction City *Union* said on October 7, "The verdict of the citizens seemed to be unanimously in support of the Marshal, who bravely did his duty." However, the city council discharged Hickok as soon as the cattle season ended in December.

In 1872, Wild Bill was often in Kansas City, Topeka, Ellsworth, and other points along the Kansas Pacific.[26] In August he served as the master of ceremonies in a Wild West show at Niagara Falls, featuring three wild buffalo chased by Sac and Fox Indians. The Niagara Falls *Gazette* of August 28 referred to the entrepeneur as "the most celebrated Scout and Hunter of the Plains." Bill apparently made his living also as a gambler and special policeman. The Topeka *Daily Commonwealth* of September 28, under the heading of "PLUCK SUPERIOR TO PISTOLS," reported that Wild Bill had squelched a disturbance by some pistol-wielding Texans at the Kansas City fairgrounds.

In the early months of 1873, his activities again become obscure. The range of possibilities is indicated by the heading of a *Commonwealth* article on March 1: "WILD BILL. Lionizing in New York, Visiting Friends in Springfield, Mo., Killing Indians in the West, Killed in Galveston, and Riddled with Bullets at Fort Dodge." The Springfield location is the most credible, since Hickok wrote a letter to the St. Louis *Democrat* from Springfield on March

[25] Letter from Charles Gross to J. B. Edwards, June 15, 1925, in the KSHS. Gross was a room clerk at the Drovers Cottage and had suggested that Hickok be brought to Abilene as marshal.

[26] Connelley, *Wild Bill and His Era,* chap. 25.

13 denying a story in the paper that a Texan had killed him. The *Democrat* promised to consult Hickok before printing any stories about his death.

In the summer, Buffalo Bill offered him a role in the play *Scouts of the Plains:* "Thinking that Wild Bill would be quite an acquisition to the troupe, we wrote him at Springfield, Missouri, offering him a large salary if he would play with us that winter. He was doing nothing at the time, and we thought that he would like to take a trip through the States, as he had never been East."[27] Hickok accepted the offer, but he had a tempestuous career with the show. He played rough pranks on the other actors, taking especial delight in burning the legs of the "Indians" by firing blank cartridges quite close to them. He got into barroom fights during the tour. And despite his naturally theatrical appearance, he hated the declamatory speeches, typical of the melodrama of the day, which he was required to recite. In the spring of 1874, he was back on the plains after an amicable parting with Buffalo Bill, who took more readily to posturing before the footlights.

During the next two years Hickok spent a great deal of time in Cheyenne. The Cheyenne *Leader* of July 22, 1874, reported that "Mr. William Haycock, more familiarly 'Wild Bill,' is in town." On May 3, 1876, the *Leader* said that it had received circulars from St. Louis announcing that Wild Bill was organizing a gold-seeking expedition to the Black Hills. On June 8 the paper reported that Hickok was back in town, presumably managing the Black Hills trip. It was in Cheyenne also, on March 5, 1876, that Hickok had married Mrs. Agnes Thatcher Lake. He had first met the widow when she brought her "Hippo-Olympiad and Mammoth Circus" to Abilene in 1871.

During the Cheyenne years, Hickok was a man living on his reputation. In the *Ellis County Star* for June 29, 1876, a correspondent reported having seen Hickok in the town earlier in the month: "The notorious Wild Bill is stopping here, and I have been told from a pretty reliable source that he was arrested on several occa-

27 Cody, *Autobiography*, 329.

sions as a vagrant, having no visible means of support." The correspondent's choice of words is significant. Wild Bill is now "notorious" rather than "famous." The *Leader* in its obituary on August 16 also said that "of late years Wild Bill seems to have been a very tame and worthless loafer and bummer. Our city Marshall ordered him out of town by virtue of the provisions of the vagrant act only a few months ago."

In any case, Hickok soon left for the Black Hills in an attempt to recoup his finances. He rode into Deadwood Gulch accompanied by "Colorado Charlie" Utter and Calamity Jane Cannary, who is said to have followed him "as a dog follows its master."[28] Hickok made sporadic attempts to locate mining claims, but he spent most of his time playing poker. While engaged in one of these games, on August 2, 1876, he was shot through the back of the head by Jack McCall. Clutched in Bill's lifeless hand, according to tradition, was the "dead man's hand" of aces and eights.

Some historians have said that the criminal element in Deadwood plotted Hickok's murder. Afraid that he would become town marshal, they made McCall their tool. However, there is no evidence that Hickok was ever considered for city marshal and no indication that he would have accepted the post.[29] It seems unlikely that the gambling fraternity would plot his death. He was one of them, and his actions at Abilene indicated a tolerant attitude toward public gambling. McCall's own explanation was that Hickok had killed a brother of his at Hays City. He was clearly suffering the delusions of a paranoiac.

With the exception of the one appearing in the Cheyenne *Leader,* newspaper obituaries were generally favorable to Wild Bill. The Hays City *Sentinel* said on August 16:

During his residence in Hays, Hickok was one of the best citizens of the town. He never commenced a muss; but he was always in at the close, and, as a general thing there was a procession to "Boot Hill"

---

[28] John S. McClintock, *Pioneer Days in the Black Hills,* 106.

[29] Edward L. Senn, *"Wild Bill" Hickok, "Prince of Pistoleers," A Tale of Facts and Not Fiction and Romance,* 13.

on the same day. . . . All concede that he was a kindhearted, gentle-mannered gentleman, and only when aroused was he dangerous. Many of his old friends now reside in Hays, and all express great sorrow at his untimely end.

Perhaps his end had not been as untimely as the *Sentinel* thought. Since the frontier was passing, Hickok's actual value was now less important than his symbolic value. In fact, Wild Bill died just in time to rescue his own legend. The time and manner of his death were appropriate to the frontier epic that was to be fashioned in biographies, novels, and films.

CHAPTER XI

The Pistol Dead Shot

WILD BILL is a monumental figure in the tall-tale mythology of the West. The tales made him a hero to that vast popular audience which has been most receptive to the Western legend. In these stories Bill fights Indians and bears, outwits or outshoots the "bad" gunfighters, and performs other exploits thought to be appropriate to his fancy clothing and Olympian reputation.

Many of the heroic potentialities in Hickok's career were first exploited by George Ward Nichols in his famous story for *Harper's*. Nichols can be described as a "local-colorist," referring to a literary style which demanded picturesque characters who spoke in dialect. Nichols decided that Hickok was picturesque enough, and the fact that he did not speak in dialect could be easily corrected by literary surgery. Hence we have Wild Bill saying, "I allers shot well; but I come ter be perfeck in the mountains, by shootin' at a dime for a mark, at bets of half a dollar a shot." But Nichols made more lasting contributions to the Hickok legend than simply giving his hero a phony dialect. His tales of Wild Bill's exploits in the Civil War and of his desperate battle against the ten-man "M'Kandlas gang" are famous in frontier mythology.

Two of Nichols' dubious war stories concern Bill's escapes through the Confederate lines after spying missions. On one occasion as the two armies face each other, Bill and his partner are seen to gallop out from the Rebel lines. Bill's mate is shot down from behind, but Bill jumps his horse over a twenty-foot ditch and rides to safety. When asked why he had not stolen in at night, Bill replies: "I wanted to show them cussed rebs what a Union soldier could do." In another heroic episode, Bill challenges a Rebel ser-

121

geant to see who could ride closest to the Union lines. As they near the Yankees, the sergeant suddenly suspects Hickok of being a spy, but Bill shoots him and then escapes across a river through a hail of Confederate bullets.

The newspapers in Kansas and Missouri were skeptical about these reputed exploits. The editor of the Springfield *Patriot* on January 31, 1867, reported that Hickok's partner in the first of these exploits, "swore yesterday that Nichols' pathetic description of his untimely murder in 1863, in that article, was not true." The Leavenworth *Conservative* remarked that "the river adventure would hardly be credited among those on the army staff in the fall of 1864." But these papers were seldom read east of the Mississippi.

Nichols' story of the "M'Kandlas" fight was also discredited in the newspapers. The story incorporates two legends which tend to justify Hickok's actions in that affair: McCanles was the local bully whom all the settlers feared and hated; he was a Confederate conspirator. As the account opens, Wild Bill learns from a "Mrs. Waltman" (Mrs. Horace Wellman) that the M'Kandlas gang have threatened to kill him and are now dragging the Union-loving "Parson Shipley" around on the ground with a lariat. This reference to the first printed report of the episode (see above) identifies M'Kandlas as the "secesh" villain and Wild Bill as the Unionist champion. The gang soon ride up to Mrs. Waltman's cabin, and when Bill refuses to come out, they attack him. Bill shoots six of the desperadoes with his rifle and pistol and in hand-to-hand combat slays another four with his knife and fists. Wild Bill is badly wounded himself, but "that blessed old Dr. Mills pulled me safe through it, after a bed siege of many a long week."

This fable, illustrated in the magazine with garish prints, made Hickok a national hero. It was reprinted with little change by a score of biographers and journalists who did not bother to check the facts.[1] Indeed, it was sixty years before a magazine printed

---

[1] Some of the more widely known narratives in which the legend appears are: J. W. Buel, *The Life and Marvelous Adventures of Wild Bill* (1880), 13; D. M. Kelsey, *Our Pioneer Heroes and Their Daring Deeds* (1883), 481; Clarence E. Ray,

definitive statements about McCanles' true Union sympathies and his equable relations with the other settlers.[2] Only in the local press were the distortions in the Nichols article noted at the time it was published.

The Atchison (Kansas) *Daily Champion* of February 5 got somewhere near the truth in its comments on the story:

> The McCandlas gang consisted of only the leader and three others, and not of fourteen as stated in the magazine. Of these "Wild Bill," in the fight referred to, shot McKandlas through the heart with a rifle, and then stepping out of doors, revolver in hand, shot another of the gang dead; severely wounded a third, who ran off to a ravine near by, and was found there dead, and slightly wounded the fourth, who ran away and was not heard of afterwards. There was no grudge existing between the McKandles gang and "Wild Bill," but the former had a quarrel with the Stage Company, and had come to burn the station "Bill" was in charge of.

The Springfield *Patriot* (January 31) was also concerned about the article:

> We are sorry to say also that the graphic account of the terrific fight at Mrs. Waltman's, in which Bill killed, solitary and alone, "the guerrilla McKandlas and ten of his men"—the whole bilen of 'em—is not reliable. The fact upon which this account is *founded* being, that before the war, and while yet out in the mountains, Wild Bill did fight and kill McKandlas and two other men, who attacked him simultaneously. These little rivulets in the monthlies, weeklies, and dailies, all run into and make up the great river of *history* afterwhile; and if

Famous American Scouts (1890), 149; Emerson Hough, *The Story of the Outlaw* (1907), 172; William F. Cody, *True Tales of the Plains* (1908), 53; Harry Young, *Hard Knocks* (1915), 45; Hough, *North of 36* (1923), 317; Fred E. Sutton (as told to A. B. MacDonald), "Fill Your Hand," *Saturday Evening Post,* Vol. CXCVIII (April 10, 1926), 14; Wilbert E. Eisele, *The Real Wild Bill, Famous Scout and Knight Chivalric of the Plains* (1931), 43. For a more detailed analysis of the evolution of this legend, see Ramon Adams, "With Our Rocking Chair Historians," Denver *Westerners Brand Book* (1952), 17–35.

[2] George W. Hansen and others, "Wild Bill–McCanles Tragedy, a Much Misrepresented Event in Nebraska History," *Nebraska History Magazine,* Vol. X (April–June, 1927), 94, 103, 117.

many of them are as salty as this one, the main stream will be very brackish at least. We must, therefore tell the truth to "vindicate history."

The editor's fears were justified. In fact, he was writing a classic description of the legend-making process. The Nichols story was reprinted in the weeklies and dailies, and by simple repetition became "history."

Henry M. Stanley was another scribe who, possibly assisted by the hero himself, helped to build the legend. In the St. Louis *Democrat* article of April 4, 1867, there is this story:

> The following dialogue took place between us: "I say, Mr. Hickok, how many white men have you killed to your certain knowledge?" After a little deliberation, he replied, "I suppose I have killed considerably over a hundred." "What made you kill all those men? Did you kill them without cause or provocation?" "No, by heaven! I never killed one man without good cause." "How old were you when you killed the first white man, and for what cause?" "I was twenty-eight years old when I killed the first white man, and if ever a man deserved killing he did. He was a gambler and a counterfeiter, and I was then in a hotel in Leavenworth City, and seeing some loose characters around, I ordered a room, and as I had some money about me, I thought I would retire to it. I had lain some thirty minutes on the bed when I heard men at my door. I pulled out my revolver and bowie knife, and held them ready, but half concealed, and pretended to be asleep. The door was opened, and five men entered the room. They whispered together, and one said, 'Let us kill the son of a ———; I'll bet he has got money.' I kept perfectly still until just as the knife touched my breast; I sprang aside and buried mine in his heart, and then used my revolver on the others right and left. One was killed, and another was wounded; and then, gentlemen, I dashed through the room and rushed to the fort, where I procured a lot of soldiers, and returning to the hotel, captured the whole gang of them, fifteen in all."[3]

Stanley was either a credulous journalist whom Bill hypnotized or a shrewd publicist who invented the story to spice his copy.

[3] Reprinted in *My Early Travels and Adventures in America and Asia*, I, 5–8.

In his *Autobiography* (1879), William F. Cody also contributed to the Hickok legend. Cody's books must be used with extreme care, especially when he is relating episodes which have reached him secondhand. His garbled version of the McCanles affair does not inspire confidence in his historical accuracy. He has Wild Bill as a pony express rider and states that the desperadoes killed the stock-tender (Brink) and assaulted his wife! In another Cody story, Hickok learns that a Wild West drama is advertising him as the leading star, though using another actor. He goes to see the melodrama but is so disgusted with the performance that he hurls the bogus Wild Bill through the nearest pasteboard scenery.[4] While the story may typify Bill's customary method of handling problems, it is not verified. Of similar nature is the tale of Bill's run-in with a gambler at a faro game in Cheyenne:

> "I'll just play that fifty dollar bill as it lays. If it loses, its yours; if it wins, you'll pay me fifty dollars, or I'll know the reason why."
>
> "I am running this game, and I want no talk from you, sir," said Boulder.
>
> One word brought on another, until Boulder threatened to have Bill put out of the house. Bill was carrying the butt end of a billiard cue for a cane, and bending over the table, he said: "You'd rob a blind man." Then he suddenly tapped Boulder on the head with a cane, with such force as to knock him over. With another sweep of the cane he tumbled the "look out" from his chair, and then reaching over into the money drawer he grabbed a handful of greenbacks and stuck them in his pocket.[5]

This story, like others in the Cody repertoire, comes completely equipped with dialogue and other convincing details. But like so many episodes in the Hickok biography, there are no eyewitness accounts to verify it.

The first biographer to capitalize on the Hickok legend was a St. Louis newspaperman named J. W. Buel. Buel knew that a biography would sell, because the reading public had become familiar

[4] *Autobiography,* 333–34.
[5] *Ibid.,* 335.

125

with Hickok's name and more sensational exploits through the writings of Nichols, Stanley, Cody, and other authors. The martyred General Custer, in *My Life on the Plains* (1874), had drawn a sketch of Hickok, "a Plainsman in every sense of the word, yet unlike any other of his class."[6] Captain Jack Crawford, the "Poet-Scout of the Black Hills," had written a laudatory poem, entitled "Under the Sod," which had appeared in New York newspapers and in a collection of Crawford's writings.[7] All Buel had to do was piece together the various printed tales about Wild Bill, put in some additional anecdotes which would typify his prowess, and write the book in a style sufficiently florid to satisfy the literary tastes of the period.

The biography, published in 1880, contributed greatly to the legend of Wild Bill Hickok. Buel claimed to be working from Bill's "diary," though none actually existed. He undoubtedly talked with Hickok in Kansas City at one time or another, but the biography reveals no evidence of research. The title is the give-away: *The Life and Marvelous Adventures of Wild Bill, the Scout, Being a True and Exact History of All the Sanguinary Combats and Hair-Breadth Escapes of the Most Famous Scout and Spy America Ever Produced*. Justification of this grandiloquent title required the inclusion of many fictional and/or inflated episodes.

Several of Buel's invented anecdotes became part of the Hickok mythology. At Independence, Missouri, Jim Hickok acquired his name of "Wild Bill" when he "dispersed a dozen infuriated men" who were going to lynch a friend of his. (The likeliest origin of the nickname is the "Duck Bill" appellation at Rock Creek.) As a sharpshooter during the Civil War, Bill mows down whole regiments of the enemy. At the Battle of Pea Ridge, he kills thirty-five men, including the Confederate General McCulloch. And he fights a knife duel with an Indian chief, who acquires the name of "Conquering Bear" in subsequent biographies. Those familiar with Wild

[6] Page 33.

[7] The poem is reproduced in Frederick E. Pond, *Life and Adventures of "Ned Buntline"* (New York, Cadmus Book Shop, 1919), 91–92.

Bill's career know that he had the ability to kill an Indian in hand-to-hand combat, but for this particular story there is not a shred of evidence.

Buel's tales about Hickok have something of the quality of an early Mark Twain story with the ironic title of "The Dandy Frightening the Squatter." An elegant young dandy, equipped with two horse pistols, attempts to frighten a brawny woodsman for the amusement of his lady friends. Unfortunately the woodsman is not frightened, but instead plants a huge fist between the eyes of his astonished antagonist and ends up by possessing himself of the dandy's pistols. With important modifications, this is the plot of many of the Wild Bill stories. Bill is the brawny frontiersman, and he is victorious. Yet he also has the stylish dress and polished speech of the dandy. These in fact mark him as a "rube" to the uncouth rowdies of the frontier saloons. After a standardized repartee involving insults or provocations to the well-dressed stranger, Bill's lighting-like use of his pistols or fists convinces them of their mistake.

One day in the spring of 1867, reports Buel, Wild Bill rides up to a saloon in Jefferson County, Nebraska. Four insolent cowboys at the bar take the well-dressed stranger for a "dude." They jostle him, insult him, and bump him as he is about to take a drink. When Bill slaps the nearest rowdy, the others begin to pull their weapons. But Hickok expostulates: "Gentlemen, let us have some respect for the proprietor. You are anxious for a fight, and I will accommodate you if you will consent to step outside. I will fight all four of you at fifteen paces with pistols." With the proprietor acting as referee, the five men all blaze away on the signal. Bill is severely wounded in the right arm, but he kills three of the four louts and disables the survivor.

This preposterous tale has been accepted by most biographers,[8] although it rests upon nothing more substantial than Buel's statement that he had "heard the details from eye-witnesses." Fortunately, Hickok's activities in the spring of 1867 are well docu-

[8] Wilstach, *Wild Bill Hickok*, 139–41; Richard O'Connor, *Wild Bill Hickok*, 109.

mented. Stanley's dispatches on Hancock's campaign report Wild Bill scouting from Fort Harker in April, and the records of the Quartermaster General show that in May and June he was "scouting with 7th Cavly in the field."[9] He would hardly have been engaged in scouting had he been shot through the arm. And when Stanley saw Hickok at Junction City in May, he surely would have picked up this marvelous story. The three-out-of-four exploit is a classic tale in folklore, and the outlines of this story resemble the equally legendary account of Billy the Kid's shooting three of the four cowboys at John Chisum's line camp.

Another specimen of folklore among Buel's anecdotes concerns Jack Mulrey. As Wild Bill is patrolling the streets of Hays City, he suddenly encounters Mulrey, who covers him with drawn pistols. It looks like the end for our hero, but glancing behind Mulrey, he calls out, "Boys, don't hit him." As the startled ruffian turns to face this threat, Hickok draws and puts two bullets through his slow-witted adversary. This story has a classic appeal; it is the kind of clever exploit expected of most folk heroes. But it is simply an imaginative reconstruction of the episode. The lone newspaper reference on this shooting yields no information about how Mulrey died.[10]

At Hays, also, Bill has his epic battle with no less than fifteen troopers of the Seventh Cavalry. This story has a factual basis, for Hickok did shoot two soldiers at Hays, one of whom died the next day. But Buel characteristically inflates the episode by free use of the multiplication table. One of the soldiers insults Wild Bill, and a fist fight ensues. The other fourteen soldiers rush in when they see their companion being thrashed. A friendly bartender throws

[9] Miller, Nyle H. and Joseph W. Schnell, "Some Notes on Kansas Cowtown Police Officers and Gun Fighters," *Kansas Historical Quarterly,* Vol. XXVI (Winter, 1960), 419.

[10] The first record of dialogue in this episode is in the *North Topeka Times,* August 31, 1876, in which Bill says: "Don't hit him. He is only fooling." The *Times* had copied this story from the St. Louis *Globe-Democrat.* Buel was a newspaperman in St. Louis at the time, so he may have written the original anecdote, or he may have copied it later when writing his biography.

Bill his pistol, and in the resulting melee, he kills four troopers
and is himself struck by seven bullets. After his bloody scrapes
with the McCanles gang, the four cowboys in Nebraska, and the
troopers in Hays, Hickok is certainly the most bullet-riddled hero
in Western mythology.

Buel originates other anecdotes which exemplify Bill's character. One day as Hickok is eating oyster stew in a restaurant at
Ellsworth, he sees a frightened look on the face of the waiter.
Swiveling about, he sees the desperado Bill Thompson pointing a
gun at him. Thompson's bullet shatters the soup bowl, but Hickok
draws quickly and kills the intruder. He then calmly orders another
bowl of stew from the paralyzed waiter. Hickok actually was in
Ellsworth some time in 1872, according to Colonel H. C. Lindsay.
He and Wild Bill witnessed a fist fight between Bob Dunlap and
Gill Thompson.[11] This may have been the anecdote which Buel
puffed up into another shooting affray.

At the time of Bill's disastrous attempts to produce the Wild
West show at Niagara Falls, he has an encounter whose plot resembles that of Twain's story about the dandy:

> Among the many spectators was a party of English snobs, one of whom
> seeing Bill dressed in buckskin breeches and generally frontier style,
> asked him if he were an Indian or a white man. The question was
> addressed in a cockney way peculiar to English *haute tons,* and gave
> such offense that Bill replied: "This is the kind of man I am," at the
> same time striking the impertinent fellow a blow in the face which
> sent him sprawling into the street.[12]

A similar tale is set in Chicago, where "seven roughs" begin
bantering Hickok about his buckskin clothes. An exchange of insults is followed by an epic battle in which Bill clears out the
roughs by using his pistols as billy clubs. Buel gives the date of
this purported episode as 1874, although other writers shift it
to 1869.

[11] Connelley, *Wild Bill and His Era,* 178–79.
[12] *Life and Marvelous Adventures,* 34.

Buel not only invented many fresh anecdotes, he also improved upon the older stories. In reworking the McCanles affair, he identifies Bill's opponents as horse thieves who came to the Rock Creek station to run off stock for the Confederacy. Since horse stealing was the most heinous offense in the West, this new dimension makes McCanles a double-dyed scoundrel and adds to Bill's heroism in resisting his "gang."

The Life and Marvelous Adventures of Wild Bill is thus an important landmark in the legend. Buel appropriated a name which Nichols and others had made well known, added to it enough exploits to keep biographers happy for half a century, and thus guaranteed Wild Bill a place in the pantheon of American heroes. The biography was popular enough to be reprinted in 1891, and a condensed version even appeared in 1946.[13] Most of the same legends also appeared in Buel's *Heroes of the Plains* (1882), a popular anthology sold by subscription. These books have remained standard sources, despite their glaring inaccuracies. Biographers, magazine writers, and even historians have been understandably reluctant to part with the appealing anecdotes which Buel improvised.

Other classic legends appeared in Prentiss Ingraham's *Wild Bill, the Pistol Prince,* published by Beadle and Adams in 1881. Although represented as a biography, this paperback is actually a series of fictional adventures imperfectly tied to Hickok's chronology. One of the most enduring of these adventures is Bill's arrival in Leavenworth:

> His first landing in Kansas convinced him that he had struck the right field of adventure, for a fight was in progress as he went ashore, which ended in the death of a number of participants.
>
> Failing in an effort to secure employment at once, Jimmy sought to enlist himself with the "Red Legs," an anti-slavery command under the leadership of the noted Jim Lane.

He is accepted into the band after a sensational display of shoot-

[13] J. W. Buel, *The True Story of "Wild Bill" Hickok,* ed. by J. Brussel (New York, Atomic Books, 1946).

WILD BILL AND THE CINNAMON BEAR
"This kind of face-to-face struggle with animals is an item
in the mythology of most frontier heroes."

WILD BILL HICKOK AND THE INDIANS
Prentiss Ingraham contributed to the snowballing legend of Wild Bill.

ing skill. While engaged in a rifle contest with one of the Redlegs named "Shanghai Bill," Wild Bill shoots a crow flying over the heads of the crowd. The feat "set the crowd wild with enthusiasm," but it enrages Shanghai Bill. He draws his revolver, but Wild Bill is quicker and kills the bully.

In lieu of any documented information about Hickok's early days in Kansas, these anecdotes were accepted by most biographers and historians. But they rest upon nothing more substantial than Ingraham's imagination. General Lane never had military headquarters in Leavenworth, and in fact the Red Legs were not organized until the beginning of the Civil War.[14]

Ingraham also invented Hickok's knife fight with a bear. Near Santa Fe, Bill is thrown from his horse and forced to grapple with the enraged beast. This kind of face-to-face struggle with animals is an item in the mythology of most frontier heroes. Many of these tales appear to have been inspired by the Davy Crockett *Autobiography* and almanacs. Crockett typically out-grins bears and performs other comic exploits. Hickok is not a comic figure, but his shout of defiance is clearly drawn from the Crockett tradition: " 'Chew away, old lady, for this is the arm that does the work,' shouted Bill, as he again drove his knife to the hilt." This bear story appears in virtually every printed account,[15] yet its falsity is proved not only by its conformity with the classic folk pattern, but also by its origination in one of the most unreliable of the Hickok narratives.

Wild Bill's escapes from the Indians also conform to the well-known folkloric pattern. Daniel Boone had escaped from the Shawnees by leaping off a sixty-foot cliff. Wild Bill performs a similar exploit when trapped by Blackfeet:

> Upon arriving at the spot the foiled redskins discovered that he had been standing on the edge of a precipice, which overhung a foaming torrent, rushing at its base, sixty feet below.

[14] Connelley, *Wild Bill and His Era*, 216.

[15] For recent examples, see O'Connor, *Wild Bill Hickok,* 56; *Pony Express Courier* (Placerville, Calif.), Vol. XXVII (January, 1961).

From this dizzy height Wild Bill had boldly taken the leap, and the rushing waters had received him in their bosom and hurled him on unhurt down the stream, and out of sight of his foes.

In the *Pistol Prince* and in a dime novel entitled *Wild Bill, the Pistol Dead Shot* (1882), Ingraham also contributed to the snow-balling legend of the McCanles affair. Footnotes rarely appear in dime novels, but on page fourteen of the latter, Ingraham reveals his sources by quoting from Buel's *Life:*

This combat, of one man fairly killing ten acknowledged desper-adoes, has no parallel in any authentic history. The fight has been described more than a hundred times in newspapers and periodicals, and was illustrated in Harper's Magazine, but all accounts heretofore have been marred by much fiction and gross inaccuracies. The par-ticulars as here recorded are unquestionably correct, for they were obtained from Capt. Kingsbury, who heard Bill's recital of the facts.

Ingraham's account is also borrowed from Captain Kingsbury and is thus no more accurate than that of his predecessors. But the citation does reveal the kind of uncritical repetition of legends which characterizes most popular nineteenth-century narratives.

In the twentieth century, generic tales continued to be attached to Hickok's name. Harry Young, who claimed to have known Wild Bill in both Hays City and Deadwood, contributed one old chest-nut which had been told of Jim Bridger[16] and half a dozen other frontiersmen. While scouting for Custer in Kansas, Hickok is trapped by Indians in a box canyon. He kills five of them, but when his ammunition is exhausted, the remaining savages close in on him. When asked by his breathless listeners what had finally happened, Bill replies, "By God, they killed me, Boys."[17]

Other stories continued to embody the dandy-versus-rubes theme:

A bar-keeper at Cheyenne . . . remarked to him one day, "And how did you leave the Kansas cows, Mr. Wild Bill?" The sentence was

[16] Botkin, *A Treasury of Western Folklore,* 646.
[17] *Hard Knocks,* 216.

barely finished before said Bill shot the whiskey decanter from the bar-keeper's hands, and quietly remarked:

"Son, the next time you get fresh we won't waste good whiskey, but it wouldn't surprise me if there was one less fool in these parts."[18]

Typical of the stories which became attached to Hickok are those to be found in Wilbert E. Eisele's *The Real Wild Bill, Famous Scout and Knight Chivalric of the Plains* (1931), which is Wild West fiction of the old school. Eisele repeats all the conventional stories, including the five-handed duel in Nebraska, the bear story, and the fight with fifteen troopers in Hays. When five desperadoes hold up the stage near Deadwood, Bill shoots four of them and crushes the skull of the fifth by hurling a pistol at the man's head. And Eisele adds a new story which symbolizes his admiration for the "Knight Chivalric." While journeying on a Mississippi river-boat, Wild Bill sees a cotton planter fleeced of his money by crooked gamblers. He wins back the money, kills the chief crook in a derringer duel, and woos the planter's beautiful daughter. Ned Buntline and Zane Grey could scarcely do better.

The stories of Wild Bill's shooting skill quite naturally bordered on the miraculous. Actually, there are several reports of his shooting at targets with remarkable accuracy.[19] He was assumed to have been equally skilled in ventilating humans, but it should be remembered that at Rock Creek he only wounded Woods and Gordon. Perhaps the key factor in Hickok's gunfighting success was not accuracy with the unwieldy pistols of frontier days, but rather his lightning-fast reflexes and instant readiness to kill. Sometimes he was over-quick, as the death of Mike Williams at Abilene proves.

Nichols had told of Bill's putting six bullets through the letter "O" of a sign "more than fifty yards away," without even sighting his pistol. This became something of a standard test, although the distance tended to become longer. Wyatt Earp remembered that at Kansas City in 1871 he had seen Hickok put ten bullets through

[18] George T. Buffum, *On Two Frontiers*, 332.

[19] Robert Kane, "The D.A. vs. S.A. Controversy," *Outdoor Life*, Vol. XVII (June, 1906), 589–92; reprinted in Connelley, *Wild Bill and His Era*, 9.

the "O" of a sign "possibly one hundred yards away."[20] By the rules of arithmetic progression, there should be an account of his putting fifteen bullets through an "O" 150 yards away.

J. W. Buel related how his hero had cut a rooster's throat at thirty paces without touching the head or body, and had driven a cork into a bottle without breaking the neck.[21] An article in the New York *Sun* in 1884 reported that he could drop an apple from a tree by cutting the stem with a bullet and then put two more balls through it as it fell to the ground.[22] One may be permitted to doubt these feats, as well as that persistent legend which concerns Hickok's ability to shoot forward and backward simultaneously. In his popular lectures in the late seventies, Captain Jack Crawford used to demonstrate how Bill might have performed this feat by firing over his shoulder, as Crawford claimed he had done while battling the troopers at Hays City.[23] The legend took printed form in O. W. Coursey's *Wild Bill* (1924). Two gunmen had decided to kill Hickok by closing in on him from opposite ends of a restaurant. But a friendly waitress warns Bill of the plan, and he proves equal to the occasion:

> Wild Bill, facing the desperate character who entered the front door, had shot him with a revolver in his left hand, while with his right hand he had thrown the other gun back over his left shoulder and shot the man coming from the rear. History does not record a more dare-devil act, a more astute piece of gun-work, or a cleaner fight.[24]

One can only agree with Mr. Coursey that history does not record such a performance.

A variant of this story was printed in William E. Connelley's biography of Hickok in 1933. At Solomon, Kansas, Wild Bill emerges from a restaurant and fires simultaneously at two desperadoes running in opposite directions, bringing them both down.

[20] Stuart N. Lake, *Wyatt Earp, Frontier Marshal*, 43.
[21] *Life and Marvelous Adventures*, 86–87.
[22] Clipping at the Colorado State Historical Society.
[23] Connelley, *Wild Bill and His Era*, 25–26.
[24] Page 25.

The WPA guide to Kansas repeats the story, although moving the location to Abilene.[25] Connelley heard this story from an old-time resident, but it is clearly a generic tale rather than an authentic occurrence.

Although Connelley wrote the most useful Hickok biography, he was rather uncritical in his acceptance of the traditional stories. In discussing the encounter with Jack Mulrey in Hays City, Connelley unconsciously reveals the kind of reasoning that results in the aceptance of questionable events: "That the incident is genuine there is no question, and it illustrates the poise, coolness, and quick-thinking of Wild Bill." It is authentic because it illustrates certain of the hero's qualities. The anecdote has indeed been retained because it symbolizes appropriate personal qualities and not because it is historically accurate. Nor does Connelley recognize the folkloric parallels between some of his stories. He describes Wild Bill's dash into the Union lines from a scouting mission in April, 1863. In the hail of fire his partner, John Allen, is killed. In September, 1864, Bill again performs the identical feat. "The whole rebel command fired at him, and his companion Stone was killed." By such repetition is the legend built.

[25] *Kansas: A Guide to the Sunflower State* (1939), 355.

CHAPTER XII

The Civilizer

HICKOK'S LEGENDARY GUNFIGHTING EXPLOITS are more than just dramatic displays of shooting prowess. They are also connected with his role as the agent of civilization on the Plains frontier. His guns serve society by bringing law and order to a lawless land. Even as biographers and journalists were casting Hickok in this grandiose role of "civilizer," they were beginning to sketch the portrait of the idealized and composite gunfighter who is now a familiar figure in Western legend. This mythic hero lives by a chivalric code, possesses admirable personal traits, and serves society even though he kills other human beings.[1] In tracing the supposed traits and historical role of Wild Bill, one is simultaneously describing the evolution of a classic type-figure in Western mythology.

The typing process began with George Ward Nichols' seminal article in *Harper's*. Nichols was trying to create a character who would fascinate Eastern readers; he was also trying to create a type-figure of the frontiersman. As he said: "My object here has been to make a slight record of one who is one of the best—perhaps the very best—example of a class who more than any other encountered perils and privations in defense of our nationality." As a result of the article, "Hitchcock" became the name writers used when they wished to personify the whole class of Western fighting men.

Although Wild Bill is typed as a scout in this article, the classic

[1] For a portrait of the prototypic "Gentleman Killer," see Robert Byington, "The Frontier Hero: Refinement and Definition," *Publications of the Texas Folklore Society,* ed. by Mody C. Boatright, Vol. XXX (1960), 140–55.

components of the gunfighter legend are also discernible. The fight with Dave Tutt in the public square is treated romantically, ignoring the Springfield *Patriot*'s report that the "citizens of this city were shocked and terrified" by the episode. The duel is fought in chivalric fashion and involves the honor of the participants. This romanticized encounter may in fact have been the source of a similar episode in Owen Wister's *The Virginian* (1902), and the duel in that novel in turn established the "walk-down" as a rigid convention in Western fiction.

Nichols' article reveals his admiration for a character who had killed "hundreds of men." In fact, this was the first in a long succession of admiring sketches of Western fighting men turned out by Eastern writing men. To convert the gunfighter into an ultra-heroic figure, it was only necessary to connect his pistolry with a broader social purpose. This link was forged by later biographers, but the possibilities of such a development are foreshadowed in Nichols. Wild Bill is admirable not only because of his honest and dignified character, but also because he has used his six-guns for the right purposes. His heroic defeat of the McCanles gang is a preview of the socially desirable uses to which his weapons would be put in his later career as a peace officer.

Henry M. Stanley and George Armstrong Custer also helped Wild Bill to gain notoriety in his initial role as the type-figure of the scout. Stanley was in fact searching for a Leatherstocking figure, a hero who would symbolize the Plains frontier just as Cooper's fictional character had represented an earlier West.[2] General Custer, who always had a sharp eye for the dramatic, quickly singled out Hickok as the leading character among the scouts:

> Among the white scouts were numbered some of the most noted of their class. The most prominent man among them was "Wild Bill," whose highly varied career was made the subject of an illustrated sketch in one of the popular monthly periodicals a few years ago. "Wild Bill" was a strange character, just the one which a novelist might

[2] Theodore Davis MS, "Stanley's Indian Campaign," Chicago *Westerners Brand Book,* Vol. II (1946), 97–106.

gloat over. He was a Plainsman in every sense of the word, yet unlike any other of his class. In person he was about six feet one in height, straight as the straightest of the warriors whose implacable foe he was; broad shoulders, well-formed chest and limbs, and a face strikingly handsome . . . . Add to this figure a costume blending the immaculate neatness of the dandy with the extravagant taste and style of the frontiersman, and you have Wild Bill, then as now the most famous scout on the Plains.[3]

Hickok's typology shifted from scout to gunfighter when Buel's biography appeared in 1880. Since "gunfighter" was not quite a respectable title, Buel preferred "civilizer":

Wild Bill, as a frontier character of the daring, cunning and honorable class, stands alone, without a prototype; his originality is as conspicuous as his remarkable escapades. . . . Wild Bill was a necessary character in the Far West during the period which marked his career. He was essentially a civilizer, in the sense of a vigilance posse. . . . When Bill drew his pistol there was always one less desperado to harass the law-abiding, and his presence served to allay the hunger of cut-throats and rapacious plunderers.

The implications of the passage are clear. Hickok in his character and career was the ideal plainsman and the perfect type-figure of the lawman. His combats are to be recorded not only for their intrinsic value; they are also to be viewed within the more imposing context of the westward march of civilization in the United States. If Hickok did indeed facilitate the settlement of the Plains, then continued homage to his legend is justified. Buel says that "an appreciation of the services Wild Bill rendered the civilizers and pioneers of the West belongs to those who come after us," but he cannot resist expressing his own laudatory evaluation: "Wild Bill played his part in the reformation of pioneer society more effectively than any character in the annals of American history."

Similar praise for Wild Bill appeared in the dime novels by

[3] *My Life on the Plains*, 34.

Ingraham and Cody that were published in the eighties and nineties. The gunfights that occur in these novels are uniformly represented as chivalric affairs. The *code duello* is punctiliously observed, and Bill and his opponents wait politely for the signal before beginning to shoot. This is true of Hickok's gunfight with the vicious Dagger Don in Ingraham's *Wild Bill, the Pistol Dead Shot* and of his shoot-out with Mephisto Mike in Cody's *Wild Bill, the Wild West Duelist* (1894). But this glamorization misrepresents the gunfights of history, which were usually the spontaneous climax of some drunken saloon brawl. At least such was the actual background of the Strawhim and Coe shootings at Hays and Abilene.

Romanticizing the gunfighter, the popularizers ignored the results of his skill. There seems nothing romantic about Monroe McCanles' being an orphan at twelve or about Phil Coe's groaning in agony for three days until he died from the slugs in his intestines. The death of innocents like Mike Williams was the price that was paid for Hickok's quickness with weapons. But the dime novels helped to popularize man-killing as the most significant feature of Plains history, just as movies and television do today. Hickok's success in this primitive art made him, in Cody's words, "known by reputation, as his deeds in Kansas and Missouri had spread over the whole border, and wild prairie-men looked upon him as a hero of heroes."

Since Cody was a good friend of Wild Bill's, there is a great deal of editorializing in the dime novels authored by "Buffalo Bill" (though these possibly were ghostwritten by Prentiss Ingraham). In the *Wild West Duelist,* the author defends Hickok's reputation: "He was in no sense of the word a bravado, and though many stories have gone the rounds of his personal difficulties, some told by those who should have known better, he was not a man to seek trouble, but rather to avoid it." Hickok is also given speeches in his own defense: "Let a man kill a few desperadoes, in the discharge of duty, and to save his own life, or the lives of others, and

139

before long he is branded as a man-killer, a name that no one who has a true heart cares to hear; but like the official executioner must stand ready to take life when the occasion demands it."

Hickok's identification with the westward movement, as the type-figure of the gun-toting peace officer, was also cemented in the many popular histories and anthologies of the border. Buel's *Heroes of the Plains* (1882), Cody's *Story of the Wild West* (1888), Kelsey's *Our Pioneer Heroes and Their Daring Deeds* (1883), and Clarence Ray's *Famous American Scouts* (1890) all placed him after Boone and Carson in the succession of Western pioneers. The journalists, historians, and novelists who drew upon these books accepted such an evaluation along with the legendary stories which they printed. As a result, Hickok by the end of the century "has a secure place in the history of the frontier; and any relation of cattle-trail days that omits his deeds and misdeeds is incomplete."[4]

Magazine writers soon took up the job of proving that Hickok was indeed a suitable symbol of law and order. In an article published in 1901, E. C. Little eulogized him as the outstanding figure among the border peace officers. "As Wild Bill Hickok was the original, so was he the first of his class." Comparisons with the Knights of the Round Table run through the essay: "Hickok's morals were much the same as those of Achilles, King David, Lancelot, and Chevalier Bayard, though his amours were hardly as frequent as David's or as inexcusable as Lancelot's. In a way he was a reincarnation of Lancelot, the renaissance of the knight-errant."[5] This idealized portrait was used as an argument for giving Wild Bill and his comrades a "statelier history" than they had thus far received in the dime novels. The suggestion to lionize Wild Bill by writing an epic that would highlight his historical significance and grandiose achievements was later implemented by William E. Connelley.

---

[4] Georgetown (Colo.) *Herald,* November 10, 1899 (clipping in Western History Collection, Denver Public Library).

[5] "A Son of the Border," *Everybody's Magazine,* Vol. IV (June, 1901), 578–87.

Emerson Hough in his widely read *Story of the Outlaw* (1907) devoted one essay to "Wild Bill Hickok—The Beau Ideal of the Western Bad Man; Chivalric, Daring, Generous, and Game—A Type of the Early Western Frontier Officer." Among Bill's chivalric qualities was his habit of paying the funeral expenses of his victims. This bit of folklore originated in the New York press and was then publicized by General Custer.[6] But there is no documentary evidence to support the claim. Hough feels that Hickok's biography is an adequate summation of all law enforcement west of the Missouri: "To describe the life of one Western town marshal, himself the best and most picturesque of them all, is to cover all this field sufficiently."

In his novel *North of 36* (1923), Hough also used Wild Bill as the symbolic peace officer. The story concerns a cattle drive from Texas to Abilene and the adventures along the way of the trail boss and the lady heroine, Taisie Lockhart. As sheriff of Abilene in 1867 [*sic*], Bill helps the hero capture a band of rustlers. It is stated that Hickok killed nine of the ten men in the "McCandless gang" when they came to run off stock for the Confederate Army east of Abilene [*sic*] in 1860 [*sic*]. The historical errors are typical of Hough's work, but they may be excused on the grounds of poetic license. More basic questions were raised about the value of the book as an authentic representation of the cattle frontier.

The novel is essentially an idealized version of the Chisholm Trail and of life in the Kansas cow towns. Although Hough claimed that his story was true to the spirit of the frontier, Stuart Henry attacked it both for its factual inaccuracies and for its sugar-coating of an essentially drab way of life.[7] Henry's criticism of the great Western legend provoked an uproar. Texans, who seem to have a vested interest in the romance of the cattle trails, were par-

[6] The New York *Post* published a statement, copied in the Junction City *Union* of November 11, 1871, that Hickok "paid for the funeral of a man whom he had shot." See also *My Life on the Plains*, 34.

[7] *Conquering Our Great American Plains*, 357–62. (Much of the material cited here is a recapitulation of a book review which Henry published at the time Hough's novel first appeared.)

ticularly incensed. The *Saturday Evening Post* presented their side of the story on June 7, 1924, in an editorial headed "Texas Versus Henry." And many Kansans were upset by Henry's deglamorization of early-day Abilene. One pioneer declared himself "profoundly grieved that Stuart Henry doesn't remember things as they were in that fairyland of adventure and romance."[8] The whole controversy indicated the depth of feeling attached to the Western legends, including that of Wild Bill Hickok.

Also in 1923, the motion picture actor William S. Hart gave the world a sentimental version of the hero in the film *Wild Bill Hickok*. Much of the sentiment was drawn from the theme of Hickok's going blind. (There are several contemporary references to Hickok's having eye trouble.)[9] Wild Bill works as a gambler at Dodge City [*sic*], with Calamity Jane acting as the "look-out." The central episode was a legendary reconstruction of the McCanles battle, although in deference to the McCanles relatives the name was changed.[10]

In 1926, Frank Wilstach published a biography entitled *Wild Bill Hickok, the Prince of Pistoleers*. Wilstach, a theatrical manager from Indiana, idolized his subject. He described him as being "in his time and in his environment, this country's greatest peace officer." As to his role in Western history, he "brought order out of chaos and made life endurable for the rightfully disposed who lived in his jurisdiction." His traits are those of the classic gunfighter: courtly manners, personal honesty, and devotion to duty. Instead of Nichols' crude dialect—"I come ter be perfeck in the mountains"—Wilstach has Wild Bill speaking like this: "I understand you cheap, would-be gunfighters from Montana have been making remarks about me. . . . I want you to understand unless they are stopped there will shortly be a number of cheap funerals in Deadwood. I have come to this town, not to court notoriety,

[8] Letter from E. C. Little to H. L. Humphrey, March 21, 1924, in "Dickinson County Biographical Sketches," Vol. I, 102, in KSHS.

[9] Russell, *Lives and Legends of Buffalo Bill*, 207.

[10] George N. Fenin and William K. Everson, *The Western: From Silents to Cinerama*, 106.

but to live in peace, and do not propose to stand for your insults."[11] Wild Bill was "neither a bad man nor a killer in the sense that Billy the Kid was a taker of human life." He was, in short, a suitable symbol of civilization. Tributes from Cody, Custer, and other friends of Wild Bill round out this picture of a frontier hero.

Wilstach's examination of Hickok's career was not wholly uncritical. He wrote the first widely known revision of the McCanles affair, pointing out that only three men had died and that McCanles had been "preposterously maligned by border historians." Wilstach even traced the mysterious Kate Shell to get her version of the fight, although she really added nothing to the story. Wilstach himself confessed that talking to her was like "opening an oyster with a blade of grass." However, by carefully examining the local annals of Kansas and Nebraska, Wilstach was able to scale down the epic proportions of the battle and restore the whole affair to something nearer historical truth.

Unfortunately the promising start that was made in the analysis of the Rock Creek episode was not fulfilled in the rest of the book. Wilstach insists upon describing Wild Bill's Illinois boyhood in some detail. Stories about any hero's early years are seldom authenticated, and the wise biographer inspires confidence in his work when he refrains from attempts to reconstruct this period. But Wilstach tells of how Hickok read Peters' *Life of Carson* at fifteen and then modeled his own life on Kit's. Unfortunately, Wild Bill was fifteen in 1853, and the Peters book was not published until 1858. Wilstach also says that Wild Bill had fled to Kansas because of a presumably fatal fist fight with one Charles Hudson. This episode appears in a number of accounts, but repetition does not make it a true story. There is not a shred of documentary evidence for this affair, nor is there even a strong oral tradition concerning it. Finally, Wilstach repeats most of the traditional anecdotes drawn from Buel and Ingraham, including the quadrangular duel in Nebraska and the "oyster stew story." It is evident that Hickok's reputation is built upon these exploits, and if they are legendary,

[11] Page 275.

then Hickok's role is more the product of folk process than of history.

In 1927, the *Nebraska History Magazine* published several articles that were critical of Wild Bill. In one of these, George Hansen defended the character of David C. McCanles and described Hickok as a "cold-blooded killer without heart or conscience." This bitter indictment provoked a thunderous response from William E. Connelley, secretary of the Kansas State Historical Society. Connelley's impassioned defense, in the pages of the Kansas historical journal, made it quite clear that the state of Kansas had a vested interest in Hickok's heroism. Said Connelley in rebutting Hansen's "preposterous account" of the Rock Creek affair: "It was necessary to make a plain, emphatic statement of this historic event because of these misrepresentations. Kansas reveres and honors her heroic pioneers. And James Butler Hickok was one of the greatest of these."[12]

Connelley fashioned his defense by pointing to David McCanles' unsavory reputation. He was a "bad" man, a Southern sympathizer, and hated Hickok because of the latter's attentions to Sarah Shull (Kate Shell). These tragic flaws justified the conclusion of the affair: "If ever a man deserved killing, it was McCanles at Rock Creek Station." Connelley moved from this negative argument to a positive exposition of Wild Bill's virtues. His wartime services as a spy were authentically heroic. He had repudiated the grosser distortions of the Nichols article in *Harper's*. He loved children, protected the weak or aged, and killed only in the line of duty. Finally, he "contributed more than any other man to making the West a place for decent men and women to live in—a place in which they could have homes and cities and farms and churches and schools." Connelley obviously had no doubts whatsoever about Hickok's value in facilitating settlement of the Plains or about his worth as a symbol of frontier virtues.

---

[12] "Wild Bill—James Butler Hickok," *Kansas Historical Collections,* Vol. XVII (1926–27), xi.

Connelley's final answer to the critics came when his biography of Hickok was published in 1933. Wild Bill is viewed as the harbinger of civilization, the ideal symbol of the Plains settler. The key statement about Hickok's epic significance occurs in this passage:

> Any man who by his own force and fearlessness beats the dark forces of savagery and crime, so that civilization may be free to take another step forward on her march to progress—is he not the greatest and truest type of the frontiersman? Such a man was Wild Bill. . . . He typified the pioneer, enduring danger and hardship that in his wake might follow peaceful farmers and merchants; that where he had passed might spring up villages and towns.[13]

The statement crystallizes an important assumption about Wild Bill. He was self-conscious about his role as the agent of civilization. He endured hardship and danger, not for money or notoriety, but because he knew that his services were necessary if civilization was to come to the Plains. This assumption is doubtful at best.

Connelley's portrait is really that of an idealized gunfighter of legend, rather than the actual Wild Bill. This is evident from a comparison of his statements with firsthand information about the real Hickok. "Wild Bill found relaxation and enjoyment in cards, but he seldom drank." The independent testimony of the two newspaper correspondents quoted above, as well as Cody's *Autobiography,* indicate that Wild Bill drank quite frequently. "One of Wild Bill's most persistent traits was his liking for children." The archetypal gunfighter must of course like children, animals, and old people, but this particular statement must be qualified. Stuart Henry's remembrance of a childhood in Abilene was that Wild Bill was a bogeyman, whose very name was enough to terrify children. Perhaps in Abilene Bill had little opportunity to display his affection for children. "But he became at once shy and inarticulate on the subject of his own bravery and skill. Faced with admirers, he

[13] *Wild Bill and His Era*, 7.

blushed and stammered and fled." This statement does not square with newspaper and magazine reports of his behavior; for example, those of Theodore Davis and Henry M. Stanley cited above. His style of dress and the pride he took in his personal appearance do not support the view that he blushed and stammered when his own virtues were under discussion.

Connelley was evidently so dazzled by his vision of an epic gunfighter that he could not face up to some of his hero's faults. When he ran across what he considered to be damaging material, he omitted it. In quoting the following letter, Connelley omitted the italicized portion:

> *He always had a mistress. I knew two or three of them, one a former mistress of his was an inmate of a cottage in McCoys addition. Bill asked me to go with him to see her to be a witness in an interview, I believe she was a Red Head but am not sure, she came to Abilene to try and make up with Bill. He gave her $25.00, and made her move on. There was Nan Ross, but Bill told her he was through with her. She moved on.* When Mrs. Lake the Widow of Old Lake of circus fame came to Abilene she set up her tent Just West of the D Cottage on the vacant ground. Bill was on hand to keep order. Bill was a Handsome man as you know & she fell for him hard, fell all the way clear to the Basement, tried her best to get him to marry her and run the Circus. Bill told me all about it. I said why don't you do it—He said "I know she has a good show, but when she is done in the West, she will go East and I don't want any paper collar on, & its me for the West. . . .[14]

In his treatment of the McCanles affair, Connelley was unwilling to admit that some of his hero's actions were questionable. As his articles in the *Kansas Historical Collections* demonstrated, the reputation of Wild Bill became an emotional issue and a matter of state pride rather than a problem in objective history. Connelley

[14] Letter from Charles F. Gross to J. B. Edwards, June 15, 1925, in KSHS; Connelley, *Wild Bill and His Era*, 155; Nyle H. Miller, "Kansas Frontier Police Officers Before TV," Kansas City *Westerners Trail Guide*, Vol. III (March, 1958), 13–14.

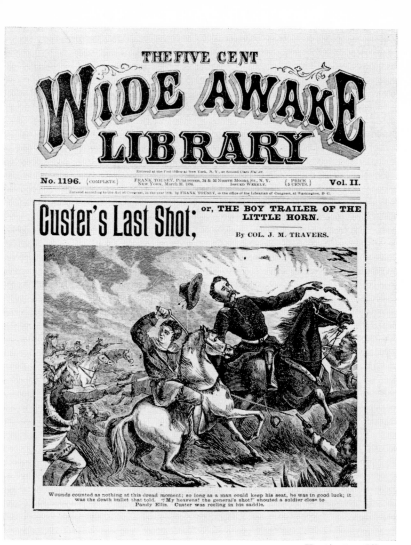

Huntington Library

CUSTER'S LAST STAND
"Of course dime novelists were under no obligation to write
with accuracy."

GENERAL GEORGE ARMSTRONG CUSTER, 1875
"He wore the flamboyant costume which the public and
press expected of him."

apparently felt that any downgrading of Wild Bill would imperil personal, state, and national ideals. This attitude is quite understandable in view of the fact that Hickok's epic stature and achievements are the theme of the biography. And biographers of other gunfighters have also treated their heroes in similar fashion. Wyatt Earp was for his biographer the "epitomizing symbol" of Western America. "The Old West cannot be understood unless Wyatt Earp is also understood."[15]

Nevertheless, Connelley's biography has shaped the contemporary image of Wild Bill Hickok. One finds his interpretations embodied in most printed accounts, including the standard reference works. The *Encyclopedia Americana* echoes a favorite Connelley theme when it explains that Hickok "never killed but in self-defense or line of duty."[16] Stewart Holbrook in a magazine article described Wild Bill as being "quiet and courteous. He seldom swore, drank even less, and was a little quicker with Mr. Colt's Patent Revolving Firearm than any of the many ugly customers he found it necessary to shoot in the process of civilizing the frontier."[17]

In 1936, Hollywood produced a supercolossal "epic" starring Gary Cooper as Wild Bill. One significant fact about the film was that it had the generic title of *The Plainsman,* indicating how the individual and the type had merged into one figure. The script writers appropriated some of the most honored old legends, including the five-handed duel in Nebraska. They also wrote in a romance between Bill and the beautiful Calamity Jane.

The Wild Bill–Calamity Jane legend is rooted in her presence at Deadwood during the last months of Hickok's life, in her burial next to him, and in printed stories which linked the two romantically. An early example of the latter is "Calamity Jane, Queen of the Plains," which was printed as a serial in Street and Smith's *New York Weekly* early in 1882, and which featured tender love

---

[15] Lake, *Wyatt Earp, Frontier Marshal,* viii.
[16] (1960), XIV, 166.
[17] "There Was a Man: Wild Bill Hickok," *Esquire,* Vol. XXXIII (May, 1950), 64.

scenes between the two.[18] This romantic tradition has been kept alive in popular magazines and in films like *The Plainsman,* which imprinted the legend upon the minds of millions of viewers in highly dramatic fashion. Anti-Hickok writers have claimed that Calamity Jane was Wild Bill's paramour in Deadwood.[19] There have even been claims that the two were married,[20] but there is no satisfactory legal evidence to support this tradition. Pro-Hickok writers like Wilstach have indignantly rejected the thesis that Wild Bill regarded Calamity Jane with anything more than genial tolerance. They point out that Bill was happily married to Mrs. Agnes Thatcher Lake, and that even had he strayed from the path, he would have picked a handsomer woman than Calamity Jane. The existing photographs of Miss Cannary tend to support this interpretation.

Juvenile books also make Hickok the prime civilizer of the West. Stewart Holbrook's *Wild Bill Hickok Tames the West* (1952) repeats the Connelley theme by praising Hickok as one "who more than any other had brought civilized order to the frontier." In the process of describing how Hickok pacified the border, Holbrook is guilty of ignoring history. The McCanles "gang," for example, are all armed when they appear at Rock Creek. McCanles draws a gun and takes a step into the house before Hickok fires on him. A jury finds Wild Bill not guilty of murder. In reality, McCanles was not armed, and there was no jury trial—merely a hearing before Justice Coulter. Holbrook says that at Abilene Hickok "asked to be relieved of his post as marshal." To put it more bluntly but more accurately, the city council fired him. Hickok also visits the dying Phil Coe, a sentimental legend which belongs with those about his paying for the funeral expenses of his

---

[18] Reckless Ralph, "Calamity Jane, Queen of the Plains," *New York Weekly,* Vol. XXXVII (January 16–March 13, 1882).

[19] One of these was John S. McClintock in his *Pioneer Days in the Black Hills,* 106. The best study of this legend is in Roberta Beed Sollid, *Calamity Jane: A Study in Historical Criticism* (Montana Historical Society, 1958).

[20] Kathryn Wright, "The Real Calamity Jane," *True West,* Vol. V (November-December, 1957), 22.

victims. There are also legendary stories about Hickok in Dodge City and his encounter there with an imaginary bad man named "Jake Jones." Such anecdotes explain why this book is classified under "Fiction" in most libraries.

Recently the national symbol of Plains history has been the virtuous and smooth-faced hero of the television series, "Wild Bill Hickok." This program, initiated in 1953, was one of the first to use a pseudohistorical framework for fictional adventures. The technique was so successful that it was subsequently applied to other gunfighters, including Wyatt Earp and Bat Masterson. Programs of this type are in the same tradition as the quasi-biographical dime novels written by Prentiss Ingraham in the nineteenth century. In both cases the result is an addition to legend at the expense of history. One suspects that the real Wild Bill would have snorted with derision had he seen the television plays produced under his name. And if one believes the legendary stories, he might even have hurled his impersonator through the nearest pasteboard scenery.

Biographers have continued to find Hickok a popular and profitable subject. Richard O'Connor's *Wild Bill Hickok* (1959) is a well-written but undocumented reworking of the standard episodes. O'Connor faced the same problem that Connelley and Wilstach did: subtract any of Hickok's more sensational adventures on the grounds that they are unauthenticated, and he ceases to stand as the most picturesque example of the general class. Thus biographers, to prove the epic stature of their heroes, must continue to assign to them the traditional traits and exploits. The Mulrey affair, the bear fight, and the "oyster stew" story are some of the familiar tales that O'Connor includes. However, he is somewhat more critical of his subject's character than was William E. Connelley. And he quite correctly doubts that Wild Bill was a fervent disciple of law and order.

So Hickok emerged from the confusing variety of "Comanche Bills," "Cherokee Bills" and others to become the symbolic typefigure of the plainsman and gunfighter. Was Hickok really any different from the hundreds of similar types who populated the Wild West? A description of "Comanche Bill," for example, might well fit Wild Bill:

> I knew Comanche Bill very well indeed for several years. He drifted into Ft. Dodge in the spring of 1867—was Scout here for several years, from here went to Fort Harker, but spent most of his time in Ellsworth. Was killed one night in a drunken row in Nick Lynche's saloon, I think by Tom Atchison, another scout. He was quite a character, always dressed in frontiersman style, long hair, a wide brim slouch hat, high heeled boots, tucked in trousers, big flowing black neck tie, with open shirt, wide collar and never without a belt and six shooter, but this time he did not draw quick enough.[21]

The only difference between the two Bills was speed in drawing their weapons, which is some claim to distinction, and the fact that Wild Bill happened to be in Springfield, Missouri, when George Ward Nichols was looking for a character to put into a magazine article. Without a key publicist, many frontiersmen have remained in obscurity.

[21] Letter from R. M. Wright to Herbert Myrick, July 13, 1904 (Herbert Myrick MS Collection, Huntington Library, San Marino, Calif.).

CHAPTER XIII

"A Bold, Bad Man"

THERE HAVE BEEN MANY who have thought that Wild Bill was not a suitable symbol for the Western pioneer. They have regarded him not as the advance agent of civilization, but rather as an unsavory gambler-gunman. Their views have provoked a debate over Hickok's actual merits, and the vigor of the debate has helped to keep his legend alive.

There are a number of uncomplimentary references to Wild Bill in the contemporary newspapers. The *Saline County Journal* of January 18, 1872, in discussing a rumor that Hickok was in Boston, spoke as him as "the man who has shot men down in cold blood by the scores and is as big a criminal as walks the earth. If it is pleasure for those down-easters to welcome a gambler, a libertine and a rowdy, we can furnish those of the same ilk, just as deserving, by the hundreds, from our 'wicked plains.' " Much of the adverse comment appears to have been of Southern or Confederate origin. The Topeka *Kansas Daily Commonwealth* of May 11, 1873, carried a statement whose source was given as Colonel Norton of the *Arkansas Traveler*. Colonel Norton pricked the bubble as follows:

It is disgusting to see the eastern papers crowding in everything they can get hold of about "Wild Bill." If they only knew the real character of the men they so want to worship, we doubt if their names would ever appear again. "Wild Bill," or Bill Hickok, is nothing more than a drunken, reckless, murderous coward, who is treated with contempt by true border men, and who should have been hung years ago for the murder of innocent men. The shooting of the "old teamster" in the back, for small provocation, while crossing the plains in 1859, is one fact that Harper's correspondent failed to mention, and being

151

booted out of a Leavenworth saloon by a boy bar tender is another; and we might name many other similar examples of his bravery. In one or two instances he did the U.S. government good service, but his shameful and cowardly conduct more than overbalances the good.

In the historical literature of the eighties, there are also a number of anti-Hickok statements. William E. Curtis remarked that Wild Bill was "at one time not only a famous, but a worthy, character, as worthy as men of his class often are, but dissipation and gambling turned a skillful guide and a brave scout into a worthless desperado."[1] Frank Triplett characterized Bill as a bully and a coward, "a red-handed murderer without a single redeeming trait," whose death by assassination was simply poetic justice.[2] And A. T. Andreas, in his monumental *History of the State of Kansas* (1883), regarded Hickok as anything but a hero. At Hays, he was "the dread of others equally bad and reckless of life as himself . . . and the only way he answered admonition or brooked interference was with the revolver." He then went to Abilene, where he continued his "murderous practices," being "a bold, bad man," who "thought no more of killing a man than he would a dog."[3] Such moral judgments seem to come naturally to anyone writing about Wild Bill.

In dime novels, oral tales, and novels, Hickok is occasionally the villain. *Wild Bill's Last Trail* (1892), by Ned Buntline, emphasizes Bill's heavy drinking and his gambling, criticisms which reflect Buntline's own temperance background. Wild Bill's "crowd" frequently appears in the story as a dangerous and drunken mob. The plot is built around the revenge motif. Phil Coe's sister, disguised as a man, comes up from Texas to avenge her brother's death. Wild Bill is wracked by guilt over Coe's murder, indicated by the fact that he faints whenever the sister appears. Buntline's own judgment of Hickok is expressed in this critical speech:

[1] *A Summer Scamper Along the Old Santa Fe Trail* (Chicago, Interocean Publishing Company, 1883), 58.

[2] *Conquering the Wilderness*, 537–40.

[3] Pages 1291, 688.

"Most outlaws are desperadoes, but a man can be a desperado, and yet not an outlaw. If to be always ready to shoot for a look or a word—whether his opponent is ready or not—is not being a desperado, I do not know what is." Similar judgments were to be expressed later in full-length novels, like Courtney Ryley Cooper's *The Last Frontier,* in which Wild Bill is a featured character.[4]

Some of the stories told by old-timers pictured Hickok in an unfavorable light:

> One story that used to be told in Cheyenne, but which is not authenticated, was that on one occasion at Abilene he entered a restaurant for breakfast and ordered ham and eggs "turned over." The waiter returned with the eggs fried on one side and "Bill" angrily said:
> "I told you to have them eggs turned over!"
> Whereupon the waiter playfully gave the dish a flip and turned them over. This so angered "Bill" that he shot the waiter dead, and then finished his meal, the poor waiter's body lying at his feet.[5]

Many of the fictional Wild Bill stories, including the "oyster stew" episode and the simultaneous forward-backward shooting affair, seem to be set in or about restaurants.

The first revisionist interpretation of the Hickok saga was printed in Charles Dawson's *Pioneer Tales of the Oregon Trail and Jefferson County* (1912). Dawson introduced material which could be used by those who thought that Hickok's halo was undeserved. He described the Rock Creek affair not as a heroic epic but as the "tragic drama of Jefferson County."[6] His case was built upon a study of the character of McCanles, whom he described as "a born leader, with an utter disregard of danger in any form." Dawson was also the first to add Kate Shell to the plot. It was the rivalry between Hickok and McCanles for her attentions, said Dawson, which provoked the bloody affair at the station. Although Dawson

---

[4] In Cooper's novel, published in 1923, Bill appears as a dangerous killer. He is subject to fits of violence and jealousy, and he threatens to kill the hero of the story.

[5] William F. Hooker, *The Prairie Schooner,* 110.

[6] Page 209.

did not document these assertions, his interpretation made Hickok's actions considerably less admirable than when the story had involved the protection of Union property against Confederate conspirators and horse thieves. Dawson also challenged the orthodox story by pointing out that "McCanles gang" was not a technically accurate description but merely a term used by those writers who disliked David McCanles and his friends. (Current encyclopedias still speak of the McCanles "gang.")[7] Finally, Dawson stated that young Monroe McCanles owed his life not to Hickok's kindheartedness, but to the fact that Wild Bill had to reload his pistols after shooting Woods and Gordon.

Dawson's book reached only a small local audience, and hence it did not inspire any revisions in the traditional story until Frank Wilstach discovered it in 1926. Wilstach utilized the book in writing his own account of Rock Creek, though he took issue with many of Dawson's unfavorable statements about Wild Bill. In particular, he denied Dawson's assertion that Hickok's cheating at cards had initiated the dispute with McCanles.

The Dawson book was also cited in the articles on Hickok that appeared in the *Nebraska History Magazine* in 1927. The principal article was George W. Hansen's "The Rock Creek Ranch Events and the Trial of Wild Bill." Hansen, a banker and pioneer of Fairbury, Nebraska, called Hickok a cold-blooded killer. His case was built upon a defense of the character of David McCanles. According to Hansen, the orthodox story of the fight was false. It was simple murder rather than a heroic battle. Furthermore, Wilstach's attempts to show that McCanles was a Confederate sympathizer, and that he had threatened Wild Bill for his attentions to Sarah Shull, were misguided. McCanles was, rather, a respected citizen, whose murder the Hickok crowd had managed to turn into a glorious stroke in defense of the Union. Hansen's most serious complaint was that Hickok's actual moral qualities made him an inappropriate symbol of the frontiersmen:

[7] *Colliers Encyclopedia* (1961), IX, 392; *Encyclopaedia Britannica* (1961), XI, 541.

He died in the place he frequented most and loved best,— at the gambling table and surrounded by the vile associations of the frontier saloon. Thus died the real Hickok. The mythical Hickok, the gentlemanly gun-man, still lives in fiction and on the screen, an incitement to the youth of the country for lives of crime.

This indictment was answered by William E. Connelley, and there followed a battle fought with crackling typewriters. Much of the denunciatory material that appeared was on the level of shooting exploits. Herbert Cody Blake published in 1929 a collection of "truthful" *Western Stories,* whose subtitle was "History and Busted Romances of the Old Frontier." One of the busted romances was that of Wild Bill, whom Blake decided was inexpert with a .44, "painfully slow . . . absolutely a poor shot."

More serious questions were raised by authentic pioneers who, like Hansen, questioned the Hickok myth on moral grounds. One of these was W. Monroe McCanles, who told his story in *Forest and Stream* magazine in 1927.[8] He characterized the shooting of his father as the cowardly assassination of an unarmed man and went on to develop a convincing case for the theory that McCanles and his two adult companions were unarmed. McCanles also elaborated a conspiracy theory about the conclusion of the episode, offering two explanations about why justice was not served. He says, "It suited the Stage Company to have the matter squelched," and furthermore, "the county was not organized at that time and the trial was merely a sham trial." He further stated that William F. Cody was to blame for repeating a false story of the fight in his numerous books, apparently for publicity purposes. McCanles' conclusion: "If Jim ever killed one man that had an equal chance, I would like to have the evidence."

Stuart Henry was another pioneer who had serious doubts about the contemporary glorification of Wild Bill. He conceded that Hickok had come to typify the Wild West in the public mind. Yet

[8] M. I. McCreight, " 'The McCandless [*sic*] Gang,' " *Forest and Stream,* Vol. XCVII (December, 1927), 740–42, 762–63. McCanles also told his story in the Kansas City *Journal,* December 5, 1926 (clipping in the KSHS).

Bill had been something less than the paragon depicted by his biographers. During his tenure as marshal of Abilene, he had participated in public poker games at the Alamo saloon. He took justice into his own hands, a form of lawlessness that resulted in "loose conditions" as compared with those under his predecessor, Tom Smith. "Smith, unlike Bill, was a disciplined chief of police and led a strictly moral and legal life in Abilene as judged by any code."[9] Henry also objected to Wilstach's idealized portrait of Wild Bill: "His constant life in the bosom of Abilene's criminal population as one of its steady gamblers must disprove the Wilstach thesis as relating to that period of Hickok's life."

Southern historians, and more particularly Texans, have generally been anti-Hickok. William Walton's biography of Ben Thompson in 1884 is an early example of the Texan view that Hickok was a murderer and a grafter. Thomas Ripley is one of the more recent pro-Texan writers who regard characters like Thompson and John Wesley Hardin as being worthy of more respect than Wild Bill. These authors treasure the memory of Hardin's outsmarting Hickok with the "road agent's spin" at Abilene in 1871. None of the Hickok biographers have accepted Hardin's story, and Frank Wilstach was particularly vehement in his denunciation of it.[10] (It should be noted that this is the same kind of clever exploit that Hickok presumably pulled on Jack Mulrey; it is unacceptable because the hero outwits but is never outwitted.) The dispute reflects a traditional North-South antagonism dating from the Civil War, and Wild Bill became another pawn in refighting that epic struggle.

Hollywood has also made its contribution to the anti-Hickok tradition. In the film *Jack McCall, Desperado* (1953), Hickok is portrayed as a renegade and crooked sheriff who smuggles guns to the Indians and murders Jack McCall's parents. In the final encounter between the two, McCall kills Hickok in a fair duel

[9] *Conquering Our Great American Plains*, 284.
[10] *Wild Bill Hickok*, 186.

after giving him an opportunity to draw first. This reversal of roles was a complete distortion of history, but such distortions make up the legends surrounding most frontier heroes. McCall's reward is that at the end of the film he is tried and acquitted, the script writers neglecting to add that he was subsequently hanged by the government.[11]

The result of these criticisms was that by the post-war period, historians were talking about the "dubious tradition" of Wild Bill Hickok.[12] Ramon Adams and E. B. Mann, drawing upon the Dawson book and the Hansen article in *Nebraska History,* decided that the McCanles affair had been a simple case of murder—and this now seems to be the accepted opinion among Western specialists.[13] Mann's conclusion that Wild Bill was "no Sir Galahad" probably also reflects the current view. Most of these critical articles appeared in regional publications of limited circulation. But occasionally the popular press debunks Wild Bill. Peter Lyon's story on "The Wild, Wild West," which appeared in the August, 1960, issue of *American Heritage,* emphasized that the heroism of Hickok (and other Western heroes) was mythical rather than actual. Wild Bill, concluded Lyon, was unworthy of his own legend.

So there are many questions about the relationship between the man and his legend. The consensus of informed opinion is that the real Wild Bill was somewhere in between the paragon depicted in the Buel-Connelley tradition and the heartless devil of the Andreas-Hansen school.[14] An honest citizen in one of the lawless cow towns probably welcomed a Wild Bill, despite his faults. Bill's per-

[11] F. Maurice Speed, ed., *Western Film Annual* (London, F. Maurice Speed, 1955), 116.

[12] Wayne Gard, *Frontier Justice* (Norman, University of Oklahoma Press, 1949), 243.

[13] Adams, "With Our Rocking Chair Historians," Denver *Westerners Brand Book* (1952); E. B. Mann, "The Truth Behind the Wild Bill Hickok Myth," *New Mexico Sun Trails,* Vols. V–VII (December, 1952–February, 1953); Harry Sinclair Drago, *Wild, Woolly & Wicked* (New York, Clarkson N. Potter, 1960), 90.

[14] "The Case of James Butler Hickok, Alias 'Wild Bill,'" Chicago *Westerners Brand Book,* Vol. III (April–May, 1946), 1–7.

sonal vanity and extravagant clothing can be excused on the grounds that he was simply playing the role which the times demanded of him. His habits involving gambling, drinking, and wild women were also common to the period and the place. His callous attitude toward the taking of human life, expressed in the statement that killing ruffians "shouldn't trouble one any more than killing a rat or an ugly cat or a vicious dog,"[15] is perhaps less understandable. Yet life was cheap among the class of men to which Hickok belonged and which he typified.

What are the legendary elements in the Hickok story? The legend maintains that his killings were in defense of law and order. But McCanles, Tutt, and Coe were all shot as a result of personal feuds with Wild Bill. Only in the case of Sam Strawhim (and possibly Jack Mulrey) at Hays City did Hickok appear to be acting for the community. Were these gunfights the chivalric contests which legend has made them out to be? Americans like to think so, and one President of the United States has explained how this code guided his own life.[16] Yet these shootings were usually sudden outbursts of violence in which the shots were fired first and the questions were asked much later. Hickok, as at Rock Creek, was not always scrupulous in observing the "code." And his own death at Deadwood is probably more typical of frontier shooting than the celebrated "duels." Does the Hickok saga adequately represent the history of the Plains frontier? Nowhere in its pages do we find the pioneer farmers who actually settled the Plains. The cattlemen and the sensational gunfighters associated with

15 Connelley, *Wild Bill and His Era*, 4.

16 "I was raised in a little town of which many of you may never have heard. But out in the west it is a famous place. It is called Abilene, Kansas. We had as our Marshal a man named Wild Bill Hickok. Now that town had a code and I was raised as a boy to prize that code.

"It was: Meet anyone face to face with whom you disagree. You could not sneak up on him from behind, or do any damage to him, without suffering the penalty of an enraged citizenry. If you met him face to face and took the same risks as he did, you could get away with almost anything, as long as the bullet was in front."— Dwight D. Eisenhower, in a speech at Washington, D.C., November 23, 1953.

their era were a colorful but transitory phenomena. But such imbalance is characteristic of Western history in general. Billy the Kid symbolizes the history of the Southwest, while more important men are forgotten. But even in Hickok's own field of law enforcement, admittedly a significant aspect of early Plains history, there were others more highly respected. After all, Abilene erected its monument not to Wild Bill but to "Bear River" Tom Smith.

PART FOUR

The Soldier:
George Armstrong Custer

CHAPTER XIV

Portrait of a Soldier

DURING THE NINETEENTH CENTURY, the United States Army fought many battles with the Indian tribes of the Far West. Outstanding military leaders were involved in these wars, and there were a number of memorable engagements, including some (such as the Grattan and Fetterman massacres) in which sizable bodies of troops were annihilated by the savages. But for the American public, one soldier and one battle have come to symbolize all these campaigns. George Armstrong Custer is the soldier, and his "Last Stand" on the Little Big Horn River, June 25, 1876, has become the archetypal Indian fight of the trans-Missouri West.

Close students of the battle have for three generations been debating questions which still are only vaguely grasped by the average American. Did Custer disobey orders? Did Reno "abandon" Custer? Was the Seventh Cavalry too fatigued to fight effectively? While the experts have gone on arguing these and other military questions, the amateur has been fascinated by a more dramatic and less technical feature of the legend—the character and personality of George Custer. For the layman this is the core of the legend, and indeed most attempts to analyze the military aspects of the battle are ultimately based upon a favorable or unfavorable view of Custer's character.

But finding the truth about Custer is difficult, because he was a complex individual whose words and whose actions are often contradictory. Even without the dramatic finale at the Little Big Horn, he would have been a formidable figure in Western legend because he was adept at self-dramatization. He was one of the few articulate frontier heroes. While Kit Carson could not read or write and Billy the Kid had only a painful and half-literate scrawl, George Custer possessed an educated pen. What Frémont did for Carson, Custer did for himself. Writing articles for the *Galaxy Magazine,* he entertained armchair Westerners with shrewdly selected adventures in which Custer himself played the leading role. He wore the flamboyant costumes which the public and press expected of him. Yet there was a surprisingly sensitive nature hidden within the notorious "show-off."

Custer was born at New Rumley, Ohio, on December 5, 1839.[1] From his blacksmith father, Emanuel Custer, George inherited a political allegiance to the Democrats, an independent or even rebellious temperament, and a low social status. He continued to labor under social and educational disadvantages even when he left the Custer household at the age of ten to go and live with his half sister Lydia (Mrs. David Reed) at Monroe, Michigan. The Reeds were not considered to be among the "best" families in Monroe, and Custer's difficult relations with his future father-in-law, Judge Daniel S. Bacon, perfectly reflect the social and economic handicaps which he perhaps spent much of his life trying to overcome.[2]

But Custer was ambitious. At fifteen he attended a normal school near his home town, and in 1856–57 taught in a one-room schoolhouse near Athens, Ohio. He had originally thought of becoming a lawyer, but since the best-known social escalator for boys of that period was a West Point education, he applied for admission to the Military Academy. Custer was accepted despite his seeming lack of scholarly potential, and he arrived at the Point in the spring of 1857.

Custer's career at the Military Academy revealed his exuberance, his love of practical jokes, and his disregard of "regulations." During his four years there, he spent sixty-six Saturdays doing

[1] Milo Custer, *Custer Genealogies,* 2.
[2] Marguerite Merington, *The Custer Story,* 47, 50, 64.

extra guard duty for various offenses—sloppy uniform, laughing in ranks, and failure to prepare lessons.[3] Custer received demerits for wearing his hair too long. So he had his skull shaved; and, receiving demerits for this, he wore a wig which became the butt of cadet jokes.[4] In his last half-year he accumulated ninety-seven demerits, with one hundred requiring dismissal. His ineptitude in the study of cavalry tactics is indicative of a persistent Custer trait; he did not go by the book.

Custer was finally graduated, at the bottom of his class, on June 25, 1861. Four days after graduation, he was placed under arrest for failing to stop a fist fight between two cadets while serving as officer of the guard at summer camp. Custer was only reprimanded,[5] but the episode illustrates the juvenile manner in which he often handled his responsibilities as an officer. On a number of succeeding occasions during his career he was to ignore these responsibilities, but in each case "Custer's luck" enabled him to escape the punishment which might have reformed his behavior.

During the Civil War, Custer saw action at Bull Run, Antietam, Gettysburg, the Shenandoah campaign, and Appomattox. One key to his wartime career is his innate sense of the dramatic. Custer always had a keen appreciation for the sentimental plays and melodramas of his time; his writings are sprinkled with Shakespearean quotations,[6] and one of his closest friends was the actor Lawrence Barrett.[7] He also had a flair for costumes. During the war, one of his special nonregulation outfits included a black velvet jacket trimmed with gold lace, a crimson necktie, and a white hat. His explanation for this get-up was that he wanted his men to recognize him on any part of the field, but one can also detect the expression of a natural dramatic instinct.

[3] George A. Custer, "War Memoirs," *The Galaxy,* Vol. XXI (April, 1876), 454.

[4] J. P. Farley, *West Point in the Early Sixties,* 78.

[5] Custer, "War Memoirs," *The Galaxy,* Vol. XXI (April, 1876), 455.

[6] George A. Custer, *My Life on the Plains; or, Personal Experiences with Indians,* 161.

[7] Frederick Whittaker, *A Complete Life of Gen. George A. Custer,* 632–40.

Custer was also adept at the necessary art of self-praise. The military report was a vehicle for promotion, and Custer's reports on his own operations are seldom lacking in the required superlatives. Of an attack which he led at Gettysburg he said, "I challenge the annals of warfare to produce a more brilliant or successful charge of cavalry."[8] As one contemporary remarked, "He was apt to exaggerate in statement, not from any wilful disregard of the truth, but because he saw things bigger than they really were."[9] But this habit often led him to claim credit for accomplishments that belonged to others.[10]

Custer did, however, excel as a cavalry leader. He loved combat, particularly the saber-wielding charges whose heroism he had first appreciated as a cadet reading the romantic novels of William Gilmore Simms. He had absolutely no fear of death or injury, even though a dozen horses were shot out from under him during the war. He took chances, but his audacious tactics were usually successful. He liked to take the initiative, even when such action involved violation of orders. In 1865, he pursued the remnants of Lee's army to Appomattox station, despite orders that he halt and rest his troops.[11] Once arrived at the station, he divided his division, another dangerous but characteristic strategy which he practiced later in warfare on the Plains.

Because of a combination of combat ability, favorable publicity, and popularity with influential generals, Custer was rapidly promoted. He was made a brigadier general in June of 1863, a meteoric rise for the twenty-three-year-old captain whom newspapermen dubbed "the Boy General." The title was an appropriate one for

8 *Ibid.*, 178.

9 Capt. William Ludlow in Frances F. Victor, *Eleven Years in the Rocky Mountains,* 134.

10 "As soon as the enemy hoisted the white flag, Gen. Custer's division rushed up the hill and turned in more prisoners and battle flags than any of the cavalry, and probably had less to do with their surrender than any of the rest of us." (Battle of Sailor's Creek, 1865). *General George Crook: His Autobiography,* ed. by Martin F. Schmitt (Norman, University of Oklahoma Press, 1946), 139.

11 Whittaker, *Life,* 305; H. Edwin Tremain, *The Closing Days about Richmond* (Edinburgh, privately published, 1884), 222–23.

a grown man who signed letters to his future wife as "your devoted Boy Autie." Custer's lifelong boyishness accounts for much of his appeal and explains many of his faults.

On February 8, 1864, Custer married Elizabeth Bacon at Monroe. "Libbie" had become increasingly interested in the dashing young officer, even though she had seen him staggering down the street dead drunk one day in the fall of 1861.[12] (Custer gave up drinking after this episode and used neither liquor nor tobacco for the remainder of his life.)[13] A formidable obstacle had been overcome when Judge Bacon consented to his daughter's marriage. The Bacons and the Custers belonged to different social classes in a town where class lines were quite sharp, but Custer's rapid rise from raw country boy to brigadier general apparently convinced the reluctant judge that his prospective son-in-law had some chances of success.

Because of his youth, his spectacular costumes, and his flamboyant personality, the correspondents gathered around Custer like bees around honey. His activities were fully reported in *Harper's Weekly* and the *New York Times*. The cover of the *Weekly* for March 19, 1864, pictured Custer leading an attack during his deep raid on the enemy supply depot at Charlottesville. Custer's victorious charge at Cedar Creek in the Shenandoah campaign of 1864 (after which he was brevetted major general of volunteers) was also lauded by the press. Said E. A. Paul, writing in the *Times* of October 27, "Custer, young as he is, displayed judgment worthy of a Napoleon." Of Custer's raids south toward Appomattox in the spring of 1865, Paul wrote (March 20), "General Custer deserves the credit for planning and executing one of the most brilliant and successful fights in this or any other war." Such glowing newspaper and magazine reports satisfied Custer's craving for recognition and helped to make him into a national figure.

Following the war, Custer faced the problem of reconversion

[12] Whittaker, *Life,* 90.
[13] Lawrence Barrett in Whittaker, *Life,* 635.

to peacetime status. He spent six dreary months on occupation duty in Texas. Then, in January of 1866, his commission as major-general of volunteers expired, and he reverted to his 1862 rank of captain in the Regular Army. Custer cast about for some other occupation, but the army was clearly his life and blood. A new phase of his career began on July 28, 1866, when he was commissioned lieutenant colonel and made second in command of the newly created Seventh Cavalry regiment.[14] (He was also given the brevet or honorary rank of major general in the Regular Army, hence his courtesy title of "General.") Custer served as actual commander of the regiment most of the time until his death, since the commanding colonels were usually on detached service elsewhere.

The regiment suffered from many of the classic problems of the post-war army. Among the officer corps the usual jockeying for position was intensified by the limited opportunities for promotion in a shrunken peacetime army. Many officers with fine combat records were unhappy with their subordinate commands, and they were jealous of Custer's success. Frederick Benteen, for example, who had been a lieutenant colonel and regimental commander during the war, was now a captain and troop commander. Nor was the Seventh Cavalry completely an American outfit. There were many foreign professionals and immigrants among its personnel. A typical example was Captain Myles Keogh, an Irishman who had served with the Papal Guards in Italy. The enlisted men included a heavy quota of Irish, German, and Italian immigrants. There were also the "winter birds," enlistees who deserted for the gold mines when spring came. Life was grim on the frontier army posts. Dust storms and floods were common hazards. The fact that food, quarters, and equipment were often inferior tended to soften morale and encourage desertions.

The regiment was posted to Fort Riley, Kansas, where Custer

---

[14] Melbourne C. Chandler, *Of Garry Owen in Glory: The History of the Seventh United States Cavalry Regiment*, 3.

spent the winter of 1866–67 training his troops for an Indian campaign in the spring. The campaign was led by General W. S. Hancock, who had orders to sweep the Sioux and Cheyennes from the path of the transcontinental railroad. On Custer's first view of the Plains Indians, he noted with heavy irony that each warrior "was supplied with either a breech-loading rifle or revolver, sometimes with both—the latter obtained through the wise foresight and strong love of fair play which prevails in the Indian Department."[15] The Indians managed to slip away from Hancock, and Custer spent a fruitless spring and summer chasing them through the sea of grass.

In July, Custer made a series of forced marches along the Republican River in search of the hostiles. These marches, plus the proximity of the area to the Colorado gold fields, resulted in wholesale desertions. At noon on July 7, fifteen men broke away from the column and headed for the Denver stage road. Custer ordered his officers in pursuit, explaining subsequently that "there was no limit fixed to the measures which they were authorized to adopt in executing their orders."[16] To use the more blunt language of the subsequent court-martial orders, he "did order the said party to shoot the supposed deserters down dead, and to bring none in alive."[17] Five deserters were recaptured, three of them having been wounded by the pursuing officers. The episode is a commentary on both Custer's blindness to the limitations of those serving under him and the nature of those limitations. Custer's own explanation for the desertions was the lure of the mines and the poor food.[18] His conclusions were corroborated in *Harper's Magazine* by Theodore Davis, who reported that the men were suffering from scurvy and were deserting at the rate of fifty a month.[19]

15 *My Life on the Plains*, 26.
16 *Ibid.*, 73.
17 Chandler, *Of Garry Owen in Glory*, 5.
18 *My Life on the Plains*, 72.
19 "A Summer on the Plains," *Harper's Magazine*, Vol. XXXVI (February, 1868), 298.

Even after this unfortunate episode, Custer continued to push his men. He was searching for a courier party of ten men under Lieutenant Lyman S. Kidder, which was presumably on the plains south toward Fort Wallace. Custer found the Lieutenant and all his companions stripped and mutilated—a classic tragedy of the Indian wars.

At Fort Wallace, Custer received orders to continue operations against the Indians from that base. He disobeyed those orders and took action which can only be characterized as impetuous and irresponsible. Since supplies were inadequate at Wallace, Custer led a wagon train east to Fort Hays. Custer said that he covered the 155 miles in fifty-five hours,[20] an example of his stamina. Near Downer's Station on the way east, Custer's rear guard was ambushed and two of his men killed by Indians. Custer, inexcusably, did not stop to investigate. As he tells it in *My Life on the Plains:*

> Here, while stopping to rest our horses for a few minutes, a small party of men, who had without authority halted some distance behind, came dashing into our midst and reported that twenty-five or thirty Indians had attacked them some five or six miles in rear, and had killed two of their number. As there was a detachment of infantry guarding the station, and time being important, we pushed on toward our destination.[21]

Custer does not explain why time was so important that he had to ignore his obligation to investigate the attack. Nor does he explain that the men who halted "without authority" probably did so because their stock horses were not equal to the pace set by Custer's specially selected mounts. It is omissions such as these which make it necessary to study Custer's reports of his own actions with great care.

Custer rushed on another sixty miles to Fort Harker. There he took the train to Fort Riley—still another ninety miles to the east. And at Fort Riley he found the true goal of his breathless though

[20] *My Life on the Plains,* 82.
[21] *Ibid.*

unauthorized expedition—"Libbie" Custer. His devotion to his wife was so great that he would risk his army career to see her for a single day.

Custer knew when he left Fort Wallace that he would probably be court-martialed.[22] The court at Fort Leavenworth in September found him guilty of all charges; he had disobeyed orders, deserted his command, failed to pursue Indians who had attacked his escort, and ordered his officers to shoot down deserters. The sentence was suspension from rank and forfeiture of pay for one year.[23] But Custer did not learn much from the penalty. His astonishment at being called to book is recorded in this ironic statement:

> And as a very fair sample of the laurels which military men may win in an Indian campaign by a zealous discharge of what they deem their duty, I will here state, in parentheses, that after engaging in the [Hancock] expedition, some of the events which I am about to relate, and undergoing fatigue, privation, and dangers equal to those of a campaign in the Rebellion, I found myself at the termination of the campaign again at Fort Riley *in arrest*.[24]

In Custer, one always notes a certain lack of receptivity to external pressures for reform.

Another reason why the sentence may not have reformed the unrepentant sinner was that General Sheridan needed him to fight Indians. A winter campaign was planned against the hostile tribes in 1868, and Custer played a prominent part in it after Sheridan had secured a commutation of his court-martial sentence. In fact, Custer's victory at the Battle of the Washita, November 27, 1868, gave the regiment its glorious reputation. Custer surrounded the Cheyenne village of Chief Black Kettle on the banks of the Washita River in Oklahoma and followed the same plan of attack that he was to use at the Little Big Horn eight years later. He divided his command into four columns to encircle the Indians and to make sure that none of them would get away. The tactic was generally

[22] Merington, *The Custer Story*, 212.
[23] Chandler, *Of Garry Owen in Glory*, 5.
[24] *My Life on the Plains*, 23.

171

successful, except for the escape of a small band of warriors who were pursued downriver by Major Joel Elliot. Custer claimed in his report that he had killed 103 warriors, captured 53 women and children, destroyed 875 ponies, and burned the hostile village to the ground.[25] General Sheridan in a special order complimented Custer for "efficient and gallant services rendered."[26]

But others bitterly criticized the "Boy General" for his actions at the Washita. Major Elliot and eighteen troopers had been cut off and massacred by Indians from neighboring villages. Custer was charged with the "abandonment" of these men. The principal accuser was a member of Custer's own command, Captain Benteen, who incorporated his accusations in a letter printed in the *St. Louis Democrat* (February 9, 1869) and the *New York Times* (February 14).[27] "Who can describe the feeling of that brave band, as with anxious beating hearts, they strained their yearning eyes in the direction whence help should come? . . . But surely some search will be made for our missing comrades. No, they are forgotten."

The semiofficial reply to this charge came from De Benneville Randolph Keim, a newspaperman who accompanied Custer and Sheridan to the scene of the battle several weeks later. Keim explained that Custer's withdrawal was "justifiable according to the laws of war"; namely, the safety of the entire command must come before a fraction of it. Custer's own force was small and without supplies. The men were without proper protection from the sub-zero cold, having left their overcoats several miles to the rear. Finally, the Indians were extraordinarily strong and were seen to be steadily increasing in numbers along the bluffs above Black Kettle's camp.[28]

Even when all the evidence has been assembled on both sides of this issue, Custer's guilt or innocence still appears to be a matter

[25] Chandler, *Of Garry Owen in Glory,* 23; Letter of the Secretary of War, communicating information on the Battle of the Washita River, 40 Cong., 3 sess. (1868–69), *Sen. Exec. Doc. 18* (Washington, Government Printing Office, 1869), 29.

[26] Chandler, *Of Garry Owen in Glory,* 24.

[27] Reprinted in W. A. Graham, *The Custer Myth,* 211–13.

[28] *Sheridan's Troopers on the Border: A Winter Campaign on the Plains,* 145–55.

of opinion rather than of legal proof. But there are certain parallels with the Downer's Station episode in that Custer left the scene without ascertaining the facts. The Elliot affair also left a legacy of bitterness within the regiment that was fully revealed among the troops on Reno Hill during the Battle of the Little Big Horn. They felt that Custer had "abandoned" them as he had Major Elliot at the Washita.[29]

Custer was also criticized by humanitarians, who called his attack a "massacre" rather than a "battle." They also claimed that the majority of the 103 "warriors" cited in Custer's report were actually women and children. The claim seems to be valid since it is supported by both white and Indian sources.[30] Custer had warned his troops before the engagement that if they failed to whip the Indians, Westerners would denounce them as inefficient and softhearted. On the other hand, if they crushed the savages, they would be assailed by horrified humanitarians.[31] Indeed, the death of Black Kettle was much regretted by many whites. General Harney said: "I have worn the uniform of my country 55 years, and I know that Black Kettle was as good a friend of the United States as I am," while Indian Agent A. G. Boone remarked that "he was a good man; he was my friend; he was murdered."[32] Custer also drew criticism from General W. B. Hazen, superintendent of the Southern Indian District, who claimed that Black Kettle's village was a peaceful one.[33] Although Black Kettle himself may have been innocent, some of his warriors had been raiding along the Kansas

[29] *The Official Record of a Court of Inquiry convened at Chicago, Illinois, January 13, 1879, by the President of the United States upon the request of Major Marcus A. Reno, 7th U.S. Cavalry to investigate his conduct at the battle of the Little Big Horn, June 25–26, 1876* (hereafter cited as *Official Record of the Reno Court*) (2 vols.), I, 33; II, 377; II, 445.

[30] Charles J. Brill, *Conquest of the Southern Plains,* 15–16; Don Russell and Elmo Scott Watson, "The Battle of the Washita, or Custer's Massacre?" Chicago *Westerners Brand Book,* Vol. V (November, 1948), 49–56.

[31] *My Life on the Plains,* 183.

[32] Victor, *Eleven Years in the Rock Mountains,* 118.

[33] *Some Corrections of "My Life on the Plains"* (St. Paul, Ramaley and Cunningham, 1875).

frontier. In the village the troops found bedding, letters, and other personal items taken from murdered Kansans.

Following the battle of the Washita, Custer continued operations against the nonreservation tribes in Oklahoma. In the winter months of 1869, he displayed his courage, his stamina, and his knowledge of Indian psychology. He traveled the frozen wastes in search of his elusive quarry, accompanied by Kansas volunteers who wanted to punish the savages for past transgressions. (The Kansans noted that Custer was quite popular with his troops.)[34] Through dogged persistence, Custer finally caught up with the Cheyenne village of Stone Forehead, where two white women from the Kansas settlements were held prisoner. He effected their rescue by seizing four chiefs as hostages for the return of the captives and forced Stone Forehead to promise to come into the reservation. Custer's achievement of his objectives without the bloodshed that the Kansans desired was an accomplishment for which he took full credit in letters to his wife.[35]

The Seventh Cavalry spent the summer of 1869 at Fort Hays, Kansas. There was time for horse racing, amateur theatricals, and parties. Mrs. Custer had an opportunity to meet such noted frontier characters as Wild Bill Hickok.[36] And the General had time to indulge his interests, which included hunting, taxidermy, and autobiography.

Custer began to write the story of his life that summer at Fort Hays, but it was not until he was assigned to Elizabethtown, Kentucky, in 1871 that he started seriously to work on it. Custer and two companies of the regiment were sent to Elizabethtown to police the activities of the Ku Klux Klan. But the town was a placid one, and horse racing occupied only part of the General's time; hence he was able to set down an interesting record of his own life and times. The narrative originally appeared as a series of articles in

[34] David L. Spotts and E. A. Brininstool, *Campaigning with Custer and the Nineteenth Kansas Volunteer Cavalry*, 72.

[35] Elizabeth B. Custer, *Following the Guidon*, 56.

[36] *Ibid.*, chap. XII.

The Galaxy, an upper-middle-class magazine of the period, and then was published as a book in 1874 under the title, *My Life on the Plains.*

The book is an important historical and literary document. It helped to transform the dreary "American Desert" into a land of romance. Custer himself was innately romantic. As Captain William Ludlow remarked, "He was a natural optimist. He took rose-colored views of everything, even of the miserable lands of the Northern Pacific Railroad."[37] His book presents an idealized view of the West, with much of the sordidness and sweat removed. Custer exults in the grandeur of mountains and plains, appreciates the gaudy colors and weird war songs of Indian captives and scouts, and has a fine eye and ear for the picturesque costumes and language of white scouts like "California Joe" Milner and Wild Bill Hickok. His essays on the geography and fauna of the plains are basically a romantic tribute to the Great West.

In one respect only does Custer strike a realistic note, and that is in his views of the Indians. While he admired their courage and fighting ability, he did not harbor any illusions that they were the Noble Red Men of James Fenimore Cooper's novels. In fact, he specifically declares his intention to educate his readers to the error of attempting to apply humanitarian doctrines to the governance of Indians. And he complains that even some of the military men on the Plains, notably General W. B. Hazen, were "completely deceived as to their real character."[38] Custer's essays on the Indians also point up the extremely difficult position of army officers during the Indian campaigns: they were constantly reviled by Easterners who apparently were still guided by Cooper-inspired delusions about the red men.

The book tells us a great deal about Custer himself. The breadth of his knowledge and interests is quite unusual for an army officer of this period. There are references to authors (Cooper and Shakespeare), to artists (Church and Bierstadt), and to actresses (Maud

[37] Victor, *Eleven Years in the Rocky Mountains,* 134.
[38] *My Life on the Plains,* 197.

Müller).[39] We get glimpses of Custer's pride in himself and his regiment, as when he says, "We had some fifteen hundred troops, a force ample to cope with all the Indians which could then, or since, be combined at any one point on the plains."[40] We learn of his tremendous physical endurance, his ability to go without sleep and to endure irregular meals while campaigning.[41] We read his formula for successful Indian fighting: never wait for reinforcements, but dash into the village at once to gain the surprise.[42] We see that Custer had a sense of humor. He includes the classic story, endlessly repeated in Western films, of the white tenderfoot enjoying an Indian meal—until he learns that it is dog meat.[43] Another subject for humorous treatment is the story of two officers caught by Indians while bathing in a stream:

> The two officers in the meanwhile were far from idle; no flesh brushes or bathing towels were required to restore a healthy circulation, nor was time wasted in an idle attempt to make a toilet. If they had sought their bathing ground from motives or retirement or delicacy, no such sentiments were exhibited now, for catching up their wardrobes from the ground in one hand and seizing the bridle reins with the other, one leap and they were on their horses' backs and riding toward camp for dear life. . . . It was a long time before they ceased to hear allusions made by their comrades to the cut and style of their riding suit.[44]

Custer also reveals compassion for the sufferings of others. As he says at the battle of the Washita:

> I turned to retrace my steps when another sound was borne to my ear through the cold, clear atmosphere of the valley—it was the distant cry of an infant; and savages though they were, and justly outlawed by the number and atrocity of their recent murders and depredations on the helpless settlers of the frontier, I could not but regret that in

39 *Ibid.*, 11, 161, 251.
40 *Ibid.*, 213.
41 *Ibid.*, 234.
42 *Ibid.*, 41.
43 *Ibid.*, 31.
44 *Ibid.*, 127–28.

a war such as we were forced to engage in, the mode and circumstances of battle would possibly prevent discrimination.[45]

Such passages might be interpreted as appeasement of the critics of his Washita campaign, but other of Custer's statements, in which no public purpose is involved, also reveal a reluctance about fighting these wars.[46]

Occasionally in *My Life on the Plains* Custer confirms in his own words exactly what his critics were to say of him. While on a solitary hunting expedition ahead of his column during Hancock's campaign, Custer accidentally killed his horse while firing at a buffalo. Being alone and unhorsed in hostile Indian country was a serious situation, and Custer in a rare moment of self-perception was able to draw the moral: "That such a course was rashly imprudent I am ready to admit."[47] Concerning other controversial aspects of his career, Custer has less to say. He dismisses Major Elliot with apparent unconcern.[48] He says little in defense of his actions in shooting the deserters or in making the unauthorized trip from Fort Wallace to Fort Riley.[49] As a man who took "rose-colored views of everything," he simply ignored the distasteful aspects of human experience.

In January, 1872, there was a break in Custer's placid routine at Elizabethtown when he was assigned to escort the Grand Duke Alexis of Russia on a buffalo hunt. By this time Custer and his fellow escort, "Buffalo Bill" Cody, had become representative figures of the frontier. The newspaper reports on the excursion helped to fix Custer and Cody even more firmly in the constellation of frontier heroes. The General and Libbie also entertained the Duke at

[45] *Ibid.*, 159.

[46] See the letter to the sculptress Vinnie Ream Hoxie, February 13, 1871: "Go on dear friend conquering, and to conquer, your victories are lasting and unlike mine are not purchased at the expense of the lifeblood of fellow creatures leaving sorrow, suffering and desolation on their track." Quoted in Jay Monaghan, *Custer, The Life of General George Armstrong Custer,* 333.

[47] *My Life on the Plains,* 37.

[48] *Ibid.*, 175.

[49] *Ibid.*, 82.

Louisville and accompanied him down the river to New Orleans.[50]

In the summer of 1873, Custer led his reassembled regiment out along the Yellowstone River as an escort party for surveyors of the Northern Pacific Railroad. The commander of the expedition, General David S. Stanley, had his troubles with Custer. He described his cavalry commander as a "cold-blooded, untruthful and unprincipled man. He is universally despised by all the officers of his regiment excepting his relatives and one or two sycophants. He brought a trader in the field without permission, carries an old negro woman, and cast iron cooking stove, and delays the march often by his extensive packing up in the morning."[51] This was not the first time that a fellow officer would resent Custer's independence and self-indulgence.

Custer for his part enjoyed the expedition. He collected fossils to be sent to the University of Michigan, and while hunting with his beloved dogs, he shot a huge elk which he stuffed and sent back to the Audubon Club in Detroit.[52] He had two scraps with the Sioux, on the fourth and eleventh of August. In the former engagement, at the mouth of the Tongue River, Custer foiled an attempt to decoy him. In describing this battle, he refers to the massacre at Fort Phil Kearny, in which Captain William Fetterman had led eighty-one men into a similarly constructed ambush.[53] Custer knew enough about Indian warfare to avoid such obvious mistakes.

When the regiment was assigned to Fort Abraham Lincoln in the fall of 1873, there began what Elizabeth Bacon Custer always remembered as an idyllic period for the Custer clan. Custer was surrounded by his loved ones. These included his wife, his brother, Captain Tom Custer, and his sister Margaret with her husband, Lieutenant James Calhoun. That irascible malcontent, Captain Benteen, was assigned to Fort Rice, twenty miles away down the

---

[50] Merington, *The Custer Story*, 246–47.

[51] D. S. Stanley, *Personal Memoirs*, 239.

[52] Elizabeth B. Custer, *"Boots and Saddles,"* 293.

[53] *Ibid.*, 280ff.

Missouri. For the next three years the Custers enjoyed such diversions as were possible in a frontier garrison, including card playing and the inevitable charades. Custer was able to read up on one of his favorite subjects, Napoleon.[54] And every day he, Tom, and Elizabeth raced up and down the stairs playing tag.[55]

The one break in the routine of garrison duty came in the summer of 1874, when Custer led a small army in an exploration of the Black Hills. One of the purposes of the trip was to discover whether or not there was gold in the region. Custer reported that there was, "from the grass roots down," and the stories of newspaper reporters who accompanied him helped to spark a gold rush into the heart of the Sioux country.[56]

These newspaper reports also helped to swell Custer's reputation. The publication of *My Life on the Plains* that same year had given him literary as well as military stature. In fact, summer excursionists in 1875 came all the way to Fort Abraham Lincoln to ogle the famous author and Indian fighter. At their appearance, the General would disappear through the nearest window, leaving Mrs. Custer to face the guests alone. One group was so persistent that Custer had to hide in the chicken coop until they had left.[57]

Indeed, Custer looked like a frontier hero. In the worshipful words of his wife:

> The general was a figure that would have fixed attention anywhere. He had marked individuality of appearance, and a certain unstudied carelessness in the wearing of his costume that gave a picturesque effect, not the least out of place on the frontier. He wore troop-boots reaching to his knees, buckskin breeches fringed on the sides, a dark navy blue shirt with a broad collar, a red necktie, whose ends floated over his shoulder exactly as they did when he and his entire division of cavalry had worn them during the war. On the broad felt hat, that was almost a sombrero, was fastened a slight mark of his rank.

54 *Ibid.,* 145.
55 *Ibid.,* 144.
56 Clement A. Lounsberry, *Early History of North Dakota,* 313.
57 Elizabeth B. Custer, *"Boots and Saddles,"* 242.

He was at this time [1874] thirty-five years of age, weighed one hundred and seventy pounds, and was nearly six feet in height. His eyes were clear blue and deeply set, his hair short, wavy, and golden in tint. His mustache was long and tawny in color; his complexion was florid, except where his forehead was shaded by his hat, for the sun always burned his skin ruthlessly.[58]

Custer and Libbie spent part of the winter of 1875–76 in New York. The General was wined and dined (though he refused the wine) by prominent social and business leaders. He spent a good deal of time at Booth's Theater, where his good friend Lawrence Barrett was playing in *Julius Caesar.*

It was at this time also that Custer became more deeply involved in politics, an area in which he was conspicuously out of place. He had been influential in persuading Ralph Meeker, a reporter for the *New York Herald,* to write a series of articles exposing corruption in the Indian agencies.[59] The evidence strongly suggests that Custer also was the author of an article in the *Herald* (March 31, 1876) on "Belknap's Anaconda," which exposed the secretary of war as a grafter of the first order.[60] In addition, Custer made statements that he "knew something" about the sale of army post traderships and the cheating that went on in the handling of supplies for the Indian agencies. As a result of these activities, Custer became the unwilling tool of Democrats who were determined to discredit the Grant administration.

The excursion into politics cost Custer the command of the spring expedition against the hostile tribes. His testimony in March and April before the Congressional committee investigating corruption in the War Department had been highly critical of Secretary Belknap.[61] His statements aroused the animosity of Presi-

58 *Ibid.,* 107–108.

59 Lounsberry, *Early History of North Dakota,* 314.

60 Oliver Knight, *Following the Indian Wars,* 197.

61 Abstracts of his testimony are in Frazier and Robert Hunt, *I Fought With Custer,* 124–30.

dent Grant, who ordered that Custer not be allowed to accompany the expedition. In fact, Grant refused to see Custer, who then left Washington without official approval from the War Department. From St. Paul, Custer sent the President a plaintive telegram, requesting permission to accompany the command and "spare me the humiliation of seeing my regiment march to meet the enemy and I not share its dangers."[62] Grant relented, apparently because the antiadministration newspapers were making a martyr out of Custer. Custer was allowed to lead the Seventh Cavalry, although General Alfred H. Terry was placed in command of the whole expedition.

Custer's public humiliation apparently affected his usually sound military judgment in the campaign that followed. If any proof is needed of the General's innate sensitivity, it is to be found in his behavior on the march toward the Little Big Horn. Lieutenant Edward S. Godfrey remembered that Custer was "abstracted." He behaved in an excited manner and solicited the opinions of his officers, an unusual action for him. "He showed a lack of self-confidence, a reliance on somebody else; there was an indefinite something that was not Custer."[63] He seems to have been under severe pressure both personal and professional, to score a smashing victory that would restore his reputation.

There is abundant evidence that Custer was prepared to go to any lengths to win this victory. Even before he was replaced as commander of the expedition by General Terry, Custer had been planning the publicity coverage of his campaign with great care. On February 26, he had written Whitelaw Reid of the New York *Tribune* to send a reporter on the march, promising that a glorious show would be put on.[64] His demotion greatly intensified the need for press coverage of the victory which he expected to win.

---

[62] Edgar I. Stewart, *Custer's Luck*, 135.

[63] "Custer's Last Battle," *Century Magazine*, Vol. XLIII (January, 1892), 365.

[64] John C. Hixon, "Custer's 'Mysterious' Mr. Kellogg," *North Dakota History*, Vol. XVII (July, 1950), 153.

In fact, a newspaperman did accompany the column, despite Sherman's telegram to Terry: "Advise Custer to be prudent, not to take along any newspapermen, who always make mischief, and to abstain from personalities in the future."[65] Custer ignored all these injunctions, and Mark Kellogg (substituting for Clement A. Lounsberry) accompanied him as the correspondent of the *Bismarck Tribune, New York Herald*, and *Chicago Times*.[66] Kellogg made an ideal publicist, since he lauded Custer in dispatches to the papers. In a typical letter to the *Herald*, published (posthumously) on July 11, he called Custer "the most peculiar genius in the army. . . . a man possessing electrical mental capacity and of iron frame and constitution; a brave, faithful, gallant soldier . . . one respected and beloved by his followers, who would freely follow him into the 'jaws of hell.' "[67]

Custer also planned to cut loose from Terry's main command, "swing clear of Terry," apparently in order to win the lion's share of the expected victory for himself. That this was his intention is clear both from his actions and from a statement to this effect which he made to Captain Ludlow in St. Paul.[68] On the march up the Rosebud, Custer told his officers that "he intended to follow the trail until we could get the Indians, even if it took us to the Indian agencies on the Missouri River or in Nebraska."[69] The action which followed this statement violated Terry's order that should the Indian trail "turn towards the Little Horn, he [Terry] thinks that you should still proceed southward."[70] Custer did not proceed southward but turned and followed the Indian trail toward the

[65] Hunt and Hunt, *I Fought With Custer*, 135.

[66] Knight, *Following the Indian Wars*, 198.

[67] Reprinted in Graham, *The Custer Myth*, 235.

[68] The statement originally appeared in the article by Col. Robert P. Hughes, "The Campaign against the Sioux in 1876," *Journal of the Military Service Institution of the United States*, Vol. XVIII (January, 1896), and is reprinted in Graham, *The Story of the Little Big Horn* (New York, Collier Books, 1962), 79–126.

[69] Godfrey, "Custer's Last Battle," *Century Magazine*, Vol. XLIII (January, 1892), 365.

[70] Graham, *Story of the Little Big Horn*, 105.

Little Horn. The picture of Custer on the march is that of an impatient, even desperate man, making unwise decisions under apparently intolerable pressures.

The plan of the campaign was to encircle the hostile tribes by a three-pronged offensive. General Crook was to move north from Fort Fetterman to cut off any escape of the hostiles southward. (Crook's defeat by Crazy Horse on June 17 at the Rosebud thwarted his participation in the movement). Colonel Gibbon was to move east from Fort Ellis in Montana to cut off retreat in a northwesterly direction and was to work in close co-operation with Terry's Dakota column coming from the east. The Dakota column, nine hundred strong, left Fort Abraham Lincoln on May 17. They moved slowly westward, reaching the Powder River on June 7. Here Major Marcus A. Reno was sent out with six troops of the Seventh Cavalry to scout the Tongue River. Reno, disobeying his orders, scouted the Rosebud Creek Valley, where he found an Indian trail half a mile wide leading upstream.[71] He was criticized by Custer for not following this trail and attacking the village, even though doing so would have been an even greater violation of orders. An anonymous letter, bearing the earmarks of Custer's style, appeared in the *New York Herald* of July 23 under the heading of "Reno's Contempt of Orders." The letter stated that Reno's "blunder" in not attacking the hostiles warranted a court-martial.[72]

Terry decided to send Custer up the Rosebud to follow the trail. On June 21 he issued orders to this effect and also directed Colonel Gibbon to march up the Big Horn. By this co-operative action the hostiles would be caught between the two columns and would be unable to escape. Custer was ordered to move south and to continue toward the headwaters of the Tongue River even if the Indian trail turned westward toward the Little Big Horn.[73] This would give Gibbon's slower-moving infantry a chance to work in conjunction with the cavalry. Custer ignored these orders, and his im-

[71] Stewart, *Custer's Luck*, 234.
[72] Graham, *The Custer Myth*, 237.
[73] Graham, *Story of the Little Big Horn*, 105.

patience to catch up with the Indians may well be imagined. In a letter to his wife dated the twenty-first, he wrote: "I am now going to take up the trail where the scouting party turned back. I fear their failure to follow up the Indians has imperilled our plans by giving the village an intimation of our presence. Think of the valuable time lost! But I feel hopeful of accomplishing great results."[74]

Custer led twelve troops of the Seventh Cavalry up the Rosebud on June 22. He had with him approximately 31 officers and 585 enlisted men.[75] He also took along a large corps of scouts, including Arikara and Crow Indians, the half-blood Sioux "Mitch" Bouyer, and several whites, including "Lonesome Charley" Reynolds and George Herendeen. Herendeen was sent along by Terry to report back on Custer's scout of the upper reaches of Tullock's Creek, another part of his instructions which Custer ignored.

On the evening of the twenty-second, Custer held the memorable conference with his officers. He discussed his plan of operations, startlingly unusual behavior for him. As Sergeant F. A. Culbertson recalled: "I heard Capt Weir ask Capt. Moylan if, when he was Adjutant, Gen. Custer gave him any particular orders about doing anything. Capt Moylan said 'No,' that when he was Adjutant, Gen. Custer never told him what he was going to do; he would order him to tell the company commanders to go to such and such places and that was all."[76] Custer also solicited the opinions of his officers, another aberration which startled them and which revealed a timorousness uncharacteristic of their hitherto bold and self-assured commander.

On the twenty-third and twenty-fourth, the column continued its march up the Rosebud, continually finding signs of large bodies of Indians. On the night of the twenty-fourth, the command rested while Custer sent Crow scouts ahead to find out in which direction the Sioux village was moving. When told that it was heading over

[74] Elizabeth B. Custer, *"Boots and Saddles,"* 312.
[75] Stewart, *Custer's Luck*, 245.
[76] *Official Record of the Reno Court*, I, 332.

the divide into the valley of the Little Big Horn, Custer ordered a night march to reach the summit of the divide before dawn. The plan was to hide at the divide during the twenty-fifth and then launch a surprise attack at dawn on the twenty-sixth.[77]

Custer's scouts reached the Crow's Nest, a rocky summit from which they could see a huge Indian village some fifteen miles away in the valley. When Custer rode up to the spot, he was unable to see the village through his field glasses, probably because of the early morning heat haze.[78] But the scouts told him that the Sioux had undoubtedly learned of the presence of the troops.[79] In addition, a detail riding the back trail to recover some lost food packs found Indians breaking the boxes open.[80] Hence, Custer decided to change his plan and to attack immediately instead of waiting until the twenty-sixth. He believed that unless he acted at once, the village would escape.[81] And its escape would mean further punishment and humiliation for Custer, who had criticized Reno for failing to exploit a similar situation.

Custer led his regiment over the crest of the divide at noon on the twenty-fifth. He then divided his force into three battalions. One was composed of troops H, D, and K under Captain Benteen, who was to march to the left at an angle of forty-five degrees, scour the country for Indians, and "pitch in" to any that he came across.[82] Major Reno was also placed in command of three troops, M, A, and G, but was given no specific orders at the time.[83] Custer re-

[77] Godfrey, "Custer's Last Battle," *Century Magazine,* Vol. XLIII (January, 1892), 366.

[78] *Official Record of the Reno Court,* II, 355.

[79] Lt. Charles Varnum's letter to his parents, published in the Lowell (Mass.) *Weekly Journal,* August 21, 1876, and reprinted in Graham, *The Custer Myth,* 342–43.

[80] Godfrey, "Custer's Last Battle," *Century Magazine,* Vol. XLIII (January, 1950), 368.

[81] *Ibid.*

[82] Report of Captain Benteen in *Annual Report of the Secretary of War for 1876,* I, 479; *Official Record of the Reno Court,* II, 356, 371.

[83] Report of Major Reno, in *Annual Report of the Secretary of War for 1876,* I, 476.

tained five troops under his own command. Captain McDougall was assigned one troop to guard the pack train. The Custer and Reno battalions moved down Reno Creek some eleven miles until they reached a spot called the Lone Tepee. Here Custer ordered Reno to cross the Little Big Horn and attack the Indians. Reno said Custer told him that "the whole outfit would support me."[84] The plan of operations does not appear to have been clear in Custer's mind. In fact, four officers at the subsequent court of inquiry testified that there was no definite plan of attack.[85] By inference, one can see that Custer intended to follow the same tactics that had succeeded at the Washita—split the regiment to attack the Indians from different directions and prevent any of them from escaping. The cardinal fault in Custer's "plan," and on this point all students of the battle agree, was that he failed to gather sufficient information about his enemy.[86] Dividing his force in the face of an unknown number of Indians was a professional error of the gravest kind.

Reno headed toward the valley about two in the afternoon. He charged the village, which was obscured behind clouds of dust stirred up by the savages as a kind of smoke screen. Reno began to fear that he was being decoyed into a trap, and in addition "the very earth seemed to grow Indians."[87] Hence he halted his charge and dismounted his battalion. Whether Reno overestimated the strength of the Indians opposing him is a subject of debate. George Herendeen and the interpreter Fred Girard both said that there were few Indians opposing Reno when he halted.[88] Reno had had little experience in fighting Indians, and his dismount order may have reflected an exaggerated idea of the forces opposing him. The

[84] *Ibid.*, I, 477.

[85] *Official Record of the Reno Court*, I, 37; I, 151; II, 377; II, 502 (testimony of Wallace, Varnum, Benteen, and Reno).

[86] Colonel T. M. Coughlan, "The Battle of the Little Big Horn," *Cavalry Journal*, Vol. XLIII (January–February, 1934), 13–21.

[87] *Annual Report of the Secretary of War for 1876*, I, 477.

[88] *Official Record of the Reno Court*, I, 82; I, 214.

Indian pressure on Reno increased at this point, and he was forced back into the timber along the river. From here, Reno ordered a withdrawal to the bluffs on the other side of the Little Big Horn. This retreat, or "charge" as Reno preferred to call it, was not well led, and many casualties were suffered as the troopers floundered across the river and up the hill. Benteen joined Reno on the bluffs at about four o'clock, and shortly afterward Captain McDougall rode in with the pack train. An attempt was made to reach Custer, but at "Weir Point" the troops were forced by heavy enemy fire to return to their original position. The command was besieged until the Terry-Gibbon column reached it on the morning of the twenty-seventh.

Custer meanwhile had ridden northward along the bluffs on the east side of the Little Big Horn. There are many conflicting versions of his actions during the main part of the battle. He apparently changed his plan to support Reno "with the whole outfit" in the belief that the Indians were fleeing and that a flank attack farther down the river would completely smash them.[89] From an observation point on one of the bluffs, Custer finally saw the extent of the village, and realizing the need for all the ammunition packs he sent Trumpeter John Martin back with a message: "Benteen—come—big village—be quick—bring packs. W. W. Cooke, P.S. Bring pacs."[90] As Martin turned back, he saw Custer lead the battalion down a ravine toward Medicine Tail Coulee, at the mouth of which was a ford across the river. From this point on, there were no survivors of the fight except the Indians. The Indians swarmed out from the village and forced him back into the bluffs to the east, where the terrain was highly unsuited to cavalry. Using the cover of the ravines and deep gullies, they were able to surround him, stampede his horses, and pour a deadly rain of arrows and bullets into the embattled column on "Custer Hill."

[89] Stewart, *Custer's Luck,* 330.

[90] Milton F. Perry, "Come On! Be Quick!" *True West,* Vol. IV (March–April, 1957), 14–15, 40.

Thus perished "the Boy General" and the 231 men[91] with him. These included his two brothers, Tom and Boston (the latter working as civilian forage master), his brother-in-law, James Calhoun, and his teen-age nephew, Autie Reed. The extent of the tragedy stunned the survivors on Reno Hill, to whom "Custer's luck" had been a byword ever since the creation of the regiment. Reno and the other officers said they thought that Custer had simply ridden down the river and joined Terry.[92] Both the army and the nation demanded an explanation for Custer's defeat.

General Sheridan and Major Reno framed classic explanations for the disaster in their official reports on the battle. Sheridan concluded that Custer had based his whole plan of battle upon a completely erroneous assumption, that the village would attempt to escape rather than fight. He decided that Custer's men and horses were too tired to fight effectively, having ridden about seventy miles with few halts. He also cited the division of the regiment as a major error: "Had the Seventh Cavalry been held together, it would have been able to handle the Indians on the Little Big Horn."[93] Reno agreed with Sheridan that the "unfortunate" division of the regiment and the rapid marching for two days prior to the battle were major causes of the defeat. But he added another cause which was often overlooked in the furious debates which have raged ever since the battle occurred—there were too many Indians.[94] The "ifs" and "buts" of the military historians shrink beside the monumental fact that Custer attacked what was probably the largest congregation of Indians ever assembled on the North American continent.[95]

But even in defeat, Custer "found the one thing needed to com-

[91] Robert M. Utley, *Custer and the Great Controversy,* 27n.

[92] *Official Record of the Reno Court,* I, 138; II, 405.

[93] *Annual Report of the Secretary of War for 1876,* I, 444.

[94] *Ibid.,* I, 477–79.

[95] Estimates of the number of Indians range as high as ten thousand. For a summary of various views on this subject, see Stewart, *Custer's Luck,* 309–12.

plete his character as an ideal hero of romance—a glorious and terrible death on the battlefield."[96] The controversial nature of the battle and of its central figure invited myth-making. By means of song, story, and screen, General Custer became one of America's best-known legendary heroes.

[96] Frederick Whittaker, "General George A. Custer," *Galaxy*, Vol. XXII (September, 1876), 371.

CHAPTER XV

The Dead Lion

THERE WERE MANY REASONS why the Custer legend flourished.
Sitting Bull, popularly regarded as the Napoleon of the Indian
forces, remained at large in Canada for several years and later
joined Buffalo Bill Cody's Wild West Show.[1] The disaster became a political issue, with President Grant being accused of hav-
deliberately sent Custer to his death. There was a court of inquiry
in 1879 to determine whether Major Reno was responsible for his
commander's demise. Mrs. Custer issued a series of books which
kept the General's name before the public. But at the heart of the
legend is the fascinating personality of George Custer, and the
attempts to solve the riddles of his career have used up many tons
of paper.

In the Civil War and on the Plains, Custer was known as "the
Dashing Cavalier." The popular picture was that of a brave, reckless, dashing trooper, willing to charge at any opportunity, and
always depending upon his famous "luck" to get out of tight
scrapes.[2] This figure was an ideal hero for romantic treatment in
novels, biographies, and dime novels. But the image also had
negative connotations which were gleefully pointed up by Custer's critics. "Dashing" and "romantic" suggest impetuosity and
imprudence. The General's death at the Little Big Horn, so his
critics said, was ultimate proof of his reckless irresponsibility.

The *Chicago Tribune* of July 7, 1876, made such an evaluation
in its editorial on the battle:

[1] Russell, *The Lives and Legends of Buffalo Bill,* 316.
[2] Whittaker, *Life,* 609.

190

Custer . . . was a brave, brilliant soldier, handsome and dashing, but he was reckless, hasty and impulsive, preferring to make a dare-devil rush and take risks rather than to move slower and with more certainty, and it was his own mad-cap haste, rashness and love of fame that cost him his own life, and cost the service the loss of many brave officers and gallant men. . . . He preferred to make a reckless dash and take the consequences, in the hope of making a personal victory and adding to the glory of another charge, rather than wait for a sufficiently powerful force to make the fight successful and share the glory with others. He took the risk and he lost.[3]

This and similar criticisms following the battle were vigorously denied by the Custer admirers. But in shaping their defense they became caught in an apparently unsolvable dilemma. Custer was an attractive figure because he was daring and dashing; yet his defenders also had to prove that the defeat was not his fault because he was always careful, prudent, and levelheaded. Mrs. Laura Webb, for example, wrote a poem on "Custer's Immortality" short-ly following the battle, in which she lauded her subject as "the prince of cavaliers," the "pink of chivalry," who was "dashing, daring, brave." This exalted evaluation led her into certain errors of fact, including a statement that Custer had graduated from West Point "with the highest military honors."[4] But she sensed that her interpretation might suggest madcap haste and irrespon-sibility. So she added an essay which argued that the General had always been careful: "Men have dared to whisper that it was a blunder. Let no man whisper it again. The general who made no blunder through four years of almost daily fighting would not be apt to blunder in a skirmish."

The chief job of defending the dead hero fell to Frederick Whit-taker, whose 639-page *Life of Gen. George A. Custer* was designed

[3] Reprinted in E. A. Brininstool, *The Custer Fight, Captain Benteen's Story of the Battle of the Little Big Horn* (Hollywood, privately published, 1933), 1.

[4] *Custer's Immortality. A Poem, with Biographical Sketches of the Chief Actors in the Late Tragedy of the Wilderness* (1876), 23.

191

to "vindicate the reputation of a noble man from unjust asper-
sions." The book's length is explained by the fact that it is heavily
larded with quotations from Custer's own reports and published
writings, but Whittaker used a lot of space in expressing his own
views on the controversies which surrounded his subject. He said
that Reno and Grant were to blame for Custer's death, that the
General was cool and levelheaded, and that in fact he had never
made a mistake in his career. Whittaker's general thesis was that
Custer was "far from being the harum-scarum cavalier of public fancy."[5]

The biography is typical of the ultra-eulogistic treatments which
were conventional in the nineteenth century. The superlatives fly
thick and fast. Custer is compared with Napoleon, Cromwell, Caesar, and Hannibal.[6] He is described as "one of the few really great
men that America has produced." One wonders how thorough
Whittaker's research was when he states that "the closest inquiry
fails to reveal a single instance of ill-temper during Custer's boyhood."[7] This is a largely unprovable assertion in any event, but it
reflects an attitude of idealization which resulted in many legends
about Custer's childhood.

Whittaker stated that Custer was early imbued with a passion
for soldiering and that as a schoolboy he made up his mind to go
to West Point.[8] Most boys of that period were intrigued by soldiering, but recent and more reliable research has shown that Custer
had planned to study law after completing his West Point education.[9] Whittaker also described a childhood encounter between his
hero and Elizabeth Bacon as "the beginning of Custer's first and
last love." When Elizabeth said, "Hello, you Custer boy!" the
General "recorded an inward vow that some day the little girl
would be his wife."[10] Custer was in fact regarded as something of

[5] Whittaker, *Life,* 608.
[6] *Ibid.,* 610–11.
[7] *Ibid.,* 5.
[8] *Ibid.,* 8.
[9] Jay Monaghan, *Custer: The Life of General George Armstrong Custer,* 11.
[10] Whittaker, *Life,* 11.

a Don Juan in Monroe, and he went out with a number of women. In addition, Mrs. Custer later denounced this story as a legend.[11] The fact that she did so casts suspicion upon the usual view that Whittaker wrote his book under her guidance. Or perhaps the bereaved widow was in no condition to read copy carefully and catch such obvious errors as this one.

Whittaker's treatment of Custer's mature life is no more convincing. He does admit grudgingly that Custer erred momentarily while he was home on leave in 1861: "Briefly, this period was the one little spot in Custer's career, the one fault in a perfect life. He fell in with the prevailing habits, drank as deep and swore as hard as any man in the army."[12] But the author makes no concessions on other controversial points in the General's career. There is a labored defense of Custer's actions which precipitated the court-martial in 1867.[13] His aberrations at West Point are viewed as the careless enthusiasms of a vigorous youth. And Whittaker repudiates the view that Custer was depressed on the march to the Little Big Horn or that his humiliation might have caused him to act rashly—statements which should have been checked by the officers who rode with Custer.

The book is not only a defense of the dead hero; it is also an arraignment of Grant and Reno, whom Whittaker (and other Custer partisans) regarded as the villains of the story. Grant had in fact charged that Custer had exceeded his orders and thus sacrificed his command. Goaded by antiadministration newspapers who blamed him for the tragedy, Grant told the *New York Herald* on September 2, "I regard Custer's Massacre as a sacrifice of troops, brought on by Custer himself, that was wholly unnecessary— wholly unnecessary." A common view among the Whittaker group was that Grant had resolved to humiliate Custer for the latter's bold testimony before the Clymer committee about corruption in the Indian agencies. Whittaker went one step further by charging

11 Merington, *The Custer Story,* 47.
12 Whittaker, *Life,* 89.
13 *Ibid.,* 408.

that the President, moved by private revenge, caused Custer's death.[14] The implication seemed to be that Grant knew what was coming and arranged to have Custer on the fatal spot just at the right moment.

Major Marcus A. Reno is also indicted, the key charges being that he "betrayed" and "deserted" Custer. Anthropologists tell us that it is human nature to seek a scapegoat when a mistake has been made.[15] Reno became the leading candidate for this unenviable office even before Whittaker had launched his attack. Thomas Rosser, a former Confederate general and close friend of Custer, wrote a critical letter printed in the St. Paul *Pioneer Press* of July 8 and in the *New York Herald* of July 11. Rosser objected to a *Pioneer Press* editorial which blamed the defeat upon the reckless indiscretion of Custer. He argued that Custer would have succeeded if Reno had passed through the Indians and joined him, but Reno "abandoned Custer and his gallant comrades to their fate."[16] Reno replied through the pages of the *Herald* that there had been no plan of attack and that he had been lucky to escape with the survivors he had. Rosser's final statement, printed in the *Herald* of August 16, reaffirmed his criticism of Reno for not charging the village and for disobeying Custer's order to "come on, bring packs." This exchange foreshadowed the kind of bitter crimination and recrimination that would fill the pages of the *Army and Navy Journal*, the biographies, and the military histories for years to come.

Whittaker demanded a court of inquiry, claiming that the "nation demands such a court, to vindicate the name of a dead hero from the pitiless malignity, which first slew him and then pursued him beyond the grave."[17] When there was little response to his demand, Whittaker took steps to stir up sentiment for such a court. On May 18, 1878, he wrote a letter to the Congressional delegate from Wyoming, W. W. Corlett, demanding that Congress investi-

[14] *Ibid.*, 607.

[15] Sir James G. Frazer, *The Golden Bough*, abridged ed. (New York, Macmillan, 1942), 574–77.

[16] Reprinted in Graham, *The Custer Myth*, 225.

[17] Whittaker, *Life*, 608.

gate the charges against Reno. In June, Whittaker gave this letter full publicity by releasing it through the Associated Press. Reno himself responded by petitioning the President for a court of inquiry, which was duly convened at Chicago in January of 1879.

Whittaker's activities before, during, and after the court were not very admirable. At the court, he acted as "the accuser of Major Reno," but he produced little evidence to support his accusations. His chief contribution was to have brought before the court the civilian packer John Frett, who testified that Reno had been "very drunk" on the night of June 25.[18] Frett's testimony was refuted by the army officers who appeared. Whittaker had also pestered Captain Thomas Weir for a statement accusing Reno of being responsible for the massacre.[19] When this attempt failed, Whittaker had to confine himself to suggesting questions to the prosecutor which were designed to prove Reno's cowardice. After the court cleared Major Reno on the grounds that "there was nothing in his conduct which requires animadversion from this Court," Whittaker charged that the whole affair had been a whitewash. In a lengthy letter to the *New York Sun* of February 26, 1879, he called the court a "mockery of justice." Some of his charges were quite scurrilous. He said that Reno, Benteen, and their counsel (Lyman Gilbert) "ate and drank together at all times, and the hotel loungers said they frequently slept three in a bed, though this we cannot vouch for." Whittaker proved himself to be a poor loser and a spiteful critic of those who disagreed with his pet theories.

Despite Whittaker's complaints, the court of inquiry did help to clarify some of the issues involved in the Last Stand. Most of the officers who testified agreed that Reno's retreat to the bluffs, badly managed though it was, had undoubtedly saved what was left of the regiment.[20] They agreed that there was no plan of attack, or if there had been one, it had died with Custer himself.[21] It also

[18] *Official Record of the Reno Court,* II, 450.

[19] Graham, *The Custer Myth,* 330.

[20] *Official Record of the Reno Court,* I, 46; I, 205.

[21] *Ibid.,* I, 37; I, 151; II, 377; II, 502.

became clear that both officers and men, instead of "abandoning" Custer as Whittaker charged, were under the impression that Custer had joined Terry and had abandoned them.[22] And while the court revealed that Reno was not an outstanding military leader, it pretty well scotched the idea that he had deliberately abandoned Custer to his fate. Yet Whittaker's "abandonment" theory prevailed for many years. It is to be found in newspapers, novels, biographies, and other media, usually in the form of a dramatic depiction of Custer and his dwindling band looking upriver for sign of Reno's approach.[23]

In his biography, Whittaker helped to disseminate certain popular legends about the battle. One of these involves the escape of an "only survivor," the Crow scout Curley. The Curley legend was a product of faulty newspaper reporting and of wishful thinking, since when history does not supply a survivor, legend usually does. The Bismarck *Tribune* in its special issue on the battle (July 6) first reported this story: "We said of those who went into battle with Custer none are living—one Crow scout hid himself in the field and witnessed and survived the battle. His story is plausible [*sic*], and is accepted, but we have not room for it now." Other newspapers did have room, and with all the trimmings added. The *New York Times* of July 9 and the Helena *Herald* of July 15 both reported that Curley had escaped through the lines by disguising himself in a Sioux blanket—a story that appears to have originated through inept translation of Curley's statements.[24] As W. A. Graham pointed out, a Crow amongst the Sioux would be about as inconspicuous as a man in white tie and tails among a crowd of one-

[22] *Ibid.*, I, 33; II, 377; II, 445.

[23] J. W. Buel, *Heroes of the Plains* (1881), 388; Cody, *Story of the Wild West* (1888), 670–71; Randall Parish, *Bob Hampton of Placer* (novel) (Chicago, A. C. McClurg Company, 1906), 372–75; letter from M. D. Kelly in Springfield (Mass.) *Sunday Republican*, December 19, 1920; Charles Francis Bates in *New York Times*, June 20, 1926; Frazier Hunt, *Custer: The Last of the Cavaliers* (1928), 200; Charles Francis Bates, *Custer's Indian Battles* (1936), 35–36; Charles G. Dubois, *Kick the Dead Lion: A Casebook of the Custer Battle* (1954); Booton Herndon, "From Custer to Korea—the 7th Cavalry," *Saga Magazine*, Vol. XXII (September, 1961), 60.

[24] Graham, *The Custer Myth*, 7.

piece bathing suits.[25] But Whittaker added some artistic touches of his own to this basic legend. He said that Curley had offered to help Custer himself escape, but the brave commander "waved him away and rode back to his little group of men, to die with them."[26] With added embellishments from time to time, the Curley story passed from Whittaker's book into a number of histories, dime novels, biographies, and popular magazine articles.[27]

Whittaker also publicized the Rain-in-the-Face legend by naming that warrior as Custer's slayer.[28] Other Indian candidates for this honor have included Appearing Elk, Brave Bear, White Bull, and about a dozen others.[29] History cannot tell us which Indian killed Custer. As Thomas Marquis said, "None of the Indians knew who killed Custer. None of them knew until long afterward that he was there."[30] But a specific Indian name had to be attached to the feat in order to personify the legend. Many of the Indians themselves finally settled upon Brave Bear, as an exemplification of poetic justice. Brave Bear had been among the Cheyennes routed by Custer at the Washita in 1868, had passed the peace pipe to

[25] *Ibid.*, 9.

[26] Whittaker, *Life*, 599.

[27] T. M. Newson, *Thrilling Scenes Among the Indians* (1884), 174; J. P. Dunn, *Massacres of the Mountains: A History of the Indian Wars of the Far West* (1886), 615; *Custer's Little Dead Shot; or, The Boy Scout of the Little Big Horn,* by "An Old Scout" [Lu Senarens] (1888), 30; Captain Charles King, "Custer's Last Battle," *Harper's Magazine,* Vol. LXXXI (August, 1890), 385; Henry D. Northrop, *Indian Horrors, or Massacres by the Red Men* (1891), 409; Frederick Dellenbaugh, *George Armstrong Custer* (1917), 184; Eli Huggins, "Custer and Rain in the Face," *American Mercury,* Vol. IX (November, 1926), 341.

[28] Whittaker, *Life*, 601.

[29] "He Killed Custer" (Appearing Elk), Kansas City *Weekly Journal,* November 6, 1902 (clipping in Myrick MS Collection); Thomas Marquis, *Which Indian Killed Custer?* (Hardin, Mont., 1933); Stanley Vestal (Walter S. Campbell), "The Man Who Killed Custer" (White Bull), *American Heritage,* Vol. VIII (February, 1957), 9ff.; Edgar I. Stewart, "Which Indian Killed Custer," *Montana,* Vol. VIII (July, 1958), 26–32; David Humphreys Miller, *Custer's Fall* (1957), 210–13. Stanley Vestal had presented White Bull's case earlier, in the Chicago *Westerners Brand Book,* Vol. IV (October, 1947), and the number of revisions which were made in the story for publication in *American Heritage* cast doubts upon its historical validity.

[30] *Which Indian Killed Custer?*

him at Stone Calf's village in 1869, and then had been present at the Little Big Horn. They decided that he was the appropriate choice for the honor, since "the avenging warrior must have been one who had been in personal touch with both the first and last phases of Custer's perfidy."[31] Rain-in-the-Face, however, has always been the white man's choice.

Rain-in-the-Face first entered the Custer saga in 1874, when a scout at the Standing Rock Agency heard him boasting about the murder of two civilians who had been with Custer's Yellowstone expedition. General Custer ordered his arrest and sent a party including Tom Custer to bring him back to Fort Abraham Lincoln. Rain escaped after several months at the fort and then sent back word that he was awaiting revenge for his imprisonment.[32] This story bore legendary fruit when the newspapers began speculating about various details of the battle. The *New York Herald* of July 13, 1876, maintained that Rain-in-the-Face had cut out General Custer's heart, put it on a pole and then done a dance around it.[33] The *Herald* of August 1 reported that soldiers of the Seventh had detected him among the warriors fighting them.[34] And on October 6, the newspaper carried Captain R. E. Johnston's interview with the Sioux warrior Kill Eagle, in which the Captain asked if "Rain in the Face cut out the heart of a dead officer and showed it around the camp on a stick."[35] Kill Eagle denied that Rain had done so, but the newspaper repetition of the story laid the groundwork for a growing legend.

One version of the legend involves the mutilation of Tom Custer, and Mrs. Custer herself accepted this version.[36] But the poet Henry Wadsworth Longfellow connected the mutilation story with George Custer in his "Revenge of Rain-in-the-Face," published shortly after the battle:

[31] *Ibid.*
[32] Elizabeth B. Custer, *"Boots and Saddles,"* 205.
[33] Utley, *Custer and the Great Controversy,* 126.
[34] Graham, *The Custer Myth,* 357.
[35] *Ibid.,* 55.
[36] *"Boots and Saddles,"* 215.

The Dead Lion

But the foemen fled in the night,
And Rain-in-the-Face, in his flight
  Uplifted high in air
As a ghastly trophy, bare
The brave heart, that beat no more,
  Of the White Chief with yellow hair.[37]

This poem was quite popular, and it undoubtedly convinced many whites that Rain-in-the-Face was the individual who had dispatched the great hero. As one contemporary critic said, "It is thought by some that he was the identical Indian who killed Gen. Custer, and that he did it by way of revenge for his long imprisonment. There seems to be no real foundation for this theory; but the 'Revenge of Rain in the Face' will probably go down to posterity as an historical truth, as it has already been immortalized in verse by one of our most gifted poets, who seems, however, to have overlooked the fact that Gen. Custer's body was not mutilated."[38] But the poem is almost as good a piece of evidence as any other when it comes to determining the Indian who really did kill Custer. Moreover, Rain-in-the-Face, partly because of his catchy name, has become a classic Indian stereotype along with Hiawatha, Uncas, and Tonto. Since Hollywood in the mid-1950's produced movies about *Sitting Bull* and *Crazy Horse,* it only remains for them to turn out one entitled *Rain-in-the-Face.*

Whittaker's biography is thus a rather shoddy performance. As one latter-day student remarked, "A single twenty-five page chapter of Whittaker, upon a very cursory examination, reveals seventy-five errors of fact."[39] Basically the book is a nineteenth-century

[37] *The Complete Poetical Works of Henry Wadsworth Longfellow* (1880), 272.

[38] Victor, *Eleven Years in the Rocky Mountains,* 123. The army officers who visited the field following the battle reported that the General's body had not been mutilated. See statement of Lt. Winfield Scott Edgerly, August 18, 1881, in Graham, *The Custer Myth,* 220–21, and Stewart, *Custer's Luck,* 471. For later versions of the Rain-in-the-Face legend, see W. Kent Thomas, "The Personal Story of Rain-in-the-Face," *Outdoor Life,* Vol. XI (March, 1903), 20–27; Cyrus Townsend Brady, *Indian Fights and Fighters,* 279–89; George Creel, "To the Last Man," *Collier's,* Vol. LXXIX (January 22, 1927), 43.

[39] Fred Dustin, *The Custer Tragedy,* 216.

version of the medieval saints' lives. The saint is born in glory, suffers persecution, and then dies for the Cause, which in Custer's case is not God but Country. The canonization of this military saint was confirmed by the many adulatory books which followed Whittaker's *Life*.

William F. Cody played a self-consciously grandiose role in further dramatizing the Custer legend. On July 17, 1876, while serving as a scout with the Fifth Cavalry in Kansas, Cody shot and then scalped the Cheyenne chief, Yellow Hand, proclaiming the dripping trophy to be "the first scalp for Custer." This factual incident, with considerable embellishment, was featured in a dime novel which appeared in Street and Smith's *New York Weekly* and was entitled *The Crimson Trail; or, On Custer's Last Warpath.*[40] It also became the basis of a stage melodrama, *The Red Right Hand; or, Buffalo Bill's First Scalp for Custer.*[41] When Cody published his *Autobiography* in 1879, he included still another melodramatic version of this encounter, accompanied by a garish illustration which must have shocked even the most hardened armchair Indian fighters back east. Cody also printed a poem on Custer's death by Captain Jack Crawford, "the Poet Scout of the Black Hills," whose scouting was better than his poetry. It reads in part:

> *Did I hear the news from Custer?*
> *Well, I reckon I did, old pard;*
> *It came like a streak of lightnin',*
> *And you bet it hit me hard.*
> *I ain't no hand to blubber,*
> *And the briny ain't run for years;*
> *But chalk me up for a lubber,*
> *If I didn't shed regular tears. . . .*

Cody also exploited the Custer battle in a number of dime novels published under his name in the eighties and nineties (see Chapter XVI below). In his voluminous *Story of the Wild West* (1888),

40 Russell, *The Lives and Legends of Buffalo Bill,* 268.
41 Dixon Wecter, *The Hero in America,* 359.

he incorporated an account of the fight (copied word for word from J. W. Buel's *Heroes of the Plains*) which contained such grandiloquent passages as this: "Custer was there at the head like Spartacus fighting the legions about him, tall, graceful, brave as a lion at bay, and with thunderbolts in his hands."[42] Finally, Cody staged Custer's Last Fight as the climax of his Wild West show, which played before thousands in this country and in Europe.[43]

Cody was not the only one to appreciate the pictorial qualities of the Last Stand. A number of artists attempted to capture the episode on canvas. John Mulvany in 1881 painted "Custer's Last Rally," which was displayed throughout the country for a dozen years. But the most widely distributed of the numerous representations of the fight, though it appeared in somewhat changed form later, was that which Cassilly Adams painted in 1886. This picture was eventually purchased by the Anheuser-Busch Brewing Company, which had it lithographed and sent out to saloons as an advertising device. Thus while Henry Wadsworth Longfellow and John Greenleaf Whittier[44] were acquainting poetry lovers with the Last Stand, the nation's beer drinkers were also being treated to an imaginative reconstruction of the episode.[45] Most paintings of the battle contain gross historical errors, and they probably did more to perpetuate certain legends than any of the books. Custer is often shown with long hair (he cut it before leaving Fort Abraham Lincoln),[46] wielding a saber (sabers were left behind),[47] and wearing a dress uniform (he wore buckskins).[48] Furthermore,

[42] Page 670.

[43] Russell, *Lives and Legends of Buffalo Bill,* 339.

[44] "On the Big Horn," *Atlantic Monthly,* Vol. LIX (April, 1887), 433–34.

[45] Don Russell, "Sixty Years in Bar Rooms; or 'Custer's Last Fight,'" Chicago *Westerners Brand Book,* Vol. III (November, 1946), 61–68; Robert Taft, "The Pictorial Record of the Old West—Custer's Last Stand," *Kansas Historical Quarterly,* Vol. XIV (November, 1946), 361–90; "Speaking of Pictures . . . Artists Had a Field Day with Custer's Famous Stand," *Life Magazine,* Vol. XXIV (June 21, 1948).

[46] Statement of Lt. Edgerly, reprinted in Graham, *The Custer Myth,* 221.

[47] *Official Record of the Reno Court,* I, 39; I, 147.

[48] Mark Kellogg in the *New York Herald,* July 11, 1876, reprinted in Graham, *The Custer Myth,* 234.

there is no evidence that Custer was one of the last to die. There is even an Indian story, which cannot be disproved, that Custer was killed at the Minneconjou ford while attempting to lead his troops across.[49] But the artists responded to a subject that cried for artistic treatment—a naturally colorful episode, packed with action and dominated by the well-known central figure.

In the 1880's, Elizabeth Bacon Custer joined Whittaker, Cody, and Cassilly Adams in the circle of hero makers. In her books, notably *"Boots and Saddles"* (1885) and *Following the Guidon* (1890), she eulogized her dead husband. "Libbie" always saw Custer as larger than life size. She described him as "nearly six feet tall," whereas the West Point records tell us that he stood only five feet, eight and one-eighth inches.[50] She wrote with sentimental touches that made the General a sympathetic figure to her readers —he loved music; his troops affectionately called him "Old Curley"; he would change the regiment's line of march to avoid a meadow lark's nest. But the picture was incomplete. There was little information concerning the more controversial aspects of the General's character and career. This was to be expected in a widow's memoirs, especially in the case of the Custers, for whom conjugal love seems to have been intensified as a substitute for parental love.[51] The net effect was to create a saint whose virtues outshone even those of Whittaker's idealized hero. In addition, it is pretty well agreed that Mrs. Custer exercised an inhibitory influence upon criticism of the General.[52]

Romantic and sentimental views also characterize the many frontier anthologies and histories of the Indian wars which appeared in the eighties and nineties. These contain imaginative versions of the battle and stylized accounts of Custer's death, usually describing him with saber in hand. Custer is found to be innocent of his own defeat; Reno's incapacity and Sitting Bull's brilliance

[49] Miller, *Custer's Fall*, 128.

[50] Norman Maclean, "Custer's Last Fight as Ritual Drama," Chicago *Westerners Brand Book,* Vol. XV (October, 1958), 58.

[51] Merington, *The Custer Story*, 102.

[52] Graham, *The Custer Myth*, 141n.

are standard explanations of the disaster. The savages had a plan, they knew Custer was coming, and he fell into a remarkably well-constructed ambuscade.[53] Sitting Bull, Gall, and Crazy Horse were variously given credit for the Indians' masterful strategy, but Sitting Bull got most of the publicity. The Yankton *Dakotaian* and other papers maintained that he had studied the campaigns of Napoleon.[54] This legend was also preserved in W. Fletcher Johnson's *Red Record of the Sioux* (1891): "Sitting Bull has read French history carefully, and he is especially enamored of the career of Napoleon, and endeavors to model his campaigns after those of the 'Man of Destiny.' "[55]

In a few of the books there is an unromantic note—the suggestion that Custer committed suicide. This theory was first advanced by Colonel Richard Dodge in *Our Wild Indians* (1882), who argued that Custer's body was unmutilated because the Indians never touched a suicide.[56] Other authors, usually the unreliable ones, have also held this view.[57] Aside from its technical aspects— a right-handed man shooting himself in the left temple—the problem also involves character interpretation. Was George Custer the kind of man who would kill himself when his situation became desperate? The answer must be that, whatever his other faults, Custer never lacked courage. On this ground alone one may safely classify the suicide story as legendary. But the speculations about the manner of Custer's death are similar to those surrounding all heroes of mythology.

Occasionally the authors of these popular narratives introduce a generic character who appears frequently in the legend of the Little Big Horn. This is the white man who views the battle from

[53] Dunn, *Massacres of the Mountains,* 619.

[54] Edna L. Waldo, *Dakota,* 206.

[55] (1891), 28.

[56] (1882), 518.

[57] Joe DeBarthe, *Life and Adventures of Frank Grouard, Chief of Scouts,* (St. Joseph, Combe Printing Company, 1894), 262–63; Henry Inman, *Tales of the Trail* (Topeka, Crane, 1898), 278. For further discussion of the suicide thesis, consult "Did Custer Commit Suicide?" *Montana,* Vol. IX (January, 1959), 61; and "More Rumblings from the Little Big Horn," *Montana,* Vol. IX (October, 1959), 45–51.

the Indian camp. Various names are attached to this character, such as Ridgely, Walter Winnett, or Jack Cleybourne. The Minneapolis *Pioneer Press* of September 8 and the New York *Sun* of September 9, 1876, published an interview with Ridgely, an "old trapper," who claimed that he had been a prisoner in Sitting Bull's camp and had witnessed the battle and the torture of prisoners. Ridgely was subsequently cited as the authority for imaginative versions of the battle which were printed in the histories.[58] The Minneapolis *Journal* of August 15, 1920, printed the story of Winnett, a "mining prospector," who had also been a prisoner. From a hill he saw the final stages of the battle.[59] Jack Cleybourne had presumably been captured by the Indians in 1866 and given the name of "Chialla," meaning "White Cheyenne." He had witnessed many battles from the Indian side and had tried to save Indian children during Custer's attack on Black Kettle's village. In Cleybourne's manuscript account of his experiences, obtained by Herbert Myrick, he maintained that Custer was the last to fall during the battle.[60] He also claimed to have had a conversation with the dying General, in which Custer pleaded, "Don't let them butcher me." Other of the innumerable "survivors" claimed to have witnessed the fight from a tree, a hollow log, and the inside of a dead horse.[61]

Although the heroic tradition fathered by Whittaker maintained its vitality to the end of the century and beyond, close students of the battle were treated to a blistering debate over the degree of blame which should attach to the dead general. The controversy was touched off by Edward S. Godfrey's article on "Custer's Last Battle" in the *Century Magazine* in 1892. This article has become a standard source in reconstructions of the episode, although its accuracy has been challenged on the basis of Godfrey's anti-Reno bias and the fact that it did not appear in

[58] For example in Northrop, *Indian Horrors, or Massacres by the Red Men,* 408.

[59] Myrick MS Collection.

[60] *Ibid.*

[61] Dustin, *The Custer Tragedy,* 150; Stewart Holbrook, "Phonies of the Old West," *American Mercury,* Vol. LXVIII (Fall, 1949), 234.

print until sixteen years after the event.[62] Certainly Godfrey had no love for Major Reno. At the court of inquiry, he had been the only officer who failed to approve Reno's conduct, characterizing it as "nervous timidity."[63] In the article he specifically pinpointed "Reno's panic rout from the valley" as one of the major causes of the defeat, in addition to the overpowering numbers of the enemy and the defective extraction of cartridges from the carbines. "At no time during the battle was his conduct such as to inspire confidence." Godfrey also answered the charge that Custer had disobeyed his orders, by pointing out that General Terry had given his cavalry commander a free hand. This defense of Custer's actions was vigorously seconded by General J. B. Fry in a three-page commentary following Godfrey's article.

The Godfrey-Fry effort further opened the door on one of the most intriguing of the battle problems—Did Custer disobey his orders? The final answer to the question was, as Godfrey himself admitted years later, "largely one of sentiment,"[64] But Godfrey and Fry followed Whittaker in arguing that Custer's orders were discretionary rather than obligatory. Since it was impossible for Terry to give him precise orders, because of the unknown location and numbers of the enemy, Custer could not "disobey" them in any blamable sense. General Nelson Miles was also an early advocate of this theory, and Charles Kuhlman has advanced it in recent years.[65] Miles had often been Custer's hunting companion, and he quickly sprang to the defense of his old friend. In his *Personal Recollections* (1896), Miles remarked, "I have no patience with those who would kick a dead lion."[66] He went on to cite a mysterious affidavit which supported the "discretion" theory. According to this affidavit, Terry told Custer, "Use your own judgment, and do what you think best if you strike the trail; and what-

---

[62] E. A. Brininstool, *Major Reno Vindicated* (Hollywood, privately published, 1933).

[63] *Official Record of the Reno Court*, II, 443.

[64] Letter to Brady, *Indian Fights and Fighters*, 376.

[65] *Did Custer Disobey Orders at the Battle of the Little Big Horn?* 28.

[66] Miles, *Personal Recollections* (1896), 199.

ever you do, Custer, hold on to your wounded."[67] Miles never revealed the source of the affidavit, and only later was it discovered to be one Mary Adams, Custer's Negro servant, who had been hundreds of miles from the mouth of the Rosebud on June 21.[68]

Miles and other Custer partisans never satisfactorily answered charges that Custer had failed to observe certain of Terry's "suggestions." Such charges were made in an article by Colonel Robert P. Hughes, Terry's brother-in-law, who proceeded to "kick the dead lion." Though published in an obscure military magazine,[69] Hughes's article nevertheless became the principal weapon in the hands of Custer's critics for years to come. The main items in the indictment include the fact that however permissive or courteous the phrasing of an order, it is still an order; that Custer lacked sufficient reason for departing from these orders; that Custer's statements and actions before and during the march (such as his declaration to Captain Ludlow that he intended to "swing clear of Terry," or his following the Indian trail west instead of turning south as his instructions read) indicate that he deliberately disobeyed orders and had intended to do so from the very beginning.

This interpretation has enraged three generations of Custerphiles, one of whom attacked Hughes for his "comic opera ideas," "evasions," and "patent falsehoods."[70] But when one moves away from textual analysis and theories of military tactics and turns to character interpretation, the Custer case is considerable weakened. At West Point, in the Civil War, at Fort Wallace, on the Yellowstone expedition, and in his comments on the Reno scout, George Custer gave ample demonstration of his disregard for book regulations. He was by temperament an independent spirit who chafed at a tight bit. Whatever the mechanics of the Little Big Horn operation, the Custer record makes it entirely plausible that he would disregard any and all orders should his spirit so dictate.

[67] *Ibid.*, 204.

[68] Graham, *The Custer Myth*, 282.

[69] *Journal of the Military Service Institution of the United States,* Vol. XVIII (January, 1896).

[70] Kuhlman, *Did Custer Disobey Orders?* 5, 53.

But the Hughes article caused scarcely a ripple in the smooth surface of the Custer legend. Buried as it was in a technical journal, it aroused chiefly the military insiders. Poets, novelists, and motion picture producers continued to copy the picture of an idealized hero held up by Whittaker, Cody, and Elizabeth Bacon Custer. In 1896, Ella Wheeler Wilcox published a 107-stanza poem which attempted to treat Custer on Homeric scale:

> *All valor died not on the plains of Troy*
> *Awake, my muse, awake! be thine the joy*
> *To sing of deeds as dauntless and as brave*
> *As e'er lent luster to a warrior's grave.*
> *Sing of that noble soldier, nobler man,*
> *Dear to the heart of each American.*
> *Sound forth his praise from sea to listening sea—*
> *Greece her Achilles claimed, immortal Custer, we.*

Romantic and sentimental themes are built around standard legends. The story of Curley's offer to help Custer escape is put into the narrative:

> *A second's silence. Custer dropped his head,*
> *His lips slow moving as when prayers are said—*
> *Two words he breathed—"God and Elizabeth,"*
> *Then shook his long locks* [sic] *in the face of death,*
> *And with a final gesture turned away*
> *To join that fated few who stood at bay.*
> *Ah! deeds like that the Christ in man reveal.*
> *Let Fame descend her throne at Custer's shrine to kneel.*[71]

Such inspiring views of the great hero were also to be found in novels by Herbert Myrick, Randall Parish, and Cyrus Townsend Brady. Myrick's *Cache la Poudre: The Romance of a Tenderfoot in the Days of Custer* (1905) is an awkwardly written story with a conventional plot. It features two New York stockbrokers, the "unprincipled" Henry Rudolph and the "high-minded" Jerome James, both of whom go west and continue their battles for the hand of

[71] *Custer and Other Poems* (1896), 134.

the heroine and the other goods of this life. Rudolph becomes a frontier desperado, while James enlists in the Seventh Cavalry. (The plot of two stockbrokers who go west and continue their rivalry in the wide open spaces is common in dime novels of this period.)[72] James as an enlisted soldier is able to voice his admiration for the commanding general, and Myrick inserts many editorial comments: "At this time Custer was furthest from being the dashing, carefree, reckless commander his enemies had represented."[73] Reno is frequently criticized for failing to aid the embattled General. Despite the heavy doses of hero-worship, Myrick's interpretation of Custer is of more interest than the wooden love scenes between James and the heroine.

Bob Hampton of Placer (1906), by Randall Parish, introduces another stock figure who was to become all too familiar to readers of Custer fiction. This is the cashiered officer of the Seventh who attempts to restore his tarnished reputation. Hampton does indeed die with honor on the field after carrying dispatches to Custer. In fact, the honor of the regiment and the virtues of its commander are prime themes in the novel. This adulatory attitude leads Parish into certain statements that must be questioned on historical grounds. He describes the eagerness of the troops on Reno Hill to go to Custer's assistance,[74] although in fact (Weir's sally notwithstanding) many of them feared that Custer had abandoned them.[75] And there is no evidence that any officer on the hill said, "Is this the Seventh?—skulking here under cover while Custer begs for help?"

The most ambitious of the early novels was Brady's *Britton of the Seventh* (1914). Tony Britton is also a disgraced former officer, who achieves redemption by serving in the battle as a civilian scout. There is an improbably melodramatic chapter (XXVI) on

---

[72] For example, in *Kit Carson's Boys,* by "An Old Scout," No. 304 of the Pluck and Luck series (New York, Frank Tousey, 1904), in which hero Tom Gardner battles the villainous former clerk, Neal Krumage.

[73] Page 146.

[74] Page 352.

[75] *Official Record of the Reno Court,* I, 33; II, 445.

the Last Stand, with Custer reading lost love letters and performing other leisurely activities. But Brady, who had thoroughly studied the battle as history, incorporates an elaborate analysis of it in the novel. Despite the evidence of the Reno court, he insists that Custer had a clear-cut plan of attack.[76] Reno is severely criticized for his failure to support this plan: "Reno in the lead reined in his horse. Fatal indecision. The salvation of all was to press the charge home, madly to gallop on. If the woman who hesitates is lost, what of the soldier? The line wavered a little. There were lions in the line, a stag only in the lead."[77] Brady also indicts the Major for the "disgraceful scene" on Reno Hill when he failed to go to Custer's assistance. Brady's novel is interesting as an example of the attraction which this battle has had as both sober fact and imaginative fiction. The elaborate historical analysis is integrated with passages which depict how things *might* have been. It is also one of the last novels of the heroic tradition. When novelists again turned to Custer, they viewed him in a less favorable light.

The Custer saga also attracted motion picture producers. In 1909, Colonel William Selig turned out a one-reeler entitled *Custer's Last Stand*—the first of many "Last Stands" to be filmed over the next half-century.[78] By 1925, the battle was worth nine reels, in a picture entitled *The Scarlet West,* with Clara Bow and Johnnie Walker. The climax of these film versions was the ambitious 1941 production, *They Died with Their Boots On,* starring Errol Flynn as Custer. Custer is sympathetically treated as a brilliant and beloved commander, whose death was plotted by his political enemies. In the climactic battle, Custer is depicted as the final survivor, surrounded by scores of dead soldiers in freshly pressed uniforms.[79]

In biographies also, Custer continued to be viewed as the symbol of a glorious military tradition. Frederick Dellenbaugh drew heavily on Mrs. Custer's books in constructing a biography into

[76] Parish, *Bob Hampton of Placer,* 300.

[77] *Ibid.,* 321.

[78] For discussion of some of these, see George N. Fenin and William K. Everson, *The Western: From Silents to Cinerama,* 11, 57, 148, 167.

[79] *Life Magazine,* Vol. XI (December 8, 1941), 75–78.

which not one shadow of a doubt concerning Custer's actions is permitted to intrude. The same flat recital of the General's great deeds forms the substance of Frazier Hunt's biography of 1928. Hunt has had a tendency to idealize rather than explain controversial figures (see his *Tragic Days of Billy the Kid*), and so he does here. The complexities of Custer's character are not explored, nor is the battle itself examined except to castigate Reno for failing to support his commander. Hunt's title was *Custer: Last of the Cavaliers*, and the book was also the last of the laudatory biographies. Except in juvenile literature, the thirties saw a new and more critical approach to biographical interpretation. But the juvenile books have perpetuated the Dellenbaugh-Hunt tradition of uncritical glorification.

CHAPTER XVI

A Boy's Hero

"IN THE COURAGE OF CUSTER, the youth of America will always find inspiration."[1]

The heroic legend of General George A. Custer is in large part a boy's legend. The components of Custer's world—dogs, horses, uniforms, Indians, battles—are all things which boys understand. While adults become aware of the complexities of his career, to the boy he represents a simple combination of romance, action, and wish-fulfillment. Custer clearly stands as a symbol of certain traits which are particularly associated with boyhood: courage, enthusiasm, love of animals, the enjoyment of physical action. Thus the history of Custer interpretation in dime novels, juvenile biography, and boys' fiction is to some extent a record of American ideals.

Frederick Whittaker helped to process the legend for juvenile consumption. Whittaker was well known as a dime novelist, his forte being stories with such intriguing titles as *The Sword Prince* and *The Boy Crusader*. In 1882, he published a dime biography entitled *The Dashing Dragoon; or, The Story of Gen. Geo. A. Custer from West Point to the Big Horn*. The biography has a heavy pedagogical tone. The youthful readers are admonished to study hard, because this was how "Autie" got into West Point. They are told that their hero "never got into a *mean* scrape, never lied, and, what is more remarkable still, never had a single fight in all his boy life." As a boy general, Custer was quiet and modest, neither smoked nor drank, and was deeply religious. "With all his dash and reputation, he never became vain and puffed up, but was

---

[1] Bates, *Custer's Indian Battles,* 36.

as jolly and full of fun, round the camp fire, as if he were still a boy at school."

This model picture of exemplary conduct entails the omission of certain important facts and a one-sided interpretation of others. While most boys of nineteenth-century fiction and biography were expected to be "deeply religious," Custer himself was never the zealous Christian that Whittaker makes him.[2] Custer's troubles at West Point and his court-martial there are quietly dropped from the narrative. The court-martial of 1867 is mentioned, but it is described as having been brought on by a personal enemy who had determined to injure Custer. The court's decision is called, without any reasons given, "a very unjust sentence." Major Marcus Reno, whom Whittaker violently criticized on other occasions, is made to appear responsible for Custer's defeat on the Little Big Horn.

Whittaker also retailed the same legends about Custer's Last Stand that had appeared in his full-length *Life*. The Curley-escape story, the Rain-in-the-Face myth, and other historical inaccuracies may be cited. But the dime-novel writers who used Whittaker as their text did not know about these inaccuracies, nor did the majority of them seem to care. They simply copied large chunks of his narrative, language and all.[3] *The Dashing Dragoon* helped alert them to the commercial possibilities of the Custer story.

Several dime-novel versions of the Little Big Horn were published in 1883. One of them, *Custer's Last Shot; or, The Boy Trailer of the Little Horn,* by Colonel J. M. Travers (St. George Rathborne), may be taken as a model for the others. Mason Pierrepont, the "boy trailer" of the title, is trying to rescue his sister, who is in the hands of the Sioux. In this task he is aided by two old trappers, Pandy Ellis and Bolly Wherrit, and opposed by a pair of white renegades and a giant Indian outlaw named Red Goliath.

[2] Merington, *The Custer Story*, 79.

[3] Compare Whittaker's description of Reno's retreat ("Then Reno suddenly made up his mind. He saw himself overwhelmed by numbers, and determined to retreat to the river.") with the same episode in *Custer's Little Dead Shot* (1888) ("Then Reno suddenly came to a decision. He knew he had met overwhelming numbers and he determined to retreat to the river.")

The story takes place during the Custer battle, and a loose historical framework holds the plot together.

Custer appears as a romantic figure, a "dashing spirit" the author calls him, but there is also a recognition of his stubborn and reckless qualities. "None knew the reckless, dashing nature of Custer better than Pandy, and he heard the orders for a division of the regiment with dismay." Yet it is his bravery and gallantry during the Last Stand which are emphasized. Mason Pierrepont implores him to retreat, but Custer will have none of it: "Forward, men, forward. Down with the hounds;" He dies in the arms of the "boy hunter," but not before he has killed Black Sculley, one of the white renegades. Mason himself survives the battle, being buried under a pile of corpses. He crosses the river to the Sioux camp, where he sees his sister being abducted by Red Goliath. He trails the two to a cave, where he has a death struggle with the Indian, and is finally saved by Bolley Wherrit.

The characters in this novel are all stock figures in the popular boys' fiction. The boy hero who becomes Custer's companion and who accompanies the great general as a junior scout serves as the vehicle for vicarious participation in the battle. The old rangers, speaking a dialect salted with "wal" and "hyar," are straight from the Leatherstocking tradition. The Indians are all "red fiends" or "savage devils," and their character and language are just as improbable as those of James Fenimore Cooper's savages. Red Goliath leaps into a tentful of enemies with the words, "I'm the identical chap." The captive sister (or girl friend) represents the slight female influence in these novels. The girl has only a minimal role because these stories were meant for young boys who were being initiated into a world of masculine heroics.

The white renegades also represent one of the oldest conventions in popular adventure fiction. The renegade was a stock character in the paper-backed novels which preceded the dime novels. In fact, the theory that a white man had directed the Indian victory at the Little Big Horn may have arisen from the repetitious appearance of this character in frontier stories. A story printed in the *New York Herald* of August 1, 1876, is straight out of the dime novels. It said that one of the Indians shot by Reno's men was found masked, "and upon removing the mask the features of a white man were disclosed, with a long, gray, patriarchical beard."[4] Major Reno gave formal recognition to these tales in his official report, where he said, "I think we were fighting all the Sioux Nation, and also all the desperadoes, renegades, half-breeds, and squaw-men between the Missouri and the Arkansas and east of the Rocky Mountains."[5] Of course, there were squaw men and renegade whites in the West. One example was Frank Huston, an embittered former Confederate who had lived with the Sioux and who claimed that there had been white men with the Indians at the battle.[6] However, the Indians themselves all stated that there were no whites in camp.[7]

The renegades are a clue to another characteristic of these dime novels: they are riddled with factual errors. In *Custer's Last Shot*, the General wears his hair long; the Ree scout, Bloody Knife, appears with Custer up on the ridge rather than with Reno down in the valley; the troops use sabers. (The cover of the novel shows Custer and the boy trailer slashing at surrounding Indians with these weapons.) Of course, dime novelists were under no obligation to write with accuracy; but by tying their stories to actual episodes, they helped to confuse fact and fancy and to disseminate legends about Custer and his last battle.

Occasionally an adult hero replaces the boy in the novels. Such is the case in Prentiss Ingraham's *Buffalo Bill's Grip; or, Oath-Bound to Custer* (1883), in which the ubiquitous Buffalo Bill is the first to discover the tragedy at the Little Big Horn. He finds the corpse of the blond-haired General, his "sword blade [*sic*] buried in the body of a painted chief." Cody thereupon swears an oath to avenge Custer's death. But before he can carry out this pledge, he

---

4 Graham, *The Custer Myth*, 357.

5 *Annual Report of the Secretary of War for 1876*, I, 477.

6 Graham, *The Custer Myth*, 80.

7 *Ibid.*, 56, 92.

is captured on the battlefield by the renegade, Bill Bevins, who is disguised as one of Sitting Bull's warriors. (Bevins was an actual character, but he was a stage robber rather than an Indian ally.) From this old enemy Cody learns that the Cheyenne chief Yellow Hand had killed Custer. Later in the story, Buffalo Bill fulfills his oath by killing Yellow Hand and "taking the first scalp for Custer."

Custer's Washita campaign was the subject of another novel published in 1883. This was Thomas Harbaugh's *Roving Rifle, Custer's Little Scout; or, From the Plains to West Point*. A quick friendship springs up between an orphaned youth (whose only name is "Roving Rifle") and Custer, who employs him as a scout. The complicated plot involves spies and counterspies operating between Custer's camp and Black Kettle's village. Roving Rifle plays a prominent part in the campaign: "Snow or storm must not turn me back. I am Custer's soldier now. The success of the winter march depends on finding the 'Rapahoe spy." Black Kettle is characterized as a "vindictive redskin, who had given the Government more trouble than all the other chiefs combined." Thus it must have been satisfying to the young readers when Roving Rifle, after a series of escapades in the Indian village, kills Black Kettle. Custer rewards the young hero by sending him to West Point.

But most of the stories continued to be built around the climactic battle on the Little Big Horn, with the narrator being a witness and somehow managing to survive the annihilation. Ingraham, in an 1887 novel entitled *Buffalo Bill's Big Four; or, Custer's Shadow,* has Cody marching in the Dakota column with Custer. Buffalo Bill attempts to warn the General against bringing on a fight with the savages:

> "I'm afraid, General," he said, "you are underrating woefully the strength of the redskins. They are flushed with victory, and will fight like demons. They are moreover, fairly well armed, and in this case we must not reckon too much on the superiority of white soldiers."
>
> "What, Cody," cried the general, "are you, too, going to turn croaker? I shall move out with seven hundred sabers [*sic*], and I think we shall be able to cope with more savages than we are likely to meet."

At the last stand, Cody and Custer fight shoulder to shoulder with sabers. Bill survives the battle, being saved from scalping by an old Indian friend. Ingraham closely follows the Whittaker interpretation by inveighing against Reno for failing to come up to aid Custer. An indication of Ingraham's historical accuracy may be found in his statement of the causes of the Sioux War: "The Crows and the Sioux [sic] had joined together, and, inducing the neighboring tribes to join them, were sweeping all signs of civilization before them."

"A True Story of the Battle at Little Big Horn" was the subtitle of *Custer's Little Dead-shot; or, the Boy Scout of the Little Big Horn,* an 1888 novel by "An Old Scout" (Lu Senarens). The teen-age dead shot is "Yellowstone Jack" Shelby, who like Roving Rifle of the Washita affair, is a prairie orphan who looks up to Custer as a foster parent. Custer and Jack attempt to assist young Ethel Readon in finding the murderer of her father. The murderer is Barnabas Zadok, a "heavily bearded arch scoundrel," who has allied his band of white renegades with Sitting Bull. During the usual complicated tale of captures, escapes, and recaptures, the boy scout is at one point rescued just as he is about to be consumed by the fire at Sitting Bull's torture stake. At the Last Stand, Custer realizes too late that he has been led into an ambush by Sitting Bull's clever ruse. He turns to Yellowstone Jack and shouts: "Ride for your life, boy, and tell Benteen to come on. Big village! Be quick! Bring packs." Yellowstone Jack thus becomes the last living white man to see the great General. And the device of having the boy replace Trumpeter Martin becomes a standard feature in subsequent book-length fiction.

One of the earliest attempts at a full-length fictional interpretation of Custer was *Master of the Strong Hearts* (1898), by Elbridge S. Brooks. The hero of this novel is Jack Huntingdon, a sixteen-year-old student in New York City. He makes friends with the Sioux, Young Wolf, and encounters this friend many times during the story. The Jack–Young Wolf relationship complements the Jack-Custer story line and enables the author to unify his plot by presenting both sides of the Indian wars.

Jack is a city boy from the East, which means that he has to go West to find real adventure—the "uncitified adventures" with which Custer is identified. In fact, the novel incorporates an anti-school philosophy which seems quite appropriate to the Custer story. When Jack has to return to school after his adventures on the Plains, it is to the "same uneventful routine" as before. The basic appeal of the Custer legend to young boys seems to involve this contrast between the dull and stuffy schoolrooms "back East" and the action and color of life in the Far West. This appeal is both implicit and explicit in practically all the boys' novels.

The heroic image of Custer himself is fully revealed in the story. Brooks has a sense for the romantic and colorful picture that Custer makes:

> The General rode at the head of his troop, like the splendid horseman and gallant cavalier that he was. In his suit of beaver-fringed buckskin, his big sombrero and his long cavalry boots, he looked every inch the soldier, and needed only the long, floating blond locks that once had swept his shoulders and fixed his personality with the Indians (who called him sometimes "Chief Long Hair" and sometimes the "White Chief with the Yellow Hair") to be the Custer of romance and song, the Custer of the Valley, the Custer of the Grand Review at Washington. . . .[8]

He also manages to capture some of the flavor of Custer's personality, by having him quote poetry (Scott's "Lady of the Lake"), and by his cheerful interest in Jack Huntingdon. The bond between the two is established by the fact that Jack's father had served under Custer in the Civil War, a device that is to be used again in other novels. Custer writes a letter to the father, and as a result Jack is able to go with the Custer expeditions as an assistant herder. This helpfulness of course inspires Jack with even greater

---

[8] Brooks, *Master of the Strong Hearts*, 213.

admiration for Custer: "He could have hugged the General then and there if it had been allowable."

Yet the political quarrels in which Custer became embroiled are also used to shed light on his personality:

> That matter has, however, long since been sifted and settled. We know now that the great soldier-president misunderstood and misjudged Custer; we know that the dashing cavalry leader, dis-spirited by this misjudgment, acted unwisely, and brought himself into such direct antagonism to his superiors that, for a time at least, he was deprived of his command, and very nearly placed under arrest; we know that his superiors quickly relented their harshness, appreciating Custer's value as an Indian-fighter and the inspiration his presence meant to his command; but we know also that the wound to his manly pride and womanly sensitiveness, both of which had part in his high sense of honor, rankled, affected him, and led him into an over-zeal that is now history.[9]

Assignment of Jack to the Seventh Cavalry as an assistant herder is necessary to put the boy close to Custer, since the boy hero is an alter ego to the man hero. Jack is always near Custer and observes his actions without being to any great extent concerned with important official tasks. He is also able to take part in the story, and various devices are used to get him into the Sioux camp so he can be an omniscient observer. For example, when he is fighting with Reno in the valley, his horse carries him full tilt into the Sioux lines, a historically based incident.[10] He is then saved by Young Wolf in a dramatically improbable fashion that reminds one of Mason Pierrepont's escapades in the dime novel. Jack fights on the bluff with Reno and is one of the volunteers who goes for water.

By being an active participant in Custer's campaigns, the boy hero becomes an imaginative projection of Custer's exploits on the boys' level. The boy also represents all the Custerian ideals, for example the love of animals: "Jack was a lover of all pets—

[9] *Ibid.,* 126.
[10] Graham, *The Custer Myth,* 139.

especially dogs—and made himself familiar with the stag-hounds on the daily march, while they, in return, showed their fondness for this active boy."[11] This alter-identification is even more obvious when one examines Jack's personal characteristics. He is active and aggressive, an embryo Custer. The following is a typical observation on his character: "Independence sometimes breeds heedlessness, especially in a boy of active and inquisitive temperament, and Jack Huntingdon, as you know, had a pretty fair opinion of his own ability to take care of Jack Huntingdon. He felt himself as wide-awake a scout as any in the troop, and was even disposed to criticize Major Reno as over-cautious."[12] This might be a description of Custer himself, right down to the criticism of Major Reno.

So *Master of the Strong Hearts* incorporates many of the basic elements of the Custer legend: action, courage, manliness, the appeal of the West, the color and romance of Custer himself. In short, Brooks is writing more than just entertainment, he is also writing a lesson in the history of American ideals. The moral is explicitly drawn in the final page, where Jack Huntingdon, who twenty years later is now a consulting architect, tells his doctor-friend Young Wolf: "After all, Young Wolf, even death has its compensations, and the memory of General George Armstrong Custer will live as long as the story of American heroism holds him up as one of its brightest examples."[13]

Fifteen years after *Master of the Strong Hearts,* Edwin L. Sabin published his boys' book, *On the Plains with Custer.* Sabin makes much greater use of documentary material than Brooks. In fact, his book is primarily a narrative of the Custer campaigns from 1867 to 1876, with Ned Fletcher, the boy hero, kept in the background. Ned has been an Indian captive, and the opening scene pictures his escape. His sister Mary still remains in the hands of the Indians, a familiar plot-element left over from the dime novels,

[11] Brooks, *Master of the Strong Hearts,* 135.
[12] *Ibid.,* 137.
[13] *Ibid.,* 314.

and part of the story is concerned with Ned's search for her. He stays with Custer as a boy bugler and orderly at first, and later in the story enlists, serving in Captain Tom Custer's and Captain Benteen's companies as a trumpeter. He participates in all the historically-based incidents which form the thread of the narrative: Custer's meeting with Pawnee Killer on the banks of the Republican River; the massacre of Lieutenant Kidder and his men near Fort Harker; and the battle of the Washita, where Ned rescues his sister. And he is at the Battle of the Little Big Horn, where he becomes Corporal Martin, taking Custer's last message back to Reno.

Sabin expertly mixes all the appeals of the Custer legend in large doses: action, the romantic image, the boyishness of the General. The book opens with the kind of action scene which is quite appropriate to these stories. General Custer saves Ned from the charge of a wounded buffalo. This incident establishes Custer's frontier skills and also his colorful appearance: "This straight, lithe, square-shouldered figure, standing there so fascinating in face and form and garb."[14] Later on, when Ned hears that Custer is about to begin his Yellowstone expedition in 1873, he reacts in romantic fashion: "That news was enough for Ned. It set his blood to tingling, it set his thoughts to dancing, it filled his eyes with pictures of camp and of march and of an alert, lithe, soldierly figure whose keen blue eyes and long yellow hair and clarion voice no boy ever could forget, any more than he could forget the cavalry guidons waving in the charge."[15] This is really a boy's image, as Sabin well realizes when he says: "About this handsome, energetic army of-officer was an air so happy-go-lucky and boyish that Ned, another boy, found himself already loving him."

Do any of the unromantic aspects of army life appear in the book? As might be expected, they are omitted or passed over lightly. The Battle of the Washita is purged of all controversy. The slaugh-

[14] Sabin, *On the Plains with Custer*, 25.
[15] *Ibid.*, 231.

ter of the Indian pony herd at the battle is quite gently explained like this: "This was cruel, but necessary in war. What could the column do, with all those wild ponies and mules? The Indians would fight fiercely to retake them; the Indians would be badly crippled without them. So the general had set his heart hard, and had given the order. When the firing ceased, all the column was glad, for killing horses is not soldiers' work."[16] The same attitude is taken when the Seventh is assigned to protect Northern citizens and negroes against the Ku Klux Klan in the South: "This was not soldierly work such as serving on the plains. . . ." Thus, the romantic aspects of military life are stressed; it is a world of flags and music, "Garryowen," bright uniforms, and heroic death. Perhaps this is true of boys' literature in all ages and countries.

Ned Fletcher is an interesting literary hero, but the author's emphasis on historical material does not give him much room to develop Ned's character adequately. Ned's bond with Custer is strengthened by the same device used in the case of Jack Huntingdon, that is, the father had served with Custer in the Civil War. Custer's response to this revelation: "The son or daughter of any of my boys is like one of my own family." The pro-action, anti-intellect strain in Jack Huntingdon, with his lack of enthusiasm for school, is maintained in Ned Fletcher's boredom with being a quartermaster clerk in the interim between campaigns. (In view of this philosophy, it is surprising to find that the schools were using Custer material to teach American history in the elementary grades.)[17] Both boys become close friends with "Autie" Reed, the General's nephew, to provide a boys' story to parallel the main Custer story. But the continuities between the two books rest mainly on admiration for Custer and his ideals.

In 1938, Zoa Grace Hawley published her volume, *A Boy Rides with Custer*. The story covers the period 1875–76 and is concerned

[16] *Ibid.*, 221.

[17] Mary G. Kelty, *Teaching American History in the Middle Grades of the Elementary School* (Boston, Ginn, 1928), 519.

with the adventures of fifteen-year-old John Rand, a doctor's son in the Dakota territory. John's friendship with the young Sioux, Ma Chee, is temporarily broken when a local white family is massacred, and John and his brothers ride off to Fort Abraham Lincoln to enlist for Custer's final campaign. The plot, like that of *Master of the Strong Hearts,* revolves around the reconciliation between John and Ma Chee, or in broader terms the mutual understanding between Indian and white. This theme is suggested quite early in the book by John: "Listen, Ma Chee. They fight each other mostly because they do not understand each other. Each thinks the other is wrong, but there is wrong on both sides. Pa says so, and he knows this country and he's a just man. You tell this to your people if they don't know."[18] Another similarity in the plot structure is that Ma Chee rescues John when he is fighting in the valley with Reno, much as Young Wolf rescues Jack Huntingdon.

General Custer occupies less space in this story, although he is again intensely sympathetic to the boy hero's problems. When John goes to Fort Lincoln with his brothers, he is too young for the army, but Custer allows him to enlist as a civilian interpreter. The author had prepared her young readers for this eventuality earlier, by means of John's speech to his father: "General Custer likes boys. He adopted an orphan once and took him into battles. And the paper says he's got his younger brother and his nephew with him. The nephew's just a boy. They go everywhere with him." And of course John is permitted to accompany Autie Reed on the march to the Little Big Horn. Mrs. Hawley describes the battle quite accurately and is one of the few authors who correctly places Bloody Knife down in the valley with Reno. There is an unusually good description of the wounded after the battle, tied in with John's duties as a medic.

The most significant characteristic of this book is that of wish-fulfillment. The average fifteen-year-old has no chance to fight Indians or lead the glamorous life of a General Custer. This con-

18 Hawley, *A Boy Rides with Custer,* 22.

ventional viewpoint is put in the mouth of a friendly storekeeper, who tells John: "Why, son, there isn't a chance in the world of your going off to fight Indians. Of course you'd like to, but the Army can't take fellows of your age. You stay and help me until the boys come back." But the whole story is a surmounting of this kind of work-a-day limitation and the projection of the boy into a situation where these dreams reach reality.

In biography written for the boys' market, the ideals which Custer represents can be made even more explicit than in the fictional stories. Custer obviously has a place in the American tradition, and the biographer is able to make clear just what his contribution was. Quentin Reynolds undertook this job in *Custer's Last Stand,* published in 1951.

In this biography, the specifically American ideals associated with Custer are carefully woven into the narrative structure. These include democracy, the meaning of West Point, the duty of self-improvement. In a juvenile series (the Landmark series) devoted to American heroes, these little lessons are to be expected. The democratic ideal, for example, is handled like this:

> The officers in charge at the encampment never mentioned the word "democracy," but the cadets were learning the meaning of the word every day. They lived close to each other—the rich, the poor, the banker's son, the orphan, the boy from Kentucky, and the lad from Boston. At first each had thought the accent of the others strange. A boy from New England could hardly understand the slow drawl of a cadet from the South. But gradually each began to understand the others; each realized that he and his part of the country were only tiny parts of the whole United States.[19]

West Point also is an American ideal: " 'West Point!' Charles gasped. Almost every great American general had been a West Point man. In those days boys didn't have baseball players or movie stars for their heroes. Their idols were the men who led the

[19] Reynolds, *Custer's Last Stand,* 60.

fight against Mexico, the officers who had fought the Indians; and these were all West Pointers."[20]

Custer's distaste for school work is again emphasized. One of the chapters is entitled "The Boy Who Hated Homework," and as Reynolds says of Custer: "He was a real Western boy, and he hated to stay indoors." The narrative consequently centers on "Autie's" frontier skills—horsemanship, trailing, soldiering, and hunting. Nevertheless, the value of self-discipline and self-improvement is also taught. This is in connection with Custer's realization that he has to study if he wants to enter West Point. Some of the moral imperatives are little different from those to be found in Whittaker's *Dashing Dragoon*.

A significant feature of the biography is its many factual errors. Sitting Bull is depicted as an all-knowing battle commander, which is highly improbable in view of the confusion in the Indian camp when Reno attacked: "Fifteen miles away old Sitting Bull was in his lodge getting reports. He had been getting them all morning. Sitting Bull was the Supreme Commander. Every Indian now took orders from the wise old chieftain. Sitting Bull knew just where Colonel Gibbon was. He knew exactly where General Terry was."[21] There are other inaccuracies: General Terry has the Little Big Horn flowing into the Rosebud;[22] General Crook is called General Crock;[23] Bloody Knife rides with Custer up on the bluffs;[24] and the Indians are given more credit for knowledge of Custer than they deserve: "Years later the Indians would call him Autie when they were hunting him."[25] There is also a poetic stroke added to the canvas of the Last Stand, when Autie and Tom Custer die together.[26]

[20] *Ibid.*, 19.
[21] *Ibid.*, 167.
[22] *Ibid.*, 154.
[23] *Ibid.*, 156.
[24] *Ibid.*, 175.
[25] *Ibid.*, 5.
[26] *Ibid.*, 180.

But Reynolds drew a sympathetic portrait of the General, one which has been quite appealing for young boys. And the factual errors simply prove that the drama is more important than the fact. This biography is really a folk-legend, purged of uncomfortable realities and recreating a shining symbol of American ideals. As such it is characteristic of the vast body of boys' literature which has appeared over the last eighty-nine years.

CHAPTER XVII

"Glory Hunter"

THE YEAR 1933 marked the beginning of a new era in the Custer legend. The death of Elizabeth Bacon Custer in that year removed restraints upon criticism of the General. Criticism was soon embodied in Frederic F. Van de Water's *Glory Hunter,* published in 1934. The book exemplified the debunking spirit which affected much of the biographical writing of the period. Van de Water made use of the increasingly popular technique of psychological analysis to draw a portrait of an impetuous and irresponsible egotist. Custer appears as a commander who treated his dogs with more solicitude than he did his men and who was guilty of nepotism, arrogance, and incompetence. His boyishness, an engaging quality for earlier biographers, is to Van de Water a cardinal flaw. Since Custer lacked military skill, his demise at the Little Big Horn was simply the long-deferred penalty for incompetent generalship. This unflattering portrait has in the last quarter of a century become the most influential interpretation of General Custer.

Van de Water has been charged with bending the facts to fit his thesis. One complaint has been that he manipulated hunting episodes to highlight Custer's cruelty.[1] On one occasion, reported the General in *My Life on the Plains,* the dogs brought a buffalo to bay: "Drawing my hunting knife and watching for a favorable opportunity, I succeeded in cutting the hamstrings of the buffalo, which had the effect to tumble him over in the snow, when I was enabled to despatch him with my pistol."[2] Van de Water says:

[1] Don Russell, "The Battle of the Little Big Horn," Chicago *Westerners Brand Book,* Vol. I (October, 1944), 2–3.

[2] *My Life on the Plains,* 15.

"Custer was delighted with the prowess of the staghounds who tore at a snow-bogged calf until, 'watching a favorable opportunity, I succeeded in cutting the hamstrings.' "[3] The omission of the pistol shot has the effect of turning a sportsman into a sadist.

There was, however, sadism in Custer's hunting. Mrs. Custer herself records one episode which supports the Van de Water interpretation. Custer wounded a buffalo and then waited for the women of the party to come up and view the death shot. "It was a repetition of the Spanish bull-fight with the matador for a few brief moments."[4] Custer's voracious appetite for hunting was perhaps more acceptable in the 1870's than in these days of the Society for the Prevention of Cruelty to Animals.

One can hardly agree with the publisher's book-jacket claim that *Glory Hunter* is "the most fair and impartial biography." Van de Water indulges in rather heavy editorializing about his subject's sins, and it is clear that he interprets every episode and every character trait at the farthest end of the scale from Frederick Whittaker. Whittaker sees the 1867 court-martial as a conspiracy by Custer's enemies; Van de Water views it as proof of the General's egomania. Where Whittaker finds the cause of the "Custer Massacre" to lie in criminal dereliction by Custer's subordinates, Van de Water finds it in Custer's own rashness and irresponsibility. These differences measure the change that has taken place in the Custer legend since 1876.

Glory Hunter quickly became the master model for novelists, script writers, and historians. Van de Water was himself a novelist *(Fool's Errand; Thunder Shield)*, and his skill at portraiture produced a memorable interpretation which clearly influenced writers like Harry Sinclair Drago, Ernest Haycox, Will Henry, Clay Fisher, and others. All these novelists stress the same characteristics that Van de Water stressed: Custer's rashness, irresponsibility, and egotism. The question concerning whether Custer had disobeyed his orders, still lively among military historians, has been

[3] *Glory Hunter,* 190.
[4] *Following the Guidon,* 203–204.

answered in the affirmative by all recent novelists. Usually their characters make statements about Custer's error in dividing the regiment, or there is dialogue in which Reno's men curse Custer for having abandoned them as he had Major Elliott's party on the Washita.

Harry Sinclair Drago's *Montana Road* (1935) is built around the adventures of Stephen Glen, an Indian agent who later serves as a scout with Reno's battalion. The novel would hardly appeal to Custerphiles, for it is laced with frank comments about Custer's shortcomings. The General appears as a temperamental and undisciplined commander who cannot hold the regiment's loyalty. Glen as an eyewitness sees him blunder along to the Little Big Horn, disregarding the advice of his scouts that there are at least twenty-five hundred Indians in the valley. He also hears Reno's troopers curse the Boy General for having divided the regiment.

Bugles in the Afternoon (1944), by Ernest Haycox, is one of the best historical Westerns ever written and probably the best novel about the Seventh Cavalry. The plot concerns a disgraced officer who returns to the regiment as an enlisted man in an attempt to redeem himself. The pattern of interpretation follows Van de Water, with many of the episodes supporting a characterization of Custer as a glory seeker whose hunger for applause led to gross errors of judgment. For example, use is made of Custer's statement to Captain Ludlow that he intended to "pull away from Terry."[5] Similar ideas are echoed by the enlisted men: " 'There's Terry to hold him down,' said Hines. 'He'll do as he did before with Stanley. He'll listen to orders and march away and disobey 'em.' "[6]

Haycox at times seems to load his characterization too heavily against Custer: "He could be harsh and brutal for the sake of a soldierly ideal, but there was no gentle insight in him, no compassion, no deep sympathy."[7] This is straight Van de Water doctrine. As a matter of fact, Custer's comments in *My Life on the Plains* do

[5] Haycox, *Bugles in the Afternoon,* 185.
[6] *Ibid.,* 216.
[7] *Ibid.,* 215.

reveal compassion, and his letter to the sculptress Vinnie Ream Hoxie does indicate insight.[8]

Custer's requiem, which Haycox has General Terry frame, is characteristic of much recent interpretation: "He knew, as he stood so gravely here upon the scene of defeat, how that defeat had come about. His trap, designed to snap shut, had been prematurely set off by the impetuous disregard of General Custer of his orders; wanting glory and blindly believing in himself and his regiment, Custer had not waited; the power of waiting was not in him."[9] This is an interpretation which the biographers and novelists of the pre-Van de Water period would have indignantly rejected.

Will Henry's *No Survivors* (1950) utilizes the tested fictional device of a white renegade among the Indians. In this case the central figure is Colonel John Clayton, a former Confederate officer who becomes a Sioux squaw man and warrior. Clayton deserts the Indians at the last moment and attempts to warn Custer that a trap has been set for him. Custer does not take the warning, and his stubbornness provokes some strong editorial comment: "He must be held personally responsible before the bar of history for what followed. In the light of what did follow, the charges could be no less than criminal negligence, dereliction of duty, professional incompetence, and moral guilt of murder—all in search of personal glorification and aggrandizement."[10]

The changed view of Custer calls for a revised estimate of Major Reno. Henry explains that Reno's retreat to the bluffs was not a cowardly withdrawal but the only move which could have saved his command from a fate similar to Custer's. Custer, in fact, dictates a statement of responsibility for the disaster, witnessed by Clayton, who is in at the Last Stand. So in this novel the General is permitted to achieve some redemption for his tragic flaws.

The ultimate development in novelistic interpretation is a complete reversal of the roles of Custer and Reno. In Kenneth Shiflet's

[8] *My Life on the Plains,* 159; Monaghan, *Custer,* 333.
[9] *Bugles in the Afternoon,* 294.
[10] Page 270.

Convenient Coward (1961), Reno is the hero and Custer the arch-villain. Reno gets all the good lines in this book, being allowed to explain on more than one occasion why Custer was such a poor soldier.[11] Custer oppresses Reno at every opportunity, denying him a leave of absence when his wife is dying, upbraiding him for flushing but not bagging the Indians on the Rosebud, and humiliating him on the march to the Little Big Horn. Custer is depicted as an unstable and egotistical neurotic, whose errors of tactical judgment take better men to their deaths. Shiflet offers a lengthy explanation of why Reno became the scapegoat for Custer's mistakes, by means of a speech from Lyman Gilbert:

> "It is mostly the ones who talk or write, like our friend Whittaker. The minority. The talkative, unknowledgeable minority, those who don't know anything about the battle or don't try to know the truth. . . . This talkative minority needed a coward to blame it on. . . . It's the classic all-world way of excusing everyone's small or large guilt or responsibility. Find someone to be the coward and if you can't find one, *make* one. Then everybody else is brave and the man you label a coward can get all the censure. . . . You fitted their qualifications because you were the senior officer left alive and you kept to yourself and couldn't do much talking back. . . . You don't have a raft of well-entrenched friends. You were convenient. That's the most important qualification, Marcus. You were so damned convenient. It doesn't matter that you are not a coward; you conveniently will do.[12]

Novelists who interpret the characters of the Old West are especially addicted to this kind of special pleading, on one side or the other, and Custer seems to have inspired the maximal amount of editorializing. Reading Custer fiction is not only an exercise in historical imagination; it is also an experience in impassioned argumentation.[13]

[11] Shiflet, *Convenient Coward*, 38, 179.

[12] *Ibid.*, 290.

[13] For other Custer criticism in a recent novel, see William Wister Haines, *The Winter War* (Boston, Little, Brown, 1961), 59, 67, 227.

The changing nature of the Custer legend is related not only to the impact of Van de Water's book but also to a more sympathetic view of the Indians. As the frontier receded and the horrors of Indian warfare were forgotten, army officers began to lose glamour because they symbolized the oppression of the Red Man. Perhaps the formal beginning of this pro-Indian cycle dates from Helen Hunt Jackson's *A Century of Dishonor* (1881), which highlighted the white man's injustices to the Indian. Following in the footsteps of Van de Water, who was quite sympathetic to the Indians, came a succession of other pro-Indian, anti-Custer historians.

Charles J. Brill told the Indian side of the story in his *Conquest of the Southern Plains* (1938), which was subtitled *An Uncensored Narrative of the Battle of the Washita and Custer's Southern Campaign.* Brill's theme was Custer's mercilessness to man and beast, his vicious attitude toward the Plains Indians, and the deficiencies of his official reports and published writings. Brill denies Custer's published claim of having killed 103 warriors at the Washita by citing Indian testimony that there were fifteen braves killed and "several times that many" women and children.[14] Implying that the whole Washita campaign was conceived and carried out in treachery, Brill terms the battle a "massacre" and calls the death of Black Kettle "assassination." He also gave circulation to stories that Custer and his officers selected women prisoners for a "convivial night."[15] Custer was especially attracted to Monahseetah, a young Cheyenne "divorcee," who later bore a son with fair skin and yellow hair.[16]

This Indian-son legend was an item of Indian gossip which seems to have entered Custer historiography through Frederick Benteen. In 1896, Benteen wrote a series of letters to Theodore Goldin characterizing Custer as a murderer, a liar, and a libertine. He also charged that Custer had lived with a captured Indian woman (pre-

---

[14] Brill, *Conquest of the Southern Plains,* 16.

[15] *Ibid.,* 22.

[16] *Ibid.,* 46.

sumably Monahseetah) during the winter and spring of 1868–69.[17] Like the Custer-suicide theory, this legend does not match Custer's known character. Custer liked to tease his wife in letters from New York describing his flirtations with society women, but his genuine fidelity to her argues against an affair with an Indian.[18] Nevertheless, the Custer-Monahseetah legend lives on in books and newspaper articles.[19]

Other historians adopted and promoted the Van de Water–Brill thesis of Custer's treachery to the Indians. In *Fighting Indians of the West* (1948), Martin Schmitt and Dee Brown postulated that Custer "came to the West with the cold-blooded intention of making a glorious career out of the business of slaying Indians."[20] They echoed Brill in claiming that Custer had never been able to defeat the Indians in fair fight. Instead, he had to sneak up on them in their winter lodges and wipe them out en masse.

In Clay Fisher's novel *Yellow Hair* (1954), the pro-Indian sentiment which has affected the Custer legend in recent years is also quite evident. It is voiced by the chief character, Josh Kelso, a mountain man who falls in love with Monahseetah. Custer is characterized as a "vain-crazy Indian-killer," whose Washita campaign is marked by deceit and deliberate cruelty. Black Kettle, on the other hand, is depicted as a peace-loving chief, whose attempts to surrender are rebuffed because of Custer's desire for a military victory. Indeed, Custer's defects are so numerous that he becomes something of an abstraction in the novel. Many of his actual characteristics, most notably his sense of humor, are overlooked.

Historians of the Indian have generally downgraded Custer's

[17] "Letters written by Brevet Brigadier General F. W. Benteen, U.S.A. Retired to Sergeant Theodore Goldin, 7th U.S. Cavalry," Newberry Library, Chicago, 72.

[18] In addition, there are certain technical problems involved. Monahseetah was taken prisoner in November, and her child was born in January.—Monaghan, *Custer*, 328.

[19] Charles House in New York *Herald-Tribune*, June 30, 1957; Miller, *Custer's Fall*, 67.

[20] Page 42.

military reputation as well as his character. David Humphreys Miller told the Indian story of the Little Big Horn in *Custer's Fall* (1957), a narrative based on interviews with Indian survivors in their eighties and nineties. Miller characterized Custer as a "power-hungry opportunist," whose desperation led him into a reckless military gamble.[21] Alvin Josephy wrote *The Patriot Chiefs* (1961), a history of Indian leadership in which the adjectives applied to Custer are expectedly strong:

> Ever since the Civil War, in which he had had a gallant record, Custer had been a publicized hero. He had come west after the war, looking for more glory, and had led the 7th Cavalry in cruel and unreasonable warfare against southern Cheyennes and other tribes in Kansas and on the southern plains. He was an irascible, unstable man who treated his own troops so badly that they often went A.W.O.L. When he caught them he shot them without trial, and then on one occasion went A.W.O.L. himself. In 1867 he was court-martialed for his behavior, but was soon back in command of the 7th Cavalry, and in 1868, seeking headlines again, he savagely slaughtered Black Kettle's unfortunate southern Cheyennes in an unjustified attack on the Washita River.[22]

There may be some justification in the charge that Custer was "seeking more glory." Promotions were hard to get in the peace-time army, and only impressive victories over the Indians seemed likely to secure them. However, the theory that he treated his troops so badly that they went A.W.O.L. does not seem correct. Every command on the plains had a high desertion rate, independent of the personality of the particular commanding officer. Whether the Washita affair was "unfortunate" and "unjustified" is of course a subject of debate.

Motion-picture interpretations have also reflected the Van de Water–Brill tradition. With the exception of *They Died with Their Boots On* (1941), which is in the older heroic mold, recent films all stress Custer's shortcomings. *Bugles in the Afternoon* (1953) is

[21] Page 202.
[22] (New York, Viking Press, 1961), 291.

faithful to the original Haycox interpretation of Custer as rash and inflexible. *Sitting Bull* (1954) is a sympathetic picture of the great Indian leader, who is forced into battle by the double-dealing of Custer. Custer is portrayed as a rabid Indian hater who tries to block the hero's attempts to arrange a peace treaty. In Walt Disney's *Tonka* (1957), Custer again displays an intense hatred of the red men. He would even torture the Indian youth White Bull (Sal Mineo) but for the intervention of Captain Keogh. As in *Sitting Bull,* Custer disobeys orders and rushes to his doom. Similar characterizations appear in *The Fighting 7th* (1952), *Seventh Cavalry* (1957), and a number of other films featuring the Last Stand.

Some authors of the glory-hunter persuasion do not particularly sympathize with the Indians; they just despise Custer. E. A. Brininstool and Fred Dustin began to formulate anti-Custer theses years before Van de Water's biography appeared. Brininstool issued a series of pamphlets bearing titles like *Major Reno Vindicated,* in which he attacked the Custer legend. Dustin's *The Custer Tragedy* (1939) describes the General as one of the most overrated men in American history, "an idol with feet of clay." Dustin's analysis of Custer's personality follows Van de Water, who is often praised.[23] Rashness, excessive personal vanity, and an inability to profit by experience are some of the outstanding defects noted. Dustin also made an elaborate technical study of the Last Stand and decided that it would have been a victory if Custer had obeyed orders.

Because the Brininstool and Dustin interpretations were printed in limited editions by private presses, they were known only to close students of the battle, but magazines and newspapers have given wider circulation to such views of the great hero. *Life* and *Time* have been particularly critical of Custer. *Life,* in reviewing *They Died with Their Boots On,* December 8, 1941, remarked that Custer was a "confirmed glory-hunter" who was reckless with

[23] *The Custer Tragedy,* 183, 209.

other men's lives. In an article on the seventy-fifth anniversary of the Little Big Horn in 1951, headed "All His Life He Sought Glory," the magazine maintained that Custer was less devoted to duty than to glorifying himself.[24] *Time,* on August 18, 1947, carried an article titled "General Was Neurotic," which held that in World War II Custer would have been discharged as a psychoneurotic. This theory was drawn from an article by the psychiatrist Dr. Karl Menninger, who explained Custer's condition as psychopathic and "typically characterized by excessive vanity, complete disregard for the feelings and safety of others, a lack of loyalty either to cause or to friends."[25]

Posthumous psychoanalysis has been quite popular of late, though it has its dangers. There seems to be little question about Custer's vanity. His pride in his regiment and in his own accomplishments is well known. However, it seems inaccurate to charge the General with a lack of loyalty to friends. One of the contemporary charges against him was that he packed the Seventh Cavalry with his friends and relatives. Moreover, his persistent loyalty to General McClellan, even when it threatened his own career, tends to disprove the charge.[26]

Newspapermen from one end of the country to the other have also made Custer a favorite whipping boy. Charles House, writing in the New York *Herald-Tribune* of June 30, 1957, referred to his "military rashness and disobedience, his two Army courts-martial, his vanity, his cruelty, his affinity to wenching Indian maidens, his discarded Indian son, his incredibly poor scholastic record at West Point where he graduated only because of a national need for soldiery."[27] Said John Reese in the *Pasadena Star-News* of May

24 Vol. XXXI (July 9, 1951), 41–44.

25 The Menninger article orginally appeared in the official journal of the American College of Surgeons; *Surgery, Gynecology and Obstetrics,* Vol. LXXXIV (May, 1947), 1002–12. It is summarized in the Chicago *Westerners Brand Book,* Vol. IV (July, 1947), 36.

26 See Custer's "War Memoirs," *Galaxy,* Vol. XXI (May, 1876), 813.

27 Quoted by David Humphreys Miller in *Montana,* Vol. VIII (Spring, 1958), 61.

14, 1961: "For years the 'boy general,' George Armstrong Custer, was revered as a hero who died facing overwhelming enemies, like those who defended the Alamo. Only in recent years has the public come to understand that he was a military idiot who uselessly got his whole command butchered by the Sioux, fighting a battle that should never have been fought."

Some writers have compared Custer unfavorably with other great Western cavalrymen. Even Frederick Whittaker was willing to concede that Nelson Miles and Ranald Mackenzie had "developed talents of the same nature as those of Custer."[28] One recent author has pointed out that Mackenzie's Civil War record at least equaled Custer's, while his Indian-fighting record was vastly better.[29] Mackenzie fought more major engagements with the Indians, planned his attacks more carefully, and was far more successful. Yet he died in obscurity, while Custer's spectacular failure earned immortality.

The reasons for Custer's notoriety seem clear. Not only did Miles and Mackenzie die in bed, they also lacked Custer's flamboyant personality. In comparison with the Boy General, they were always calm and careful. Hence their lives lack the provocative contradictions that have made Custer a fascinating subject of study. They have not aroused the emotionalism that afflicts most students of the Custer legend. Jay Monaghan's 1959 biography of Custer was remarkable for its avoidance of both the blind hero-worship of Whittaker and the spitefulness of Van de Water. Most students belong quite positively to either the dead-lion or the glory-hunter traditions, and seldom do the twain meet.

In any case, there will be a Custer legend for a long time to come. The Last Stand has captured the imagination of the American people. It has become as much a part of American folklore as Washington's cherry tree or Daniel Boone's discovery of Kentucky. It is one of our most democratic legends; everybody has an opinion

28 *Life*, 623.

29 Edward S. Wallace, "Border Warrior," *American Heritage*, Vol. IX (June, 1958), 22–25.

about Custer, and even an Ohio grandmother who collects dolls and buttons has published a book on the Little Big Horn.[30] Novelists and film writers are still attracted to the episode—sure proof of its popular appeal. And the continuing debate over the virtues or sins of the central figure will guarantee a long life for his legend.

[30] Nelle Deex, *Glory Trek* (1959).

PART FIVE

The Western Hero

CHAPTER XVIII

The Hero in History and Legend

THE GENERAL NATURE of the heroic legends, the details of their origin and growth, and the reasons for their continued vitality seem clear. Each hero is celebrated in a wide variety of legends. The popular narratives about them are only partly historical. In fact, underlying the surface variations among the heroes is a common pattern of anecdote and characterization which is literary and folkloric rather than historical in nature. This pattern is most clearly revealed in four aspects of heroic legend: genteel qualities, clever traits, prowess, and epic significance.

Most biographers attempt to represent their subjects as being more genteel than they actually were. This is an ironbound tradition in frontier biography, from John Filson's sketch of Daniel Boone in 1784 to the latest Hickok or Carson representation on television. The hero's speech, character, philosophy, appearance, and actions are altered to conform to a preconceived ideal. The ideal is essentially metropolitan; the gentility, elegance, and moral virtue of the type-figure are superimposed upon the heroes by those not of the frontier. DeWitt C. Peters did not give his readers a true picture of Kit Carson; he purified Carson's language and behavior in order to create a figure that he felt would be acceptable to his readers. William E. Connelley carefully edited the documents he was quoting in an attempt to make the real Hickok into an ideal hero. The result of these operations is usually a stereotyped character and an inaccurate record of the individual concerned.

All heroes are given the conventional purified language. None of them smoke, drink, or use profanity. They are all required to serve good causes. They all have philosophical depth and are self-conscious about their historical roles. Lapses from the genteel pattern, such as Custer's drinking bout, Hickok's gambling, and Carson's Indian wives, are excused as temporary aberrations or justified as accepted habits of the period. One reason for this kind of purification is made clear in the preface to Buel's *Heroes of the Plains:* "While this volume abounds with thrilling adventures, sanguinary encounters and personal combats of the most startling character, yet through every page there is observed a thread of wholesome justice, upon which is strung every deed recounted, preserving a forcible and moral influence beneficial to young and old alike." To make the Western hero a model for "young and old alike" requires the excision of material which, though factual, may be of questionable moral quality.

Yet each hero also appears in a contradictory role which is unrelated either to the genteel figure or to the actual individual. The Kit Carson of the dime novels is a savage and vindictive Indian killer who lacks most genteel qualities except some elegance of speech. The Billy the Kid of some novels and magazines is a cold-blooded psychopath, quite different from the generous folk hero of most biographers. In a number of dime novels and histories, Wild Bill Hickok is a drunken bully rather than an epic law-bringer. And one may choose from several Custers: idealist, glory hunter, Indian hater, or Indian lover. These contradictions facilitate the growth of legends, because every Western fan can create a hero after his own ideas. They also vastly complicate the historian's job.

A second major feature of the legendary pattern is the assignment to the hero of "clever" traits. The hero invariably outwits his frontier adversaries, be they Indians or renegade whites. Illustrative anecdotes are gratuitously assigned to particular heroes as symbols of the necessary character trait. Most of these stories are significant as legend, although irrelevant as history. None of them meet the standard tests of historical documentation. The exploits are usually performed alone, so that no authentication is possible.

To this class belong many of the Indian-escape and gunfighting tales. Carson's escape from the Comanches near Kit Carson's Peak is typical of the clever stratagems employed by the hero. Ingraham's story of Hickok's sixty-foot leap off a cliff to thwart pursuing Blackfeet is one of the oldest tales in the frontier repertoire, having been borrowed from the Daniel Boone narratives. Hickok's outwitting Jack Mulrey on the streets of Hays City and Billy the Kid's outsmarting Joe Grant at Fort Sumner are other episodes which have a classic appeal. From the historical standpoint, however, they are simply imaginative versions of what might have happened.

Many of these "clever" tales are legendary by virtue of a distorted interpretation of the facts. One of the cleverest exploits in Western history was Billy the Kid's escape from the Lincoln County jail. The local press greeted this exploit with shock and horror rather than with applause. Yet Walter Noble Burns turned it into a heroic feat by depicting Olinger as a vicious bully who deserved just what he got. By means of dramatic writing and questionable manipulation of the facts, many of the sordid episodes in Western history become heroic.

In addition to his cleverness, the hero typifies exceptional ability in such frontier skills as trailing, marksmanship, and hand-to-hand combat with Indians and wild beasts. There is a body of generic anecdotes which is drawn upon to illustrate the hero's prowess. In these stories the hero always overcomes tremendous odds. The Indian-fighting stories usually involve ratios of ten to one, with the hero invariably triumphant. Wild Bill Hickok became a national figure by virtue of his single-handed defeat of the entire McCanles gang. In many versions of this story, one of the villains escapes to spread word of Wild Bill's prowess. Nine-out-of-ten and three-out-of-four legends abound in frontier narratives. Hickok's battle with four insolent cowboys in a Nebraska saloon yields a survivor who lives in Kansas City and willingly tells the story of the fight to all inquiring journalists. When Billy the Kid runs across four of John Chisums' cowboys at a line camp, he shoots three of them but permits the fourth to go back and spread word of the Kid's prowess.

The frontiersman also proves his skill in encounters with wild animals. There is a complete American bestiary in frontier narratives, and hand-to-claw combats with buffaloes, bears, and mountain lions are a standard fixture. This convention reflects in part tall-tale inflation of actual encounters which were, of course, a part of frontier life, although such episodes are more often a gratuitous contribution of biographers, frequently being borrowed from earlier accounts.

There is, for example, no factual basis to the stories concerning Kit Carson's hand-to-claw fight with a "Mexican lion" or Hickok's knife fight with a huge bear. Both of these stories appear to have been borrowed from the Crockett *Autobiography* and almanacs, in which Davy fights lions, bears, alligators, and assorted other fauna. In border anthologies like Buel's *Heroes of the Plains* or Cody's *Story of the Wild West,* it is evident that these classic animal-encounter tales are assigned indiscriminately to every hero represented in the collection. Such tales are a recognized badge of prowess.

A fourth connecting link in the legendary pattern is the assignment of epic significance to the hero's career. Epic claims are a convention in frontier biography. Kit Carson's biographers compared him with Hercules and Hannibal and regarded him as an agent of Providence to settle the wilderness. General Custer was described by his biographer as one of the few really great men that America has produced and was put on a par with Napoleon, Cromwell, Caesar, and Hannibal. Wild Bill Hickok "played his part in the reformation of pioneer society more effectively than any character in the annals of American history." Even such a presumably antisocial character as Billy the Kid was hailed by his earliest biographers as "the peer of any fabled brigand on record."

From the historian's point of view, these epic claims are not justified. The heroes were less important in the over-all history of the westward movement than the legend makers would have us believe. Carson was only one of John C. Frémont's many guides, and he was perhaps a great traveler rather than a great explorer.[1] George Armstrong Custer looms large in American folklore and legend, but his battles were actually minor events in American military history. Hickok did some valuable scouting for the army during the Indian Wars, but whether as a frontier marshal he helped or hindered the settlement of the plains is still a matter of debate.

Preoccupation with epic stature tends to lead the biographer into sins of omission. He will leave out of the Carson biography such episodes as Kit's cold-blooded execution of three unarmed prisoners at San Rafael in 1846. In fact, this adventure was not recorded in biographies until Edwin L. Sabin made it public in 1914. The biographer may refuse to concede that some of his hero's actions are controversial, as did William E. Connelley in his treatment of Hickok's role in the McCanles affair. Connelley viewed Wild Bill as the greatest of frontiersmen because he braved danger to clear a path for civilization. Any criticism of this idealized figure, any challenge to the legend, provoked an emotional response. Indeed, it takes a courageous biographer to peer into the dark shadows of a hero's life. And the lesson for the careful student of Western history is that he must view heroes' biographies with a great deal of skepticism.

The characteristics of nineteenth-century biographers explain much about the origin and growth of legends. For various reasons, these writers had a casual attitude toward the truth and often held imaginative appeal to be of more importance than the facts. Novelists often wrote history. Among the Carson biographers, John S. C. Abbott and Edward S. Ellis were better known as dime novelists than as historians, while Charles Burdett was first of all a creative

[1] Nevins, "Kit Carson—Bayard of the Plains," *American Scholar,* Vol. VIII (July, 1939), 338.

writer. Custer's biographer, Frederick Whittaker, was also a pro-
lific dime novelist and fictionist. These men were accustomed to
rearranging facts for purposes of narrative interest. When imaginative appeal becomes the first criterion for the selection of material, distortions may occur. The historical problem becomes a
dramaturgical one, and the narratives acquire the qualities of imaginative literature. Such an approach is often preferred even today.
Magazines employ novelists rather than historians to write essays
on Western subjects.[2] The theory is that historians always man-
age to spoil a good story.

In fact, serious historians lost the Western field by default. Few
of them bothered to pay much attention to such presumably ado-
lescent subjects as cowboys and Indians. As Burns remarked in
connection with Billy the Kid: "Historians have been afraid of
him, as if this boy of six-shooter deadliness might fatally injure
their reputations if they set themselves seriously to write of a
career of such dime-novel luridness. As a consequence, history has
neglected him."[3] And into the vacuum left by scholarly historians
marched the popularizers.

It is also significant that most of the legend makers were Easterners, or if they lived in the West, they had been reared and
educated in the East. Walter Noble Burns, whom Eugene Cunningham called a "literary stranger" in the West,[4] abandoned the
newspaper trade in Chicago long enough to visit New Mexico and
write a fictionalized biography of Billy the Kid. George Ward
Nichols left New York and spent just enough time in Missouri to
put together a magazine article that launched the Wild Bill Hickok
legend. These writers and others like them gave Eastern readers
narratives that were based upon Eastern preconceptions and expectations rather than upon the facts. They romanticized frontier

[2] For example, A. B. Guthrie, Jr., wrote the essay on Billy the Kid for the *Life*
series on "How the West Was Won," Vol. XLVI (May 4, 1959), 87.

[3] *Saga of Billy the Kid,* 69.

[4] *Triggernometry,* 147.

characters in response to literary conventions and commercial requirements. In so doing, they erected a grand edifice of legend upon the slender foundation of fact.

Once a popularizer got hold of a promising character and printed legends about him, the legends were extremely difficult to correct. They became embedded in a number of subsequent accounts and by simple repetition came to be accepted as the truth. People seem to believe that proof of the reliability of a story lies in the number of times it has been repeated, without stopping to consider the source from which it came. Thus Wilbert Eisele, in his 1931 biography of Hickok, accepted the traditional version of Wild Bill's fight with the McCanles gang on the grounds that the story had been related more than a hundred times in various publications.[5] Indeed, by 1931 this version had appeared in an autobiography (1879), a biography (1880), a dime novel (1882), a popular anthology (1907), a novel (1923), a movie (1923), a *Saturday Evening Post* article (1926), and countless newspapers. When a particular legend becomes embalmed in encyclopedias, as this one has become, it is especially difficult to correct because many people regard reference books as the final authority.

Every legend passes through a typical cycle which includes dime novels, biographies, histories, novels, juveniles, movies, and television plays. Some heroes are honored in other media. Billy the Kid and Custer have had folk songs written about them, while Carson and Custer have been immortalized in poems based upon their exploits. In fact, it is the range of mediums in which the legend appears over a period of time which entitles the hero to legendary stature. Hickok surpasses Wyatt Earp as a legendary figure because Earp was never a dime-novel hero. (The Earp legend is of fairly recent origin, dating from Stuart N. Lake's biography in 1933.) Mackenzie and Miles have not been the subject of dime novels or motion pictures as has General Custer. Neither Jim Bridger nor Bill Williams became television heroes as did Kit

[5] *The Real Wild Bill,* 52.

Carson. By the consolidating processes of legend, certain individuals become the pre-eminent type-figures for the entire class to which they belonged.

Each of the media contributes to the legend in its own way, although they all favor the pseudobiographical format. The dime novelists often claimed that their narratives were historically true, but the number of factual errors in them was limited only by the author's imagination. Some of the feats popularized in dime novels, such as the hero's shooting a pistol out of the villain's hand, have become stock exploits in motion pictures and television. Motion-picture producers have often based their scripts upon the printed biographies and simply appropriated legends from that source with little change. More frequently, they have made wholesale revisions of history to fit the demands of a particular script. The publishers of juvenile books have also been more interested in story values than in authenticity. They have continued to purvey the familiar boyhood legends, and, indeed, the Western hero makes his first appeal to the young.

It should be noted, however, that motion pictures and television have played a vital role in perpetuating the Western hero tradition. They connect the historical name with a living person. Thus Wild Bill Hickok was personified in the 1930's by Gary Cooper, in the 1950's by television actor Guy Madison. Billy the Kid has been known to us in the persons of Robert Taylor, Audie Murphy, and Paul Newman. Tyrone Power as Jesse James, Errol Flynn as Custer, and Hugh O'Brian as Wyatt Earp have put flesh and blood into some great Western legends and thus helped to keep them alive. Without Hollywood, the Western hero might not have become the dominant figure in American legend.

Oral storytellers occasionally contributed to the legends. The lengthy time span of some of the stories and their similarities with generic tales are evidence of oral elaboration. The tale of Carson's cleaning out a Taos dance, first printed by Ruxton in 1848, may originally have been an oral tale. On the other hand, Ruxton had a lively imagination, and he may have invented the story himself. In fact, colorful details were added to the legends more often by writers than by oral storytellers.[6] The frontier heroes of the Far West, because they were creatures of professional writers, are perhaps less deserving of the title of "folk hero" than such earlier figures as Mike Fink and Davy Crockett.

There are certain key authors connected with every legend. John C. Frémont's name is forever linked with that of Kit Carson, since Frémont's *Report* started Carson on the road to legendary fame. George Ward Nichols initiated the Hickok legend. Frederick Whittaker's biography helped to inflate the already growing Custer legend. And the names of Ash Upson and Walter Noble Burns will always be associated with that of Billy the Kid. Some names cut across several of the legends. J. W. Buel and William F. Cody, by means of their biographies and anthologies, had a hand in the Carson, Custer, and Hickok legends. Prentiss Ingraham also contributed to these same legends through his dime novels and dime "biographies." Identification of these key writers helps the historian, for when he sees their names attached to a particular story, he is immediately on guard.

The professional hero makers must bear only part of the responsibility for the persistence of the legends. They have simply supplied what the people have demanded. Beauty and truth are both aspects of human experience, but beauty is preferred. There is something cold and abstract about truth. Attachment to it presupposes a certain cynicism about human nature and conduct. Romance and legend, on the other hand, are warm and colorful, representing the ideal in human aspirations. Hence it is not surprising that each legend involves a highly selective process by which the beautiful eclipses the true. The ugly or unpleasant features of life are eliminated.

The historian's ruthless quest after truth frequently mars the beauty of a perfected legend. Such heartless destruction of cher-

---

[6] "Vaunted pioneers like Daniel Boone and Kit Carson live in books, not in tales." —Richard Dorson, *American Folklore* (Chicago, University of Chicago Press, 1959), 200.

ished myths is quite unpopular in some quarters. When Stuart Henry criticized Emerson Hough's *North of 36* for its infidelities to history, he came under heavy fire for daring to question the romantic myth of the Great West. Attempts to prove by historical investigation that Billy the Kid was short weight for a hero have met with fanatical resistance. The *Los Angeles Times* in an editorial on "The Wasted Motion of Debunking" (August 28, 1960) complained about such investigations. Debunkers were described as naïve latecomers, and it was maintained that people want romance and are uninterested in having their illusions dispelled. Yet the people also have a right to know whether they are reading fact or fiction, and the historian has a responsibility to draw the line which separates the two.

The historical framework around the Western hero has made many of the legends more believable. There was a factual basis for some of the stories. Wild Bill Hickok did shoot some men at the Rock Creek stage station, though not in the number or manner that the legend records. Billy the Kid did kill some men in the Lincoln County War, though not in the numbers or for the reasons that his legend proclaims. A legend built around an actual person is doubly effective, because there is always the tantalizing possibility that it *might* have happened that way. A film such as *The Plainsman* had enormous appeal because it featured a known character from history, Wild Bill Hickok, and wove around him a series of episodes which reflected every kind of wish-fulfillment. The appeal of such legends as Wild Bill's fight with the McCanles gang and his romance with Calamity Jane proves that folklore will never be eclipsed by mere fact.

The Western hero's career has thus become an American epic by virtue of the form and content of the legends rather than because of the historical importance of his activities. The biographer's ritualistic observance of what is essentially a world-wide legendary pattern guarantees his man a place in the pantheon of American heroes. The "Clever Hero," for example, is a type which folklorists have found in all nations.[7] Thus the biographer who incorporates anecdotes in which his subject cleverly outwits his enemies is working with a proved formula. Similarly, the type of prowess which the frontier hero exemplifies in his combats with Indians and wild animals is also universally admired. The editing of the hero's personal characteristics in response to cultural expectations and literary conventions is also part of the pattern. Finally, Americans share with other peoples an interest in violence. As William James remarked, "History is a bath of blood. The *Iliad* is one long recital of how Diomedes and Ajax, Sarpedon and Hector *killed*. No detail of the wounds they made is spared us, and the Greek mind fed upon the story."[8] The American mind has fed upon the famous shootings which occupy such a prominent place in the Western hero tradition. The stories of Carson and Shunan, of Wild Bill and McCanles, of the Kid and Bob Olinger, have been American equivalents of Ajax and Hector. Thus it is conformance with an age-old formula which explains the heroes' popularity.

The proved appeal of the legends also explains why they continue to be incorporated into biographies and histories. If Billy the Kid did not outsmart Joe Grant, but simply shot him down without a chance to draw, then he is so much less the hero. The biographer will continue to include the traditional version of this episode, because it serves to confirm the heroic stature of his subject. Many biographers are quite frank in stating that such legendary anecdotes are *illustrative* of their hero's abilities. This is the key to the whole process. As symbolization proceeds, as generic anecdotes and characterizations are added to the hero's biography, the actual individual who lies at the bottom of the legend tends to become irrelevant.

The history-legend pattern of popular Western narrative has been remarkably uniform over the years. The nineteenth-century biographer and the twentieth-century script writer have both

[7] Klapp, "The Clever Hero," *Journal of American Folklore,* Vol. LXVII (January–March, 1954).

[8] *Memories and Studies* (New York, Longmans, Green, 1912), 269.

worked from a pre-set formula in which history has been either ignored or expertly manipulated. The formula is recognizable through certain fixed characteristics. There is editing of the hero's career to make it conform to metropolitan literary and commercial standards. Great feats which the hero may actually have performed at some point in his life are generalized into an expected norm of conduct for his entire life. Sensational combats or escapes which may have occurred years apart are made to appear as everyday events in frontier life when compressed into a ten-page dime novel or a thirty-minute television show. The result is that what we know as frontier "history" is quite often nothing but the repetition of a well-worn stereotype.

It appears that the most characteristic form of the Western legend is a popular narrative which features a hero with a historical name, and which perhaps contains a skeletal framework of authentic biographical information. The body of the narrative commonly incorporates exploits, traits, and evaluations which are inflated and legendary. Even competent historians are seduced by the color and obvious symbolic appropriateness of materials which they know to be legendary. These legends appeal to the human imagination; if the deeds they exploit didn't occur, they should have occurred. These heroic narratives are valuable as a record of American aspirations and traditions. They are also valuable as case studies in the legend-making process, perhaps more so than as sources of factual information about the history of the West.

Epilogue

THE WESTERN HERO has continued to be a gigantic figure in American history and mythology. Following Carson, Custer, Bonney, and Hickok came Buffalo Bill Cody, who was the last personification of this heroic tradition before the official close of the frontier in 1890. Cody saw himself as the inheritor of the Boone-Carson mantle, and he idolized his predecessors in *The Story of the Wild West* and other publications. Buffalo Bill was, in fact, an appropriate symbolic figure. He had actually served as an army scout, Indian fighter, cowboy, and buffalo hunter. He had been featured in the requisite number of legendary accounts, running the gamut from dime novels to stage melodramas. He had also had the benefit of superb press-agentry. Thus he became something of a composite symbol for Western heroism.[1]

But Cody also shaped and exploited the Western legend. In the hundreds of Buffalo Bill dime novels and in his Wild West show, he proved once and for all how commercially profitable the West really was. Thousands of motion-picture producers, novelists, biographers, and television writers were to demonstrate the effectiveness of his formula. Purified heroes, fancy shooting, melodramatic rescues, and plenty of dead Indians have been the stock ingredients in Western sagas ever since Cody successfully put them together.

The pseudobiographical format has also retained its popularity. Television plays and novels continue to be "based upon the life and legend" of practically every character who left a record of his participation in frontier violence. Only the cowboy, world-wide

---

[1] Russell, *The Lives and Legends of Buffalo Bill,* 476.

symbol of the American West, has failed to be personified in a historical individual. A wholly fictional character, the Virginian, has become the best-known representative of the group. But the legends of mountain man, outlaw, soldier, and gunfighter largely remain centered upon actual persons.

The historian finds certain advantages in having an individual personify important periods of history. Consolidating the deeds of whole classes of men in a single person seems initially to result from popular incapacity to follow clearly the great stream of history in all its complexity.[2] But the well-known exploits of a Boone, a Carson, or a Custer serve as points of reference which help to clarify historical developments. The Custer legend, for example, has been useful to statesmen as well as military historians. The President of the United States, attempting to put American history in chronological perspective for a German audience, referred to the Battle of the Little Big Horn, where in 1878 [*sic*] Custer and five hundred men [*sic*] were wiped out by Sitting Bull.[3] Despite the normal inaccuracies, the name of Custer is a short-cut reference to a whole era in the national history.

In addition, the career of the legendary hero may in varying degrees accurately reflect certain historical truths. The short life of Billy the Kid illuminates several aspects of Western history. It reveals the unsettled state of society and the ambiguity of "law" on the Southwestern frontier. It tells us something about a common frontier type, the hired gunman and outlaw. The Kid was simply the most proficient and the most notorious of the renegades who swarmed into Lincoln County. The Las Vegas poster which listed him as one of the territory's undesirables also carried the names of some twenty other criminals. But William Hedges, Little Jack, the Pock-Marked Kid, and the rest have all disappeared from history. Billy Bonney lives on as the personification of the type.

[2] Gilbert J. Garraghan, *A Guide to Historical Method* (New York, Fordham University Press, 1946), 267.

[3] John F. Kennedy, Associated Press dispatch from Bonn, Germany, June 24, 1963.

Heroic legends have narrative as well as educative values. The stories of our frontiersmen have the same appeal that heroic sagas have always had. Unfortunately, the success of the Cody formula has tended to force our legends into stereotyped molds. There are occasional attempts to break the stereotype and produce fresh interpretations of the hero. Charles Neider, in *The Authentic Death of Hendry Jones,* took an old legend and attempted to give it a mature modern meaning. Perhaps there will be more experimentation of this sort. But the predominance of the formula has tended to discourage the production of great Western epics on a Homeric scale.

The heroes also personify traits which Americans have always admired. Courage, self-reliance, and physical prowess have usually been rated high on the scale. These traits may seem anachronistic in a settled and industrialized society. Indeed, much of the heroes' appeal seems to be connected with a sentimental nostalgia for the freedom of a vanished frontier. The West generally evokes romantic and sentimental moods. The wilderness setting, from Boone's Kentucky to Custer's Montana, has always intrigued and excited Americans. The gigantic figure of the legendary hero, standing in bold relief against this picturesque backdrop, represents the perennial drama of man facing the unknown.

But the basic appeal of the legendary heroes is that they served good causes. They were servants of justice and truth, defenders of the meek and the oppressed. They became actors in the great allegory of Good versus Evil, an allegory whose roots are deep in American history.[4] That service in such causes may be historically unfounded is of little relevance in the legend. Because Americans have generally cast themselves in idealistic roles, they have been able to identify with these heroic representatives of the national character.

[4] For analyses of the Western myth as a variation of Puritanism, see John Williams, "The Western Myth," *The Nation,* Vol. 193 (November 18, 1961), 401–406; Peter Homans, "The Western: The Legend and the Cardboard Hero," *Look,* Vol. XXVI (March 13, 1962), 82–89.

Bibliography

SECTION I. KIT CARSON

A. Historical Sources

Brevoort, Elias. Manuscript, Bancroft Library, Berkeley, Calif.

Brewerton, George D. "A Ride with Kit Carson," *Harper's Magazine,* Vol. VIII (August, 1853), 307–45.

Carson, Kit. Manuscript "Autobiography," Newberry Library, Chicago.

Frémont, John C. *The Exploring Expedition to the Rocky Mountains in the Year 1842, and to Oregon and North California in the Years 1843–44.* Washington, Gales and Seaton, 1845.

——. *Memoirs of My Life.* Chicago, Belford, Clark, 1887.

Garrard, Lewis H. *Wah-to-yah and the Taos Trail.* Cincinnati, H. W. Derby, 1850.

Grinnell, George Bird. "Bent's Old Fort and Its Builders," *Kansas Historical Collections,* Vol. XV (1923), 35–45.

Hafen, LeRoy, ed. "William Boggs Manuscript about Bent's Fort, Kit Carson, the Far West and Life Among the Indians," *Colorado Magazine,* Vol. VII (March, 1930), 59–70.

Meline, James F. *Two Thousand Miles on Horseback.* New York, Hurd and Houghton, 1867.

Nevins, Allan, ed. *Polk: The Diary of a President, 1845–1849.* New York, Longmans, Green, 1929.

Parker, Rev. Samuel. *Journal of an Exploring Tour Beyond the Rocky Mountains.* Ithaca, privately published, 1838.

Preuss, Charles. *Exploring with Frémont.* Norman, University of Oklahoma Press, 1958.

Rusling, James F. *Across America.* New York, Sheldon, 1874.

Sabin, Edwin L. *Kit Carson Days.* 2 vols. New York, Press of the Pioneers, 1935.

Sherman, William T. *Memoirs.* 2 vols. New York, D. Appleton, 1886.

Bibliography

Widber, J. H. Manuscript, Bancroft Library, Berkeley, Calif.

B. *The Legend*

CHRONOLOGICAL

"An Adventure of Kit Carson," *Holden's Dollar Magazine,* Vol. I (April, 1848), 209–17.

The Rough and Ready Annual; or, Military Souvenir. New York, D. Appleton, 1848.

Averill, Charles. *Kit Carson, Prince of the Gold Hunters.* Boston, G. H. Williams, 1849.

Bennett, Emerson. *The Prairie Flower; or, Adventures in the far West.* Cincinnati, Stratton and Barnard, 1849.

Ruxton, George F. *Life in the Far West.* 2d ed. London, William Blackwood and Sons, 1851.

Melville, Herman. *Moby Dick; or, The Whale.* New York, Harper and Brothers, 1851.

Stewart, William Drummond. *Edward Warren.* London, G. Walker, 1854.

Peters, DeWitt C. *The Life and Adventures of Kit Carson, the Nestor of the Rocky Mountains.* New York, W. R. C. Clark, 1858.

Burdett, Charles. *The Life of Kit Carson, the Great Western Hunter and Guide.* Philadelphia, G. G. Evans, 1860.

Ellis, Edward S. *The Life and Times of Christopher Carson, the Rocky Mountain Scout and Guide.* New York, Beadle & Adams, 1861.

J. H. Randolph [Edward S. Ellis]. *Carson, the Guide; or, The Perils of the Frontier* (Beadle's New Dime Novels, Old Series, No. 587). New York, Beadle & Adams, 1870.

Victor, Mrs. Frances Fuller. *River of the West.* Hartford and Toledo, R. W. Bliss, 1870.

Miller, Joaquin. "Kit Carson's Ride" (1871). In Norman Foerster, ed., *American Poetry and Prose.* Boston, Houghton Mifflin, 1947.

Abbott, John S. C. *Christopher Carson, Known as Kit Carson.* New York, Dodd, Mead, 1873.

Munro, George. *Kit Carson on the War-Path.* (Munro's Ten Cent Novels, No. 253). New York, American News Company, 1873.

Adams, J. F. C. [Edward S. Ellis]. *The Fighting Trapper; or, Kit Carson to the Rescue* (Beadle's Dime Library No. 68). New York, Beadle & Adams, 1879.

Harbaugh, Thomas C. *Kiowa Charley, the White Mustanger; or, Rocky Mountain Kit's Last Scalp Hunt*. New York, Beadle & Adams, 1879.

Buel, J. W. *Heroes of the Plains*. Chicago, A. G. Nettleton, 1883.

Cattermole, E. G. *Famous Frontiersmen, Pioneers, and Scouts*. Chicago, M. A. Donohue, 1883.

Aiken, Albert. *Kit Carson, King of Guides; or, Mountain Paths and Prairie Trails*. (Beadle's Half-Dime Library of Sport, Story, and Adventure, Vol. I, No. 15). New York, Beadle & Adams, 1882.

Cody, William F. *Story of the Wild West and Camp-Fire Chats*. Philadelphia, Historical Publishing Company, 1888.

Ellis, Edward S. *The Life of Kit Carson*. New York, American News Company, 1889.

Lewis, Leon [Julius Warren Lewis]. *Kit Carson's Last Trail*. New York, Robert Bonner's Sons, 1891.

Thomson, William. "On the War-path with Kit Carson," *Lippincott's Magazine,* Vol. LVII (April, 1896), 555–64.

Inman, Colonel Henry. *The Old Santa Fé Trail*. New York, Macmillan, 1897.

Drannan, William F. *Thirty-One Years on the Plains and in the Mountains*. Chicago, Rhodes and McClure, 1899.

"An Old Scout" [Lu Senarens]. *Kit Carson's Boys; or, With the Great Scout on His Last Trail* (Pluck and Luck No. 340). New York, Frank Tousey, 1904.

McNeil, Everett. *With Kit Carson in the Rockies*. New York, E. P. Dutton, 1909.

Tomlinson, Everett T. *Scouting with Kit Carson*. New York, D. Appleton, 1916.

Creel, George. "Incredible Kit Carson," *Collier's,* Vol. LXXVIII (August 26, 1926), 11–12.

Vestal, Stanley [Walter S. Campbell]. *Fandango: Ballads of the Old West*. Boston, Houghton Mifflin, 1927.

―――. *Kit Carson, the Happy Warrior of the Old West*. Boston, Houghton Mifflin, 1928.

Holbrook, Stewart. "Kit Carson," *American Mercury,* Vol. XLIX (April, 1940), 470–73.

Peattie, Donald Culross. "Kit Carson," *Reader's Digest,* Vol. XLIII (September, 1943), 91–95.

Estergreen, M. Morgan. *The Real Kit Carson*. Taos, N. M., n.p., 1955.

Gentry, Claude. *Kit Carson*. Baldwyn, Miss., Magnolia Publishers, 1956.

C. General References

Bate, Walter. *Frontier Legend, the Texas Finale of Capt. William F. Drannan, Pseudo Frontier Comrade of Kit Carson*. New Bern, N. C., Owen G. Dunn, 1954.

Blackwelder, Bernice. *Great Westerner, the Story of Kit Carson*. Caldwell, Idaho, Caxton Printers, 1962.

Cather, Willa. *Death Comes for the Archbishop*. New York, Alfred A. Knopf, 1927.

Chittenden, Hiram M. *The American Fur Trade of the Far West*. 2 vols. New York, Press of the Pioneers, 1935.

Conner, Sabra. *On Sweetwater Trail*. Chicago, Reilly and Lee, 1928.

Davis, Blanche C. *The Hero in American Drama, 1787–1900*. New York, n.p., 1950.

Estergreen, M. Morgan. *Kit Carson: A Portrait in Courage*. Norman, University of Oklahoma Press, 1962.

Hough, Emerson. *The Way to the West, and the Lives of Three Early Americans–Boone–Crockett–Carson*. Indianapolis, Bobbs-Merrill, 1903.

Nevins, Allan. "Kit Carson—Bayard of the Plains," *American Scholar,* Vol. VIII (July, 1939), 333–39.

Smith, Henry Nash. "Kit Carson in Books," *Southwest Review,* Vol. XXVIII (Winter, 1943), 164–90.

————. *Virgin Land: The American West as Symbol and Myth*. Cambridge, Harvard University Press, 1950.

Section II. Billy the Kid
A. Historical Sources

Billy the Kid: Las Vegas Newspaper Accounts of His Career, 1880–81. Waco Tex., W. M. Morrison, 1958.

Coe, George W. *Frontier Fighter: The Autobiography of George W. Coe.* Boston, Houghton Mifflin, 1934.

"A Document in the Lincoln County War: John H. Tunstall's 'Letter to His Parents,' " *New Mexico Folklore Record,* Vol. X (1955–56), 5.

Fulton, Maurice G. "Billy the Kid in Life and Books," *New Mexico Folklore Record,* Vol. IV (1949–50), 2–3.

Grant County (Ariz.) *Herald,* September 26, 1875.

Haley, J. Evetts. "Jim East—Trail Hand and Cowboy," *Panhandle-Plains Historical Review,* Vol. IV (1931), 39–61.

Keleher, William A. *Violence in Lincoln County.* Albuquerque, University of New Mexico Press, 1957.

Mesilla *Independent,* October 13, 1877.

Poe, John W. *The Death of Billy the Kid,* With an Introduction by Maurice G. Fulton. Boston, Houghton Mifflin, 1933.

Rasch, Philip J. "The Twenty-One Men He Put Bullets Through," *New Mexico Folklore Record,* Vol. IX (1954–55), 8–14.

———. "Five Days of Battle," Denver *Westerners Brand Book,* Vol. XI (1955), 295–323.

———. "Prelude to the Lincoln County War: The Murder of John Henry Tunstall," Los Angeles *Westerners Brand Book,* Vol. VII (1957), 78–96.

———. Documents Collection, Old Lincoln County Memorial Commission, Lincoln, N. M.

Santa Fe *New Mexican,* January 17, 1880.

Santa Fe *Rocky Mountain Sentinel,* April 30, 1879.

Tucson *Arizona Citizen,* August 25, 1877.

B. The Legend

CHRONOLOGICAL

Philadelphia *Times,* July 20, 1881.

Santa Fe *Weekly Democrat,* July 21, 1881.

Chicago *Tribune,* August 7, 1881.

Jenardo, Don [John Woodruff Lewis]. *The True Life of Billy the Kid* (Wide Awake Library No. 451). New York, Frank Tousey, 1881.

The Cowboy's Career, or the Dare Devil Deeds of "Billy, the Kid," the Noted New Mexico Desperado. Chicago, Belford, Clark, 1881.

Fable, Edmund, Jr. *Billy the Kid, the New Mexican Outlaw; or, the Bold Bandit of the West!* Denver, Denver Publishing Company, 1881.

Garrett, Pat F. *The Authentic Life of Billy, the Kid.* (1882). Norman, University of Oklahoma Press, 1954.

Cowdrick, J. C. *Silver-Mask, the Man of Mystery* (Beadle's Half Dime Library, No. 360). New York, Beadle & Adams, 1884.

Siringo, Charles A. *A Texas Cowboy; or, Fifteen Years on the Hurricane Deck of a Spanish Pony.* Chicago, Rand McNally, 1886.

Doughty, Francis W. *Old King Brady and Billy the Kid* (New York Detective Library, No. 411). New York, Frank Tousey, 1890.

Hall, Frank. *History of the State of Colorado.* 4 vols. Chicago, Blakely Printing Company, 1891.

Hough, Emerson. *The Story of the Outlaw.* New York, D. Appleton, 1897.

————. "Billy the Kid, the True Story of a Western 'Bad Man,' " *Everybody's Magazine,* Vol. V (September, 1901), 302–10.

Woods, Walter. *Billy the Kid* (1903). In Garrett H. Leverton, ed., *The Great Diamond Robbery and Other Recent Melodramas,* Vol. VIII of *America's Lost Plays.* Princeton, Princeton University Press, 1940.

Chapman, Arthur. "Billy the Kid—A Man All 'Bad,' " *Outing Magazine,* Vol. XLVI (April, 1905), 73–77.

Raine, William MacLeod. "Billy-the-Kid," *Pacific Monthly,* Vol. XX (July, 1908), 38–44.

Fergusson, Harvey. "Billy the Kid," *American Mercury,* Vol. V (May, 1925), 224–31.

Burns, Walter Noble. *The Saga of Billy the Kid.* Garden City, N. Y., Doubleday, Page, 1926.

White, Owen P. *Trigger Fingers.* New York, G. P. Putnam's Sons, 1926.

Walters, Lorenzo D. *Tombstone's Yesterday.* Tucson, Acme Printing Company, 1928.

Mann, E. B. *Gamblin' Man.* New York, William Morrow, 1934.

New Mexico Writers' Program, WPA, Manuscripts (1934–38), Library of the Museum of New Mexico, Santa Fe, New Mexico.

Cunningham, Eugene, "The Kid Still Rides," *New Mexico Magazine,* Vol. XIII (March, 1935), 13–15.

Otero, Miguel. *The Real Billy the Kid.* New York, Rufus Rockwell Wilson, 1936.

"Billy the Kid." In John A. Lomax and Alan Lomax, *Cowboy Songs.* New York, Macmillan, 1938.

Billy the Kid. In Rosalyn Krakova, *New Borzoi Book of Ballet.* New York, Alfred A. Knopf, 1956.

Wesley, Paul. "Bandit Samaritan," *New Mexico Magazine,* Vol. XVII (October, 1939), 57.

Nye, Nelson C. *Pistols for Hire*. New York, Macmillan, 1941.

Avery, Delos. "The Life and Death of Billy the Kid," *Chicago Sunday Tribune*, August 27, 1944.

Corle, Edwin. *Billy the Kid*. New York, Duell, Sloan and Pearce, 1953.

———. "Billy the Kid in Arizona," *Arizona Highways*, Vol. XXX (February, 1954), 34–36.

Sonnichsen, C. L., and William V. Morrison. *Alias Billy the Kid*. Albuquerque, University of New Mexico Press, 1955.

Hunt, Frazier. *The Tragic Days of Billy the Kid*. New York, Hastings House, 1956.

Neider, Charles. *The Authentic Death of Hendry Jones*. New York, Harper and Brothers, 1956.

Wiltsey, Norman. "Killer Kid," *True West*, Vol. IV (March-April, 1957), 4–8, 30–33.

Hamlin, William Lee. *The True Story of Billy the Kid*. Caldwell, Idaho, Caxton Printers, 1959.

C. General References

Adams, Ramon. *A Fitting Death for Billy the Kid*. Norman, University of Oklahoma Press, 1960.

———. "With Our Rocking Chair Historians," Denver *Westerners Brand Book* (1952), 17–35.

Adler, Alfred. "Billy the Kid: A Case Study in Epic Origins," *Western Folklore*, Vol. X (April, 1951), 143–52.

Applegate, Frank G. "New Mexico Legends," *Southwest Review*, Vol. XVII (Winter, 1932), 201–208.

Cunningham, Eugene. *Triggernometry*. New York, Press of the Pioneers, 1934.

Dykes, J. C. *Billy the Kid, the Bibliography of a Legend* (University of New Mexico Publications in Language and Literature, No. 7). Albuquerque, University of New Mexico Press, 1952.

Fishwick, Marshall. "Billy the Kid: Faust in America," *Saturday Review*, Vol. XXXV (October 11, 1952), 11–12, 34–36.

Klapp, Orrin. "The Clever Hero," *Journal of American Folklore*, Vol. LXVII (January–March, 1954), 21–34.

Steckmesser, Kent L. "Joaquín Murieta and Billy the Kid," *Western Folklore*, Vol. XXI (April, 1962), 77–82.

Bibliography

Section III. Wild Bill Hickok
A. Historical Sources

Abilene *Chronicle,* October 12, 1871.

Andreas, A. T. *History of the State of Kansas.* Chicago, A. T. Andreas, 1883.

Central City (Colo.) *Daily Register,* September 8, 1868.

Cheyenne *Daily Leader,* March 1–August 20, 1876.

Connelley, William E. *Wild Bill and His Era: The Life and Adventures of James Butler Hickok.* New York, Press of the Pioneers, 1933.

Custer, George A. *My Life on the Plains.* New York, Sheldon, 1874.

Davis, Theodore. Manuscript on "Stanley's Indian Campaign," Chicago *Westerners Brand Book,* Vol. II (1946), 97–106.

Dawson, Charles. *Pioneer Tales of the Oregon Trail and Jefferson County.* Topeka, Crane, 1912.

"Dickinson County Biographical Sketches," Kansas State Historical Society, Topeka.

Edwards, J. B. *History of Abilene.* Kansas State Historical Society, Topeka.

Ellis County Star, June 29, 1876.

Gross, Charles F. Letters to J. B. Edwards. Kansas State Historical Society, Topeka.

Hansen, George W., and others. "Wild Bill—McCanles Tragedy, A Much Misrepresented Event in Nebraska History," *Nebraska History Magazine,* Vol. X (April–June, 1927), 67–146.

Hays City *Sentinel,* August 16, 1876.

Henry, Stuart. *Conquering Our Great American Plains.* New York, E. P. Dutton, 1930.

Kane, Robert A. "The D.A. vs. S.A. Controversy," *Outdoor Life,* Vol. XVII (June, 1906), 589–92.

Leavenworth *Times and Conservative,* August 26, 1869.

McClintock, John S. *Pioneer Days in the Black Hills.* Deadwood, S. Dak., privately published, 1939.

Miller, Nyle H., and Joseph W. Snell. "Some Notes on Kansas Cowtown Police Officers and Gun Fighters," *Kansas Historical Quarterly,* Vol. XXVI (Winter, 1960), 410–35.

Rocky Mountain News (Denver), February 18, 1867.

Senn, Edward L. *"Wild Bill" Hickok, "Prince of Pistoleers," a Tale of Facts and Not Fiction and Romance*. Deadwood, S. Dak., n.p., 1939.

Springfield *Missouri Weekly Patriot*, July 27, 1865.

Tallent, Mrs. Annie. *The Black Hills; or, Last Hunting Ground of the Dakotahs*. St. Louis, Nixon-Jones, 1899.

Topeka *Kansas Daily Commonwealth*, February 8, 1870–March 1, 1873.

Topeka *Weekly Leader*, April 2, 1868.

B. The Legend

CHRONOLOGICAL

Nichols, George Ward. "Wild Bill," *Harper's New Monthly Magazine*, Vol. XXXIV (February, 1867), 273–85.

Saline County Journal, January 18, 1872.

Topeka *Kansas Daily Commonwealth*, May 11, 1873.

Cody, William F. *The Life of Hon. William F. Cody . . . An Autobiography*. Hartford, Frank E. Bliss, 1879.

Buel, J. W. *The Life and Marvelous Adventures of Wild Bill*. Chicago, Belford, Clark, 1880.

Ingraham, Prentiss. *Adventures of Wild Bill, the Pistol Prince* (Boy's Library of Sport, Story, and Adventure, No. 3). New York, Beadle & Adams, 1881.

———. *Wild Bill, the Pistol Dead Shot*. (Dime Library No. 168). New York, Beadle & Adams, 1882.

Buel, J. W. *Heroes of the Plains*. Chicago, A. G. Nettleton, 1882.

Kelsey, D. M. *Our Pioneer Heroes and Their Daring Deeds*. Philadelphia, G. O. Pelton, 1883.

Triplett, Frank. *Conquering the Wilderness*. New York and St. Louis, N. D. Thompson, 1883.

Ray, Clarence E. *Famous American Scouts*. Chicago, J. Regan, n.d. [c.1890].

Buntline, Ned [E. Z. C. Judson]. *Wild Bill's Last Trail*. New York, Beadle & Adams, 1892.

Cody, William F. *Wild Bill, the Wild West Duelist* (Dime Library No. 807). New York, Beadle & Adams, 1894.

Stanley, Henry M. *My Early Travels and Adventures in America and Asia*. 2 vols. New York, Charles Scribner's Sons, 1895.

Bibliography

Little, E. C. "A Son of the Border," *Everybody's Magazine,* Vol. IV (June, 1901), 578–87.

Hough, Emerson. *The Story of the Outlaw.* New York, Outing Publishing Company, 1907.

Cody, William F. *True Tales of the Plains.* New York, Cupples and Leon, 1908.

Young, Harry. *Hard Knocks.* Chicago, Laird and Lee, 1915.

Buffum, George T. *On Two Frontiers.* Boston, Lothrop, Lee and Shepard, 1918.

Hooker, William F. *The Prairie Schooner.* Chicago, Saul Brothers, 1918.

Cooper, Courtney Ryley. *The Last Frontier.* Boston, Little, Brown, 1923.

Hough, Emerson. *North of 36.* New York, D. Appleton, 1923.

Sutton, Fred E. (as told to A. B. MacDonald). "Fill Your Hand," *Saturday Evening Post,* Vol. CXCVIII (April 10, 1926), 14–15, 168–77.

Wilstach, Frank. *Wild Bill Hickok, The Prince of Pistoleers.* Garden City, N.Y., Doubleday, Page, 1926.

Connelley, William E. "Wild Bill—James Butler Hickok," *Collections of the Kansas State Historical Society,* Vol. XVII (1926–28), 1–27.

Eisele, Wilbert E. *The Real Wild Bill, Famous Scout and Knight Chivalric of the Plains.* Denver, Wm. H. Andre, 1931.

Lake, Stuart N. *Wyatt Earp, Frontier Marshal.* Boston, Houghton Mifflin, 1931.

Connelley, William E. *Wild Bill and His Era: The Life & Adventures of James Butler Hickok.* New York, Press of the Pioneers, 1933.

Hardy, Allison. *Wild Bill Hickok, King of the Gunfighters,* n.p., 1943.

Holbrook, Stewart. "There Was a Man: Wild Bill Hickok," *Esquire,* Vol. XXXIII (May, 1950), 64.

———. *Wild Bill Hickok Tames the West.* New York, Random House, 1952.

Rozeboom, Robert. "Hickok—Hell's Own Marshal," *Modern Man,* Vol. III (July, 1954), 31–35.

Wright, Kathryn. "The Real Calamity Jane," *True West,* Vol. V (November–December, 1957), 22–25, 41–42.

O'Connor, Richard. *Wild Bill Hickok.* New York, Doubleday, 1959.

Burkholder, Edwin V. "The Strangeness of Wild Bill Hickok," *Argosy,* Vol. 352 (March, 1961), 40–43, 108–14.

Breihan, Carl. *Great Gunfighters of the West.* San Antonio, Naylor, 1962.

C. General References

Adams, Ramon. "With Our Rocking Chair Historians," Denver *Westerners Brand Book* (1952), 17–35.

Byington, Robert. "The Frontier Hero: Refinement and Definition," *Publications of the Texas Folklore Society,* Vol. XXX (1960), 140–55.

"The Case of James Butler Hickok, Alias 'Wild Bill' " (report of a round table discussion), Chicago *Westerners Brand Book,* Vol. III (April–May, 1946), 1–7.

Cunningham, Eugene. *Triggernometry.* New York, Press of the Pioneers, 1934.

Dykstra, Robert. "Exit John Wesley Hardin," Los Angeles *Westerners Brand Book,* Vol. VI (1956), 123–29.

Lyon, Peter. "The Wild, Wild West," *American Heritage,* Vol. XI (August, 1960), 32–48.

Mann, E. B. "The Truth Behind the Wild Bill Hickok Myth," *New Mexico Sun Trails,* Vols. V–VI (December, 1952–February, 1953).

McCanles, W. Monroe (as told to M. I. McCreight). " 'The McCandless [*sic*] Gang,' " *Forest and Stream,* Vol. XCVII (December, 1927), 740–42, 762–63.

Ripley, Thomas. *They Died With Their Boots On.* New York, Doubleday, Doran, 1936.

Uhlarik, Carl. "The Myth of Wild Bill Hickok," *Prairie Schooner,* Vol. XXV (Spring, 1951), 129–37.

SECTION IV. GEORGE ARMSTRONG CUSTER

A. Historical Sources

Chandler, Melbourne C. *Of Garry Owen to Glory: The History of the Seventh United States Cavalry Regiment.* Annandale, Va., n.p., 1960.

Custer, George A. *My Life on the Plains; or, Personal Experiences with Indians.* New York, Sheldon, 1874.

———. "War Memoirs," *The Galaxy,* Vol. XXI (April, 1876), 448–60.

Custer, Elizabeth B. *"Boots and Saddles"; or, Life in Dakota with General Custer.* New York, Harper and Brothers, 1885.

———. *Following the Guidon.* New York, Harper and Brothers, 1890.

Custer, Milo. *Custer Genealogies.* Bloomington, Ill., n.p., 1944.

Farley, J. P. *West Point in the Early Sixties.* Troy, N.Y., Pafraets Book Company, 1902.

Godfrey, Edward S. "Custer's Last Battle," *Century Magazine,* Vol. XLIII (January, 1892), 358–84.

Graham, William A. *The Story of the Little Big Horn.* New York, Century, 1926.

Hughes, Robert P. "The Campaign against the Sioux," *Journal of the Military Service Institution of the United States,* Vol. XVIII (January, 1896). Reprinted in Graham, *The Story of the Little Big Horn* (New York, Collier Books, 1962).

Hunt, Frazier and Robert. *I Fought With Custer.* New York, Charles Scribner's Sons, 1947.

Keim, DeBenneville R. *Sheridan's Troopers on the Border.* Philadelphia, Claxton, Remsen and Heffelfinger, 1870.

Knight, Oliver. *Following the Indian Wars.* Norman, University of Oklahoma Press, 1960.

Lounsberry, Clement A. *Early History of North Dakota.* Washington, Liberty Press, 1919.

Merington, Marguerite. *The Custer Story: The Life and Intimate Letters of General George A. Custer and His Wife Elizabeth.* New York, Devin-Adair, 1950.

Monaghan, Jay. *Custer: The Life of General George Armstrong Custer.* Boston, Little, Brown, 1959.

Official Record of a Court of Inquiry convened at Chicago, Illinois, January 13, 1879, by The President of the United States upon the request of Major Marcus A. Reno, 7th U.S. Cavalry to investigate his conduct at the battle of the Little Big Horn, June 25–26, 1876. 2 vols. Pacific Palisades, W. A. Graham, 1951.

Spotts, David L., and E. A. Brininstool. *Campaigning with Custer and the Nineteenth Kansas Volunteer Cavalry.* Los Angeles, Wetzel Publishing Company, 1928.

Stanley, David S. *Personal Memoirs.* Cambridge, Harvard University Press, 1917.

Stewart, Edgar I. *Custer's Luck.* Norman, University of Oklahoma Press, 1955.

U.S. War Department. *Annual Report of the Secretary of War; Being Part of the Message and Documents Communicated to the Two Houses of Congress at the Beginning of the Second Session of the Forty-Fourth Congress.* Washington, Government Printing Office, 1876.

Van de Water, Frederick F. *Glory Hunter: A Life of General Custer.* Indianapolis and New York, Bobbs-Merrill, 1934.

Victor, Frances F. *Eleven Years in the Rocky Mountains.* Hartford, R. W. Bliss, 1881.

Whittaker, Frederick. "General George A. Custer," *The Galaxy,* Vol. XXII (September, 1876), 362–71.

B. *The Legend*

CHRONOLOGICAL

New York Herald, June 1–August 15, 1876.

Webb, Mrs. Laura. *Custer's Immortality. A Poem, with Biographical Sketches of the Chief Actors in the Late Tragedy of the Wilderness.* New York, n.p., 1876.

Whittaker, Frederick. *A Complete Life of Gen. George A. Custer.* New York, Sheldon, 1876.

Cody, Hon. W. F. (Buffalo Bill). *The Crimson Trail; or, On Custer's Last Warpath.* Street & Smith's *New York Weekly,* September 23–October 30, 1876.

———. *The Life of Hon. William F. Cody . . . An Autobiography.* Hartford, Frank E. Bliss, 1879.

Longfellow, Henry Wadsworth. *Complete Poetical Works.* Boston, Houghton Mifflin, 1880.

Whittaker, Frederick. *The Dashing Dragoon; or, The Story of Gen. George A. Custer from West Point to the Big Horn* (Beadle's Boy's Library of Sport, Story and Adventure, No. 36). New York, Beadle & Adams, 1882.

Dodge, Richard I. *Our Wild Indians.* Hartford, A. D. Worthington, 1882.

Travers, Col. J. M. [St. George Rathborne]. *Custer's Last Shot; or, The Boy Trailer of the Little Horn* (Wide Awake Library No. 565). New York, Frank Tousey, 1883.

Ingraham, Prentiss. *Buffalo Bill's Grip; or, Oath-Bound to Custer* (Beadle's Dime Library No. 362). New York, Beadle & Adams, 1883.

Harbaugh, Thomas. *Roving Rifle, Custer's Little Scout; or, From the Plains to West Point* (Beadle's Boy's Library No. 96). New York, Beadle & Adams, 1883.

Newson, T. M. *Thrilling Scenes Among the Indians.* Chicago, Belford, Clark, 1884.

Bibliography

Dunn, J. P. *Massacres of the Mountains: A History of the Indian Wars of the Far West*. New York, Harper and Brothers, 1886.

Whittier, John Greenleaf. "On the Big Horn," *Atlantic Monthly*, Vol. LIX (April, 1887), 433–34.

Ingraham, Prentiss. *Buffalo Bill's Big Four; or, Custer's Shadow* (Beadle's Dime Library No. 750). New York, Beadle & Adams, 1887.

"An Old Scout" [Lu Senarens]. *Custer's Little Dead-shot; or, The Boy Scout of the Little Big Horn* (Wide Awake Library No. 826). New York, Frank Tousey, 1888.

Cody, William F. *Story of the Wild West and Camp-Fire Chats*. Philadelphia, Historical Publishing Company, 1888.

Johnson, W. Fletcher. *Red Record of the Sioux*. Philadelphia, Edgewood Publishing Company, 1891.

Northrop, Henry D. *Indian Horrors; or, Massacres by the Red Men*. Philadelphia, National Publishing Company, 1891.

Miles, Nelson A. *Personal Recollections*. Chicago, Werner, 1896.

Wilcox, Ella Wheeler. *Custer and Other Poems*. Chicago, W. B. Conkey, 1896.

Inman, Col. Henry. *Tales of the Trail*. Topeka, Crane, 1898.

Brooks, Elbridge S. *Master of the Strong Hearts*. New York, E. P. Dutton, 1898.

Thomas, W. Kent. "The Personal Story of Rain in the Face," *Outdoor Life*, Vol. XI (March, 1903), 20–27.

Myrick, Herbert. Manuscript Collection (1904–1906), Huntington Library, San Marino, Calif.

————. *Cache la Poudre: The Romance of a Tenderfoot in the Days of Custer*. New York, Orange Judd, 1905.

Parish, Randall. *Bob Hampton of Placer*. New York, A. L. Burt, 1906.

Sabin, Edwin L. *On the Plains with Custer*. Philadelphia, J. B. Lippincott, 1913.

Brady, Cyrus Townsend. *Britton of the Seventh*. Chicago, A. C. McClurg, 1914.

Dellenbaugh, Frederick. *George Armstrong Custer*. New York, Macmillan, 1917.

Hunt, Frazier. *Custer: The Last of the Cavaliers*. New York, Cosmopolitan Book Company, 1928.

Drago, Harry Sinclair. *Montana Road*. New York, William Morrow, 1935.

Bates, Charles Francis. *Custer's Indian Battles*. Bronxville, N.Y., n.p., 1936.

Waldo, Edna L. *Dakota*. Caldwell, Idaho, Caxton Printers, 1936.

Brill, Charles J. *Conquest of the Southern Plains: Uncensored Narrative of the Battle of the Washita and Custer's Southern Campaign*. Oklahoma City, Golden Sage Publishers, 1938.

Hawley, Zoa Grace. *A Boy Rides with Custer*. Boston, Little, Brown, 1938.

"Custer's Last Charge" (Folk song). In B. A. Botkin, ed., *A Treasury of Western Folklore*, 745–46. New York, Crown Publishers, 1951.

Foreman, Leonard L. *The Renegade*. New York, E. P. Dutton, 1942.

Haycox, Ernest. *Bugles in the Afternoon*. Boston, Little, Brown, 1944.

Henry, Will. *No Survivors*. New York, Random House, 1950.

Reynolds, Quentin. *Custer's Last Stand*. New York, Random House, 1951.

DuBois, Charles G. *Kick the Dead Lion: A Casebook of the Custer Battle*. Billings, Mont., n.p., 1954.

Fisher, Clay. *Yellow Hair*. Boston, Houghton Mifflin, 1954.

Vestal, Stanley [W. S. Campbell]. "The Man Who Killed Custer," *American Heritage*, Vol. VIII (February, 1957), 9–12.

Miller, David Humphreys. *Custer's Fall*. New York, Duell, Sloan and Pearce, 1957.

Shiflet, Kenneth. *Convenient Coward*. Harrisburg, Pa., Stackpole, 1961.

C. General References

Brady, Cyrus Townsend. *Indian Fights and Fighters*. New York, Doubleday, Page, 1904.

Deex, Nelle. *Glory Trek*. New York, William-Frederick Press, 1959.

Dustin, Fred. *The Custer Tragedy*. Ann Arbor, Edwards Brothers, 1939.

Graham, William A. *The Custer Myth: A Source Book of Custeriana*. Harrisburg, Pa., Stackpole, 1953.

Kuhlman, Charles. *Did Custer Disobey Orders at the Battle of the Little Big Horn?*. Harrisburg, Pa., Stackpole, 1957.

———. *Legend into History: The Custer Mystery*. Harrisburg, Pa., Stackpole, 1951.

Russell, Don, and Elmo Scott Watson. "The Battle of the Washita, or Custer's Massacre?" Chicago *Westerners Brand Book*, Vol. V (November, 1948), 49–56.

————. "Sixty Years in Bar Rooms; or 'Custer's Last Fight,' " Chicago *Westerners Brand Book*, Vol. III (November, 1946), 61–68.

Utley, Robert M. *Custer and the Great Controversy*. Los Angeles, Westernlore Press, 1962.

SECTION V. GENERAL REFERENCES ON LEGEND-ANALYSIS

Blair, Walter, and Franklin J. Meine. *Half Horse, Half Alligator: The Growth of the Mike Fink Legend*. Chicago, University of Chicago Press, 1956.

Fenin, George N., and William K. Everson. *The Western: From Silents to Cinerama*. New York, Orion Press, 1962.

Fishwick, Marshall. *The American Hero: Myth and Reality*. Washington, Public Affairs Press, 1954.

Leach, Joseph. *The Typical Texan: Biography of an American Myth*. Dallas, Southern Methodist University Press, 1952.

Malin, James C. *John Brown and the Legend of Fifty-Six*. Philadelphia, American Philosophical Society, 1942.

Paredes, Americo. *With His Pistol in His Hand: A Border Ballad and Its Hero*. Austin, University of Texas Press, 1958.

Russell, Don. *The Lives and Legends of Buffalo Bill*. Norman, University of Oklahoma Press, 1960.

Smith, Bradford. *Captain John Smith: His Life and Legend*. Philadelphia, J. B. Lippincott, 1953.

Smith, Henry Nash. *Virgin Land: The American West as Symbol and Myth*. Cambridge, Harvard University Press, 1950.

Walsh, Richard. *The Making of Buffalo Bill: A Study in Heroics*. Indianapolis, Bobbs-Merrill, 1928.

Wecter, Dixon. *The Hero in America*. New York, Charles Scribner's Sons, 1941.

Index

Index

279

The Western Hero in History and Legend has been printed on paper designed for an effective life of at least three hundred years, bearing the watermark of the University of Oklahoma Press. The book has been set in eleven-point Linotype Old Style No. 7 with two-point spacing between the lines. It is a type design largely based upon a face cut by the Bruce Foundry in the early 1870's. For years, Old Style No. 7 has been one of the most popular Linotype book faces, a tribute to its even color and uncommon legibility.

UNIVERSITY OF OKLAHOMA PRESS

Norman